10/07

EUTHANASIA

A Reference Handbook

Other titles in ABC-CLIO's
**CONTEMPORARY
WORLD ISSUES**
Series

Books in the Contemporary World Issues series address vital issues in today's society such as terrorism, sexual harassment, homelessness, AIDS, gambling, animal rights, and air pollution. Written by professional writers, scholars, and nonacademic experts, these books are authoritative, clearly written, up-to-date, and objective. They provide a good starting point for research by high school and college students, scholars, and general readers, as well as by legislators, businesspeople, activists, and others.

Each book, carefully organized and easy to use, contains an overview of the subject; a detailed chronology; biographical sketches; facts and data and/or documents and other primary-source material; a directory of organizations and agencies; annotated lists of print and nonprint resources; a glossary; and an index.

Readers of books in the Contemporary World Issues series will find the information they need in order to better understand the social, political, environmental, and economic issues facing the world today.

EUTHANASIA

A Reference Handbook

Carolyn S. Roberts
Martha Gorman

**CONTEMPORARY
WORLD ISSUES**

ABC-CLIO

Santa Barbara, California
Denver, Colorado
Oxford, England

Library of Congress Cataloging-in-Publication Data

Roberts, Carolyn S., 1960–
    Euthanasia : a reference handbook / Carolyn S. Roberts, Martha Gorman.
      p.   cm.—(Contempory world issues)
    Includes bibliographical references and index.
    1. Euthanasia. I. Gorman, Martha, 1952– . II. Series.
    R726.R53   1996   179'.7—dc20   96-28833

ISBN 0-87436-831-6

02 01 00 99 98 97 96   10 9 8 7 6 5 4 3 2 1

ABC-CLIO, Inc. (1996)
130 Cremona Drive, P.O. Box 1911
Santa Barbara, California 93116-1911

This book is printed on acid-free paper ∞.
Manufactured in the United States of America

Contents

Tables

Figures

Preface

Through the ages, people have pursued a dignified, easy, or noble death for many reasons and in many ways. Such a death has been referred to as euthanasia. The *Concise Oxford English Dictionary of Current English* defines euthanasia as "the painless killing of a patient suffering from an incurable and painful disease, [or] such a death"; however, the working definition and perception of what actually constitutes euthanasia have changed repeatedly throughout history and have differed from culture to culture. Because people attach different meanings to the same words, it is very difficult to reach the consensus needed to make the important legal decisions that are under consideration in the United States and in other parts of the world today.

Over the centuries euthanasia has been debated, refined, and codified as human ideas, needs, and communities have changed. For some, changing attitudes about euthanasia have signaled a rapid decline in civilized society. Others have perceived the process of change to be brutally slow, never quite keeping pace with human suffering. For everyone, the issue of the right to die has become dramatically more prominent within the past 30 years.

But finding answers everyone can agree on can take time. Deliberation of the euthanasia debate has resembled a method of Native American decision making that allows a group to maintain the status quo if consensus cannot be reached. In his book *In the Absence of the Sacred,* author Jerry Mander quotes Chief Oren Lyons on this method:

> Discussion continues until consensus is reached, it's a very slow process. Sometimes it takes days or weeks, but we're not in a hurry, especially about important things.... If everyone has spoken and still there's no decision, then the question is put off until the next meeting. If the issue is discussed at three meetings and there's still no decision then we decide that there will be no decision. We stop discussing it. We figure it will come up again some other time.

One cannot but wonder how quickly questions surrounding the right to die would be resolved today if we still lived in small, tribal communities where those who are suffering were not hidden from our daily lives; where caring for others were a way of life, not something we paid others to do for us; and where true democracy could be practiced, with the understanding that it would, by its very nature, serve the best interests of both the individual and the community.

From the end of World War II to the present, advances in technology and medical science have been strongly supported by our society. We have developed high expectations of our health care system. We have entreated doctors and researchers to "do all you can," but we have done this without a clear understanding of what the final hours and possibly years of our lives might look like if we get what we've asked for.

Rapid advancements in medical technology have made yesterday's heroic measures today's routine care. But these advances in medicine have not always restored the quality of life we enjoyed before illness or injury struck. Sometimes we are left in unbearable pain, unable to do any of the things that once made our lives seem worth living. Doctors can keep our bodies alive, but this reprieve may come at the expense of our spirit. This is the dilemma that lies at the heart of the contemporary debate over euthanasia.

From the living room to the hospital room to the courtroom, discussions about death, particularly discussions that involve the intentional hastening of death, inevitably spark passionate opinions. As well they should, considering the debate is over what we hold to be most precious: life itself. This book attempts to bring together under one cover an unbiased portrait of the right-to-die issue. It focuses on developments during the second half of the twentieth century, a time in which the controversy over this issue has escalated. Developments in the field of medicine have propelled the debate into murky ethical waters. The questions raised by these developments have spawned the field of bioethics, which has rapidly replaced traditional medical ethics over the past three decades. Where medical ethics once allowed the doctor to unilaterally decide what the patient should know and determine how a case should be handled, the current trend is toward decision making by committee, with increased attention to the patient's wishes. This increases the likelihood that the individuals involved will come in contact with opinions conflicting with their own.

Managed care in recent years has begun to alter and further complicate the medical decision-making process in the United States. Once based primarily on ethics, with or without patient input or consent, medical decisions today are based on bottom-line business considerations. Many are made by administrators with no medical background, and some are even made by computers. Because medical developments and the ethical concerns they have generated have precipitated the current debate, these are grouped together in this book.

Debate in the medical-bioethical arena has had wide repercussions, prompting individuals, religious leaders, and society in general to examine established beliefs about the manner and timing of death. These spiritual-social-cultural facets of the debate form a second arena in which euthanasia is examined. The complexity of the issues and the passion with which they have been discussed has made it difficult for the various forums to reach consensus, so the debate in the United States has been taken to the courts. Thus, the final category explores the legal-political arena. Contemporary discussion of the issues focuses primarily on developments in the United States, with a summary of practices in other countries. Information about how to commit suicide has been intentionally excluded.

Chapter 1 provides a historical, cultural, and legal overview, summarizes the contemporary debate in the United States, and briefly reviews practices around the world. In chapter 2, a brief

chronology documents the ebb and flow of the debate throughout the ages. Biographies of key figures, both historical and
current, comprise chapter 3.

Chapter 4 is divided into three categories: statistics, documents, and quotes. The first section contains charts and tables
interspersed with facts and statistics that graphically illustrate
some of the quantitative factors involved in the debate. The second section consists of key documents on the issue from the
medical, spiritual, and legal realms. The final section of this
chapter is devoted to points of view, presenting the words of
those who have shaped the debate.

Chapter 5 is an alphabetical listing of organizations that
address issues surrounding death and dying. Chapter 6 provides an annotated bibliography of the books and journals that
have added to our understanding of the right-to-die issue. Nonprint resources are found in chapter 7. Many of these, particularly the Internet entries, change or are updated with surprising
rapidity; the most significant and the most stable are listed. And
finally, a glossary defines terms commonly used in the context
of the euthanasia debate.

Acknowledgments

We would like to thank the following people for their contributions during the writing of this book. Many thanks to Henry Rasof for patience, clarity, and deadlines. A round of applause to the entire staff of the Boulder Public Library for their kind assistance, with special thanks to Janet Carabell and Pamela Watson for their professional commitment to making the library a truly valuable resource. Our profound thanks to Reverends Stanley Stefancic and Ralph Mero and to Christy Cruzan White for sharing their stories, wisdom, and expertise. A special thanks to Bruce Thompson and Hunter Margolf for support and wisdom all along the path, and to Laura Goodman for unstinting professional generosity and friendship. Our heartfelt thanks to Jenny Cox-Steiner and Gwen Barbee for believing. Most of all, thanks to our patient families: Jim, Soren, and Owen Roberts for their loving support; and Stu, Skylar, and Starin McKeen for surviving yet another round of "the book."

Overview

1

It is hard to open a newspaper in the United States today without finding at least one article that has some bearing on the end-of-life debate. Perhaps Dr. Jack Kevorkian, a retired Michigan pathologist, has helped another person commit suicide, or a famous person with AIDS has written about the agony of the terminal stage of this devastating illness. Maybe a religious leader has threatened to excommunicate any member who joins a right-to-die organization, or a court has overturned another law banning physician-assisted suicide. We are constantly bombarded with the stories of other people's end-of-life decisions. Sometimes the issue strikes even closer to home, and we must make decisions for ourselves or for those we love.

Euthanasia, one of the words most associated with the end-of-life debate, means different things to different people. The word is loaded with historical and emotional connotations. The dictionary definition offers ample room for interpretation: "The painless killing of a patient suffering from an incurable and painful disease," but nonetheless stops short of encompassing the constantly shifting practice of euthanasia (*Webster's* 1995). Not all of those who request euthanasia today are "patients," for instance, nor are they necessarily suffering from incurable illnesses. Moreover, modern medicine has made it possible for us to keep patients alive far beyond our ability to deal with the suffering that can ensue.

The word *euthanasia* would not exist were it the same as the act of suicide; euthanasia has a distinctly different character. Suicide is the act of taking one's own life, but not necessarily because all other options have been explored. Euthanasia is the final act of a painful struggle to live with dignity in the face of great pain or suffering that cannot necessarily be relieved. It is death as release, self-inflicted or with the aid of another.

The practice of euthanasia has been accepted and considered merciful as applied to farm animals. The veterinarian knows when to stop treatment and shoot the horse to avoid unnecessary and pointless suffering. Only when euthanasia is applied to human beings does our certainty waiver. The issue becomes murky, and we do not know how to behave. On the farm, there is much regret at the loss of a fine animal, but the farmer knows that he or she has done the right thing. There is rarely such clarity in the actions of individuals, physicians, and judges today when making decisions about ending the suffering of a fellow human. Euthanasia, however, is sometimes requested by those who are not terminally ill. People who experience extreme pain or who understand that their illness will result in a painful or gruesome end sometimes choose to take their own lives before they meet the criteria for a terminal diagnosis. For instance, people with Alzheimer's disease or Lou Gehrig's disease often seek an early death because these illnesses will, at some point, limit their ability to swallow and therefore restrict their ability to take a lethal prescription. Physician-assisted suicide, in which the physician provides the patient with a lethal means to end his or her own life—but does not administer it personally for them—is not an option for these patients; therefore, physician-assisted death, in which the doctor intentionally acts to end a patient's life (usually via lethal injection), is an effort to extend the same right to die that is exercised by those who are physically able to commit the act themselves to those who are unable to do so. Both of these practices are currently being debated around the world. The Northern Territory of Australia is the only place in the world that has instituted the legal provisions that allow physician-assisted death. The United States is in the process of legally defining physician-assisted suicide. In the Netherlands the medical profession and the courts have developed guidelines so that physicians can participate in

euthanasia and escape prosecution; thus, physician-assisted suicide and death are being refined in practice without benefit of
explicit legal sanction.

Today, many terminally ill people are requesting euthanasia
because, although modern medicine has made it possible to prolong life, a way has not yet been found to maintain an acceptable quality of life for all of those saved.

For many years, death was determined by the absence of
heart function. Now that doctors can keep the heart functioning,
death is determined by an absence of brain function. The technology that has made it possible for doctors to restart the heart and
maintain the body has created as many problems as it has solved,
particularly for the terminally ill patient. Many people do not
want their bodies kept alive if they cannot enjoy the things that
give their lives meaning. Others are in such excruciating pain that
death is a welcome release. These people want the choice to end
their lives when their situation becomes unbearable.

On the other side of the debate stand those who believe that
life must be saved at all costs and that nothing should be done
to end it on purpose. They worry that the current increase in
requests for euthanasia is the result of problems in our society
that need to be addressed in other ways. They believe that
euthanasia is just a euphemism for murder.

Recently, a Canadian woman brought the issue of physician-
assisted suicide to the front pages of North American newspapers. Sue Rodriguez's story posed the question that stands at
the forefront of the debate today: Should people unable to commit
suicide have the right to physician assistance in taking their lives?

Sue Rodriguez was diagnosed with amyotrophic lateral
sclerosis (ALS), commonly known as Lou Gehrig's disease, in
the early 1990s. ALS is a disease that destroys the nervous system but leaves the mind completely intact. Rodriguez's doctor
predicted that she had between two and five years to live. She
faced a death by either choking or suffocation when her control
over the muscles in her throat eventually deteriorated.

Rodriguez decided that she wanted to fight to live for as long
as possible, but when death became inevitable, she wanted to die
with a doctor's assistance. She was hoping to avoid a frightening
and painful end. She went to court to challenge Canadian law,
under which assisting another person to commit suicide is a
crime punishable by 14 years in prison. She lost her lower-court
battles as well as her appeal to the Canadian Supreme Court.

Sue Rodriguez did not simply battle ALS, she fought the
forces in society that exercised control over her life. During the

last 18 months of her life, she was inundated with letters, calls, and opinions. She became the focal point of heated discussions and political maneuvering. She kept her fighting spirit and her humor even as she lost the ability to comb her hair, eat, and speak clearly.

Some believed that Rodriguez had the right to make a decision about the manner and timing of her own death. They believed that, because she would be unable to take her life without help, she deserved the assistance of a physician to ensure a peaceful and dignified death.

Others were concerned that Sue Rodriguez would be just the first of many such deaths and that by legally sanctioning her death, the courts would pave the way for the elderly and the disabled to be eliminated by a society that doesn't value their lives. They were also concerned that participation by a physician would diminish societal trust in doctors.

On 12 February 1994 Sue Rodriguez died. She had indicated that her death would occur with the assistance of a physician, and this was confirmed by Svend Robinson, a member of Parliament who was present at the time of her death. Identifying this health care professional, whom she considered her savior, might have meant jail, so this individual has remained anonymous. Her death further forced the question of assisted suicide and euthanasia in general out into the open.

Although the current worldwide media blitz on the subject of euthanasia is unique to the contemporary era, the subject has been passionately debated for centuries. As perceptions of death and dying have shifted and our knowledge of medicine has increased, our perspective on euthanasia has evolved as well.

Early Attitudes toward Euthanasia

The Axial Age, from 500 to 200 B.C., is named for the powerful men who shaped the thinking of generations to come: Pythagoras, Socrates, Plato, and Aristotle in Greece, Confucius in China, and Buddha in India.

Because the word euthanasia originated in ancient Greece, it is often assumed that the ancient Greeks and Romans had a single, uncontested definition of the word. It is often translated as "good death," but the original interpretation of these words is not clearly defined for us. In Athens, magistrates kept a supply of poison for anyone who wanted to die; all that was needed was official permission. In Rome, suicide was punishable only if it was deemed irrational. For a Roman, to live nobly was to die nobly, and irrational actions were not considered noble.

But euthanasia was condemned by the Pythagoreans, who valued the spiritual nature of human existence. If God willed a person into existence, it was that person's duty to continue living. Socrates and Plato, on the other hand, valued man's ability to reason. Passages in *The Republic* indicate that Plato approved of voluntary euthanasia for adults and involuntary euthanasia for infants who were sick or defective. Socrates appears to have justified the latter because the ill and deformed placed a burden on the state. In *The Laws*, Plato wrote that suicide is acceptable only for people in four categories: those who take their lives by legal order of the state, those who are incurably ill, those who are disabled, and those who, having disgraced themselves beyond any hope of self-forgiveness, choose to atone for their actions through suicide. In all other cases, suicide was to be punished by a disgraced burial without a headstone, apart from other plots and on the periphery of the state in a nameless place. Socrates himself died by drinking hemlock, but not voluntarily; he was forced to do so by the state as a form of execution.

Plato's student, Aristotle, considered suicide an offense against the state. He viewed the individual as subject to the higher needs of society and saw depriving society of one of its workers as unacceptable. It appears he felt that death was the worst possible state and that one should strive to meet it nobly, with courage only when it became inevitable.

The Stoics believed suicide was an option when life was not in tune with nature. Suicide had to be the result of a rational choice made by the individual, not the state. Stoics believed life and death to be morally equal states; one was not considered better than the other. They did believe, however, that individuals would receive a sign from God indicating the correct time for their life to come to a close, and at this time, suicide became an option. Zeno, the founder of Stoicism, hanged himself at the age of 98.

The Hippocratic Oath, attributed to the famous Greek physician Hippocrates, appears to formally forbid euthanasia. "To please no one will I prescribe a deadly drug, nor give advice which may cause his death." This phrase and the dictum to "do no harm" are frequently cited to support this interpretation. There is, however, significant scholarly debate as to when the oath came into existence, the extent of its use in ancient times, and even who wrote it. In reviewing texts available from that time, scholar Paul Carrick, author of *Medical Ethics in Antiquity*, found that most physicians in Greek and Roman societies were probably unaware of its existence. There was "a discretionary professional right to assist in abortion or voluntary euthanasia," but physicians were not obliged either to perform or refrain from offering such services. Those physicians who knew about the oath may have interpreted it to mean that ethical practitioners must never misuse the privileged information to which they had access for personal gain or in a malicious manner. Moreover, putting an end to suffering was rarely necessary when the oath was written because people usually died quickly from illness or injury.

This view of the physician as a moral person with the freedom to make life-and-death choices on a case-by-case basis is seldom mentioned by those who use the Hippocratic Oath as proof of an ancient sanction against the practice of euthanasia or by those who use the Greek origins of the word euthanasia as proof of the practice during antiquity. In early Greece and Rome, physicians were like roving craftsmen, rarely connected to a single community. Their reputations hinged on their ability to effectively alleviate suffering. Some may have embraced euthanasia in futile cases in which there was no way to ameliorate pain. Some may also have practiced a form of passive euthanasia by refusing to treat those too sick to benefit from their ministrations. Physicians were subject to punishment, including death, if they were deemed to have mistreated a patient, but there is no evidence of a common code of ethics or licensure.

The Rise of Christianity

In A.D. 330, Christianity became the official religion of the Roman Empire. The rise of the Christian church has dramatically influenced Western opinions regarding euthanasia.

Acts of suicide were called *felo de se*—self-murder—and the church made no distinction between an emotional act of suicide and choosing to die because of a prolonged, terminal condition. Suicide in any form was strictly forbidden by the church because it held that God's will alone should determine life and death, and human interference was sinful. The belongings of those who took their own lives were confiscated to impoverish their families, and they were denied a Christian burial. Often their bodies were left on the side of the road, impaled on a stake.

Neoplatonism, a third-century school of philosophy, insisted that suicide adversely affected the soul after death. This stance, combined with the attitudes promoted by the Christian church, cemented negative attitudes regarding euthanasia during this period.

The Middle Ages

In the fifth century A.D., the Christian church, which influenced much of Europe, further stigmatized the concept of euthanasia by advancing martyrdom as a spiritual virtue, associating suffering with enhanced spiritual growth. In A.D. 562, the Council of Braga in France denied funeral rights to those who committed suicide, and soon the Catholic Church began to excommunicate anyone who committed or attempted to commit suicide. The killing of innocents was condemned. Not only was euthanasia a sin, but infanticide, suicide, and killing in self-defense were also deemed unacceptable throughout most of Western Europe. Only those who killed within the context of what the church considered a just war, or those who took the life of a criminal by state execution, were within the bounds set by the church. This code was followed throughout the Middle Ages.

In the Jewish culture, euthanasia was strictly forbidden. Practices involving the dying were governed by rules outlined by the twelfth-century physician and philosopher Maimonides in *The Misneh Torah: The Book of Judges* and were called the "Laws of Mourning." In essence, any act that caused a person to die, even someone who was already near death, was considered murder.

During this same period in Europe, the doctor-patient relationship began to change. Contracts between doctors and patients were now regularly put in writing. By the twelfth century, doctors had begun to form professional associations. This allowed educational, training, and practice standards to develop. Medical schools evolved from these physicians' guilds.

The Renaissance

Explosive scientific discovery dispelled superstitious beliefs in Western Europe during the Renaissance, radically altering attitudes regarding suicide. Between the fourteenth and the seventeenth centuries, physicians began dissecting cadavers to better understand disease in the body and identified particular organs as the sources of some illnesses. This prompted a shift to a more mechanistic view of the body—and, ultimately, of the patient as well. Significantly, during this time physicians also began to use tools, hitherto only employed by barber surgeons, not the high-minded physician who had historically used his brain rather than his hands. Doctors began the practice of taking a patient's temperature and pulse to help diagnose illnesses, and the body came to be seen more as a machine than as a divine mystery.

Ethical debates during this period focused on whether or not it was appropriate for a physician to deceive a patient if it facilitated a cure. Frightening a patient with the truth was seen as counterproductive. As reason gained respect, it once again became possible to discuss the concept of euthanasia. The Catholic and Protestant Churches continued to condemn the notion, and common law in England made suicide a crime, but people in general no longer viewed voluntary euthanasia as a terrible sin. There was a renewed interest in the concept of individual choice.

As scientific discovery gave rise to new methods for treating illnesses, the dilemmas caused by these medical advances and their potential to increase suffering were first considered. This fundamental aspect of the modern debate of euthanasia was originally addressed by English philosopher Francis Bacon, English statesman and author Thomas More, and English poet and clergyman John Donne.

The Age of Reason

By the eighteenth century, European and North American doctors began to talk about their responsibility to the patient, part of which, they thought, was ensuring that patients experienced a humane death. Medical advances, previously available to only the upper classes, had begun to filter down to the masses. The stethoscope, ophthalmoscope, and laryngoscope were all invented during this century, further demystifying the inner workings of the body. Popular opinion shifted away from punishing suicide. Rationalists thought it senseless to make a crime out of a personal act. By 1798, 6 of the original 13 American colonies had abolished all penalties for suicide, and there is no record of punishment for suicide in postrevolutionary America.

The Fourteenth Amendment to the U.S. Constitution, ratified in 1868, offered Americans protection of life and liberty and currently plays an important role in contemporary legal battles regarding euthanasia. In 1889, during a speech to the Maine Medical Association, Dr. Frank E. Hitchcock recommended that doctors not ignore the suffering of their terminally ill patients but instead allow them a humane release from their suffering. Mental or physical pain was considered sufficient cause for ending one's life.

As people in Western societies came to value the idea of standardizing and measuring the world around them in efficient and objective ways, discussions of euthanasia became less academic and more concrete. Doctors and policymakers looked for ways to save people with formerly hopeless injuries and fatal diseases. Other physicians and philosophers promoted the right of individuals to make autonomous choices about their own lives. Some sanctioned euthanasia for those unable to decide for themselves due to lack of intelligence or severe disease.

The United States in the Early 1900s

In 1901 the New Jersey Supreme Court ruled that suicide should not be considered a crime, basing this decision on the fact that there was no way to punish the defendant. In 1906 a bill was introduced in the Ohio legislature to legalize voluntary euthanasia. The bill had some safeguards: The patient would need three witnesses, and three physicians would have to be consulted before any action could be taken. The bill was defeated 78–22.

Though there was widespread support for voluntary euthanasia during this time, people were generally against involuntary euthanasia, or mercy killing, which involves taking someone's life without his or her consent. Although mercy killings did occur, they were considered murder and people were prosecuted for their actions.

Another petition, this time in 1913 in the New York state legislature, provoked the president of the American Medical Association to declare that physicians who performed any type of euthanasia demeaned the profession. The number of euthanasia cases brought to trial increased dramatically between the 1920s and 1940s, forcing lawmakers and the public to wrangle regularly with the issue of legalization.

Public debate became more and more polarized as legal battles escalated. Physicians began to speak out more frequently, providing the public with accounts of patients forced to die lingering deaths in great pain. Groups formed to support voluntary euthanasia as a humanitarian act. The British Voluntary Euthanasia Society formed in 1935; the Euthanasia Society of America was founded by the Reverand Charles Francis Potter in 1938. Polls taken during this period indicate that the general public and physicians alike were nearly evenly split on the issue.

In 1920 Germans Karl Binding and Alfred Hoche wrote *Permission for the Destruction of Life Unworthy of Life*, a pivotal tract promoting euthanasia. It espoused the individual's right to die and advocated physician assistance to help end a patient's life to relieve suffering. The paper also addressed the concept that a disabled or mentally incompetent person could be considered a drain on society. The authors asserted that those who are mentally impaired or handicapped are unable to feel suffering and thus could not give consent, making their consent to die unnecessary. The actual cost associated with the care and housing of those individuals was enumerated. To a German populace reeling under the expense of World War I and having been asked to sacrifice, work hard, and contribute to the war effort in every way possible, this paper brought home the idea that some members of society were consuming scarce resources that could be redirected toward those who were contributing the most.

It took less than a decade for these ideas and actions to be transformed into a eugenics policy under which people determined to be *lebensunwerten Leben*, or "life not worthy of life," were eliminated by the state.

World War II and Nazi Germany

In Germany during the 1920s and 1930s, the killing of the handicapped, mentally ill, and others in asylums began to be covertly sanctioned by the government. This eugenics effort came to be called the "Euthanasia Programme," a name that has since haunted the right-to-die debate. What the German government called euthanasia was actually murder on a grand scale, which swayed popular opinion away from acceptance of euthanasia. Nazi propaganda had roused the German public into a state of indignation. By comparing the finest in asylum conditions with the lifestyle of an average German worker suffering under severe war shortages, propaganda films fed resentment among a citizenry already feeling deprived. The Nazis promoted a Darwinistic view of human life in which only the fittest should survive.

The phrase *unnutze esser*, or "useless eater," came into use. A typical propaganda poster depicted two midget-sized asylum residents perched on a log resting like a crucifix across the bent back of a huge German worker. Many of those eliminated early in the eugenics program were culled from the country's church-run asylums. The weakest members of society were more easily eliminated because controls, normally exerted by family members, the law, and the church, had fallen by the wayside due to harsh economic times.

Germany was a modern nation in which the law was highly structured and efficient, the people well educated and sophisticated. The calculated cruelty of the eugenics program was thus all the more unexpected. When the atrocities were revealed, people around the world realized that if murder on this scale could happen in Germany, it could happen anywhere. The real possibility of abuse by a seemingly moral people and a legal government was demonstrated with horrifying clarity. This period in history changed the way an entire generation interpreted the word *euthanasia* and spawned the slippery-slope argument, which maintains that, if a society condones voluntary euthanasia, soon people will begin to devalue all life.

Some argue, however, that the German government did not slide down a slippery slope, but rather conjured up a horrifying vision and then created the means to carry it out. According to Michael Burleigh, author of *Death and Deliverance: Euthanasia in Germany c. 1900–1945* (1994), between 1939 and 1945 the Nazis systematically murdered as many as 200,000 mentally ill or physically disabled individuals. This program provided much of the personnel and technical expertise later deployed in the Final Solution program under which 6 million Jews were systematically murdered.

Two years after the war ended, a poll of Americans revealed that there was less support for euthanasia than there had been before the war. Euthanasia had come to be viewed as immoral and anti-American.

The Age of Medical Miracles, 1940–1990

The 1940s and 1950s marked an era of explosive change in the field of medicine. Physicians acquired powerful new tools to add to their disease-fighting arsenal, including polio and measles vaccines, tetracycline, and erythromycin. Medical technology made it possible to sustain life under circumstances in which death previously would have occurred as a matter of course.

This period also marked the beginning of an increase in patient requests for death. In 1950 the United Nations received a petition from the Euthanasia Society in England signed by 387 high-ranking Britons. It requested that an amendment to the Declaration of Human Rights include the right of incurable sufferers to voluntary euthanasia. More than 2,000 doctors and clergy also signed the petition.

That same year, at the General Assembly of the World Medical Association, a discussion on euthanasia grew heated, and a vote was taken to approve a resolution condemning euthanasia in all countries around the globe. Popular opinion polls revealed that approval for euthanasia was once again on the rise in the United States. Many people felt that some form of legislation was necessary to ensure that incurably ill patients were given the opportunity to end their lives with appropriate safeguards in place.

During this same period, the subject of euthanasia began to appear in newspapers as physicians and family members were brought to trial. The first of these trials was that of New Hampshire physician Herman N. Sander, who was charged with first-degree murder in 1950 for taking the life of a female patient with incurable cancer. The trial ended in acquittal because the jury felt there was no way to conclude beyond a reasonable doubt that the woman hadn't already died. The court in this case avoided a mercy-killing ruling, which most likely would have landed Sander in jail. The acquittal added fuel to the debate outside of the courtroom.

Other physicians spoke out during meetings of the Euthanasia Society, admitting they had provided incurable patients with information on how to self-deliver, or commit, suicide. They accomplished this by indicating that ingesting the entire bottle of pain medication would be fatal. By presenting this information as a warning rather than a suggestion, they avoided accusations of coercion but were still effective in supplying patients with the information they needed to take their own lives. More than a quarter of a century would go by before the legal system would begin to address the conditions that forced doctors and patients to act on their own in order to deal with these situations.

As these questions were vigorously debated, medical progress continued. DNA's role in heredity was explored and lasers were developed in the 1950s, and the first human heart transplant took place in 1967. The physician's ability to stave off death was growing by leaps and bounds.

A New Concept of Death

Brain death was a concept first suggested by two French neuro-physiologists, Mallaret and Goulon, in 1959. Their studies, which other researchers built on throughout the 1960s, led to the release of a landmark report in 1968 by the Ad Hoc Committee from the Harvard Medical School that redefined clinical death by laying down the criteria for brain death. The state of Kansas adopted the first statute defining brain death in 1970 (1970 KAN.SESS.LAWS 378) (KAN.STAT.ANN.SS 77-202 (1971)) and during this same year began allowing organs to be taken from legally deceased patients for transplantation. Other states soon followed with their own statutes.

The need for a new definition of death had arisen because of advances in medicine that made organ transplants possible. Doctors needed concrete criteria under which they could declare the patient dead, then restart the heart and keep the organs viable until they could be transplanted.

In 1969 a mentally retarded infant with an intestinal blockage was starved to death at Johns Hopkins University Hospital when the parents of the child refused to give permission for surgery. It took 15 days for the baby to die. This was a common practice at the time, although not one about which the public was generally aware. Public awareness got a boost when doctors from Johns Hopkins released a film about the baby that was aired on national television. Some doctors were uncomfortable with the idea of silently euthanizing patients and began asking for outside input. The need for some kind of policy became acute as the general public became a more informed participant in the end-of-life debate.

This was a period of polarization in the United States. Members of the clergy formed the strongest opposition to the legalization of euthanasia. Spiritual arguments revolved around the value of suffering and the idea that no one but God should take life. Euthanasia became grist for sermons, women's club discussions, and library and university speakers. New terms such as passive and active euthanasia and ordinary and extraordinary treatments came into use as society began to come to grips with the myriad options medical technology had begun to provide. And arguments over the meanings of these words, as well as the actions they described, became more and more frequent.

In 1974 the National Conference Steering Committee of the American Medical Association released new standards for CPR and emergency cardiac care, which included a recommendation that emergency teams be allowed to perform these treatments without waiting for a formal doctor's order. These recommendations were the culmination of a series of national panels formed to set standards for this exciting and important new therapy. It was also during this period that the first "do not resuscitate" orders, or DNR orders, came into existence. Doctors realized that resuscitation was not always appropriate for terminally ill patients. The American Heart Association released a policy statement to this effect as early as 1974.

Uniform DNR Orders and Patient Consent

Hospitals had always had their own internal criteria for DNR orders, but they had rarely involved patients in the determination process. Problems arising from two New York hospitals and their questionable DNR policies brought the matter under the investigative eyes of the courts and prompted the creation of a uniform policy for DNR orders.

By the late 1970s a study by the President's Commission for the Study of Ethical Problems in Medicine and Biomedical and Behavioral Research revealed that 20 percent of all physicians and 45 percent of nurses agreed that patients had a right to be completely informed about their prognosis. The American Hospital Association published A Patient's Bill of Rights in 1973. It began the movement toward the Patient Self-Determination Act, or the PSDA. The concept of informed consent was gathering speed. Patient consent became a requirement of the formal DNR policies that began to appear in 1976.

Virtually everyone who dies suffers from cardiac arrest at some point. This means that, as far back as 1950, nearly everyone could be resuscitated as well. However, resuscitation using CPR, electrical shock, or artificial respiration often saves bodies but not necessarily lives. The social and emotional dilemmas caused by these new therapies began to punctuate the daily life of the average citizen through news reports and coffee-table conversations. People began to wonder if "doing everything possible" was what they really wanted. The tragic story of Karen Ann Quinlan only intensified the questioning.

The Case of Karen Ann Quinlan

On 15 April 1975, 21-year-old Karen Ann Quinlan was brought to a New Jersey hospital in an alcohol- and drug-induced coma. Her doctors agreed after monitoring her condition for several months that she had suffered irreversible brain damage and was in a persistent vegetative state. Her parents decided to remove the respirator (at the time considered extraordinary means) that kept her alive. Hospital officials at first agreed with the Quinlans' decision but later changed their minds. The Quinlans went to court. By the time the New Jersey court ruled in favor of the Quinlans, Karen Ann had been weaned from the respirator by her Catholic nurse and thus was able to breathe on her own. She remained in a persistent vegetative state for another eight years, nourished by food and water through a tube surgically implanted in her stomach. This medical intervention—called artificial nutrition and hydration—was considered to be an ordinary (not extraordinary) treatment. Removing food and water to hasten death was not even a consideration at the time. Quinlan died in 1985 from pneumonia.

The Quinlan case was heard in the New Jersey Supreme Court in 1976 (*In re Quinlan*, 70 N.J. 10, 355 A.2d 647, cert. denied, 429 U.S. 922: 1976). The refusal of life-saving treatment, in this case the respirator, fell under the constitutional right to privacy, a right that is held regardless of a patient's competence. The right to refuse treatment could be exercised by a surrogate, the court decided, if the individual was unable to act on his or her own behalf: "The only practical way to prevent destruction of the right is to permit the guardian and family of Karen to render their best judgment, subject to the qualifications hereinafter stated, as to whether she would exercise it in these circumstances.... In this case there is a real distinction made between the unlawful taking of the life of another and the ending of artificial life-support systems as a matter of self-determination." The qualifications asserted that the guardian would be charged with rendering the decision that would best match that of the incompetent patient: "We have no doubt in these unhappy circumstances that, if Karen were herself miraculously lucid for an interval (not altering the existing prognosis of the condition to which she would soon return) and perceptive of her irreversible condition, she could effectively decide upon discontinuation of the life-support apparatus, even if it meant the prospect of natural death." This precedent is known in the courts as the substituted judgment standard.

Advance Directives

Before the Quinlan case only five states had introduced right-to-die legislation. In the year following the first national coverage of this case, 67 pieces of legislation dealing with end-of-life issues were introduced; 8 were passed. The Quinlan case sparked the formation of hospital ethics committees to ensure that decisions in the best interests of patients were being rendered by guardians. Disturbing questions about life-preserving medical technologies also received greater attention. The number of scholarly articles and popular-press reports concerning the right to die multiplied the following year, as did the number of people requesting living wills.

A living will is a legal document designed to provide family, hospital, and physicians with an understanding of an individual's wishes for medical treatment in the event of incapacitation. This document must be signed while a person is mentally competent and in good health so that it is clear that the decisions are made when the patient is of sound mind and without coercion. A living will is only executed if a person is unable to participate in decisions involving his or her own care. This usually happens when a person is in an irreversible terminal condition with little hope for recovery, has suffered brain damage, or is in a coma. Living wills primarily cover extreme and somewhat rare situations.

The durable power of attorney, or health care proxy, is another legal instrument developed during this time. It allows an individual to designate a proxy to make decisions in the event that he or she should become unable to do so. It further allows an individual to designate the degree of authority he or she is comfortable handing over to the proxy and what form that authority will take. This document provides a great deal of flexibility and is more effective than a living will in assuring that an individual's specific wishes will be understood. Unlike a regular power of attorney, a health care proxy remains valid until and unless it is revoked by the person who signed it.

All 50 states and the District of Columbia have statutes allowing for some form of durable power of attorney. It is considered wise to have both a living will and a durable power of attorney to help assure that end-of-life wishes are followed.

These legal instruments seemed, at the time they were developed, sufficient to serve the needs of those who wished to be able to choose the right to die, but the debate was far from over. The word euthanasia began to be associated less with a "noble death" than with making a decision about the timing and manner of one's death in order to minimize the loss of dignity suffered by patients in modern medical settings. New questions and definitions would emerge as another young woman's story made history.

The Case of Nancy Cruzan

In 1983, 25-year-old Nancy Cruzan lost control of her car and crashed into a ravine on a rural Missouri road. She survived the crash but was left permanently brain-damaged. As Nancy's family dealt with this painful tragedy, their story became national news, forcing the nation to reexamine—once again—its beliefs about the right to die.

Before her accident, Nancy Cruzan was a vibrant young woman. Oxygen deprivation caused by the massive injuries she suffered in the accident had left her in a deep coma, later diagnosed as a persistent vegetative state. Her family fought to bring her out of the coma. They talked to her, decorated her room, and stroked her constantly. After four long years, with no change in her condition, they realized that she was not going to emerge from this state.

Nancy, unlike Karen Ann Quinlan, was not on a ventilator when the decision was made to end her life. The only life-sustaining treatment that could be withdrawn in Nancy's case was the artificial nutrition and hydration supplied through her feeding tube. Her parents decided to have the tube removed. People already opposed to withdrawing any treatments were inflamed by the idea that Nancy would die from starvation and dehydration.

Right-to-life groups fought the family's decision with passion, afraid of what the consequences to society would be if the Cruzans were legally allowed to take steps to hasten death by removing what was then considered an ordinary treatment. The rehabilitation center in which Nancy was housed also disagreed with the family. The Cruzans went to court, they fought for what they believed Nancy would have wanted, and they were challenged every step of the way.

Nancy had left no written instructions regarding her end-of-life wishes. Initially, the court felt that the state's interest in maintaining the sanctity of life overrode the quality-of-life arguments presented by the Cruzan family. The Cruzans appealed this decision. On 25 June 1990, in *Cruzan v. Director, Missouri Department of Health*, the U.S. Supreme Court recognized the right to die as a constitutionally protected liberty interest. Its decision maintained that the right to refuse treatment, including artificial nutrition and hydration, is guaranteed in the Liberty Clause of the Constitution.

The court, however, erected boundaries around this liberty by requiring that "clear and convincing evidence" of a person's preferences regarding end-of-life decision making be provided before any action could be taken. Each state was required to establish standards of evidence to protect individuals against abuse and thus maintain the interests of the state in preserving life.

The Cruzans returned to the Missouri state courts for a determination as to whether or not clear and convincing evidence existed in Nancy's case. The testimony of several of Nancy's friends involving conversations they had had with her about end-of-life issues prior to her accident provided the court with this "clear and convincing evidence," and it ruled that Nancy Cruzan had the right to die. Her surgically implanted feeding tube was removed on 14 December 1990. Surrounded by her family, Nancy died 11 days later.

During the 11-day death watch, right-to-life protesters stood outside the rehabilitation center where Nancy was housed, singing, praying, and holding placards emblazoned with statements like "PLEASE FEED NANCY." Some of them tried to reach Nancy's room to reconnect her feeding tube, and many had to be carried out of the stairwells when they refused to leave the premises. These people spoke out in adamant opposition to the court's decision, protesting what they called the murder of Nancy Cruzan.

And so the contemporary battle lines were drawn and the weapons of choice—words—were carefully chosen. Those who championed the individual's right to euthanasia or assisted suicide used the words self-deliverance, hastening death, or death with dignity. Those who opposed these practices used words like killing, murder, and infanticide. Both sides were referring to the same actions and believed passionately in their points of view.

The Patient Self-Determination Act (PSDA)

The case of Nancy Cruzan was one of the most significant legal battles concerning euthanasia. It revealed to a wide audience the complexity of the medical decision-making process and motivated Missouri Senator John Danforth to introduce the Patient Self-Determination Act (PSDA).

As the first legislation outlining uniform advance directives, the PSDA was a critical first step toward clarifying the responsibilities of the physician, the patient, the family, and health care facilities. It superseded all state-level living-will legislation when it went into effect on 1 December 1991, and guaranteed all individuals residing in the United States access to advance directives. In this way it provided the courts with a vehicle by which clear and convincing evidence of an individual's end-of-life wishes could be demonstrated. A month before Nancy died, in November 1990, the PSDA was passed by Congress and signed into law by President George Bush.

This legislation remains in effect today. The wording and restrictions of advance directives are different in each state, and doctors and family members may only execute those documents that are legal in the state in which they reside. In some states, family members may authorize the withdrawal of artificial nutrition and hydration from, or treatment of, an unresponsive pregnant patient; other states do not allow these measures. Almost all states require that an individual be 18 years old to complete a living will (except Oklahoma, where the age is 21, and Kansas, which does not specify an age). The definition of terminal illness also varies from state to state.

Right-to-life organizations have developed parallel directives, known as "right-to-live" documents, as an alternative form of advance directive for those who wish to be kept alive at all costs.

Euthanasia in Practice Today

The practice of euthanasia has varied over the centuries. Since 1990 acts that are considered euthanasia have fallen into three basic categories: (1) withholding or withdrawing treatment, (2) mercy killing/assisted suicide, and (3) physician-assisted suicide. These categories have, for the most part, been defined by the courts for terminally ill individuals.

Withholding or Withdrawing Treatment

Withholding or withdrawing treatment happens when patients or their proxies choose to forego life-saving medications or antibiotics, food or water, artificial respiration, or any resuscitative measure, such as CPR, that would prolong life. People make this choice, to a large extent, because their expected quality of life is unacceptable to them.

Mercy Killing/Assisted Suicide

Mercy killing occurs when someone kills a suffering individual who is unable to either request or perform the act. It is the only form of euthanasia that is involuntary. People on both sides of the debate are very concerned about the lack of consent in these deaths.

Physician-Assisted Suicide

Physician-assisted suicide, in which a doctor assists a competent adult to voluntarily end his or her own life, is the form of euthanasia that currently sits at the forefront of the debate. Large numbers of people want to die but are unable or unwilling to commit suicide by themselves; they require or would prefer a physician to assist them in dying. The numerous concerns surrounding this issue will be examined in greater detail in the following section.

The Impact of Managed Care

The health care delivery system changed dramatically during the 1990s. Managed care, which replaced traditional health insurance plans with Health Maintenance Organizations (HMOs), Preferred Provider Organizations (PPOs), and the like, radically altered the doctor-patient relationship. By the middle of the decade, the family doctor in private practice in the United States had been virtually replaced by a "designated medical provider," who more often than not, was the doctor who happened to be on call in a clinic setting, rather than a single individual. This impacts the end-of-life debate in two very important ways.

First, a doctor who only sees a patient sporadically when on call has a far more difficult time giving valid, valuable advice regarding end-of-life decisions to terminally ill patients and their family members than would a consistent, personal physician. The "gatekeeper" position given to general practitioners within managed care delivery systems attempts to provide case management for each patient, but it often falls short of engendering the close relationship that once existed between family physicians and their patients.

Second, doctors who once owned their own medical practices are now employees of managed care organizations; thus it is the corporation, rather than an individual physician, that sets treatment standards and practices and dictates priorities. The bottom line of the corporation and its responsibility to shareholders to show a profit could take precedence over the needs of individual patients. Given this context, the questions must be raised: What if it is cheaper to end a patient's life than to treat a serious medical condition, but the patient wishes to live? Were physician-assisted death legal, where would the doctor's loyalties lie—with the employer or with the patient? There are currently few safeguards in place to ensure that the desires of the patient are always honored.

The Right to Equal Protection

During the first several months of 1996, two important legal decisions advanced the practice of physician-assisted suicide and began to pave the way toward legalized physician-assisted death in the United States. Both cases were filed by the organization Compassion in Dying, along with patients and physicians.

The first decision, made in Washington State by the Ninth Circuit Court, struck down a ban on assisted suicide that had been in effect since 1854. This decision gave people in the northwest United States the right to request a physician's assistance in obtaining a lethal dose of medication for the purpose of ending their own lives. The plaintiff in the case asked the court to acknowledge that some patients were being denied equal protection under the Constitution because, although they might be suffering from a terminal illness, they had no life-sustaining interventions to withdraw and were therefore not afforded the same opportunity to die with the care and support available in a medical setting or with a physician overseeing their care. This case builds on the rights established in the Cruzan case, further delineating the boundaries of the right to die. It was the first case in which a full federal appeals court rendered a decision on this issue.

The second decision, made in New York by the Second Circuit Court, also ruled that equal protection under the Constitution entitled patients to physician-assisted suicide through prescription medications. The court saw no difference between removing life-sustaining interventions and providing a lethal prescription to hasten death.

Those who promote the legalization of physician-assisted death assert that the individual should be able to choose the manner and timing of death and that the method should be equally available to all people, regardless of their ability to self-administer a lethal prescription, for example.

Many who argue against the legalization of any form of euthanasia or assisted death do so in part because they feel that an individual's actions in this area directly impact the safety of other vulnerable members of society whose protection is also the responsibility of the courts and of society at large. Acceptance of this practice, they say, will cheapen life and pave the way for abuses to occur. Various groups have promised to appeal the above decisions to the Supreme Court for further consideration.

The Contemporary Debate

The key issues around which the debate in the United States, Australia, and the Netherlands is currently focused can be divided into medical-bioethical, spiritual-social-cultural, and legal-political concerns.

End-of-life decisions are generally precipitated by illness and/or suffering, so the most logical place to begin to explore the contemporary debate on this topic is with medical-bioethical issues. This section encompasses concerns and arguments that emanate primarily from patients and health care providers and that focus on the health care delivery system as it impacts end-of-life decisions.

However, because physicians, hospitals, and medical ethicists cannot and should not unilaterally make end-of-life decisions on behalf of individuals, the decison-making process must then enter the spiritual-social-cultural realm. Within this arena, issues having to do with quality of life, religious beliefs, cultural norms, and economic concerns come into play.

Frequently, the medical establishment with its institutionalized ethical concerns collides with the personal, cultural, or religious beliefs or desires of the individual patient. These questions then end up in the legal system, where judges are asked to mediate questions of life and death in ways that have political implications that reach far beyond the individual whose end-of-life dilemma precipitated the act or law that can result. The legal-political section includes the arguments and decisions that have been made or that are currently being deliberated in an attempt to further define the right to die, primarily in the United States, Australia, and the Netherlands.

Medical-Bioethical Concerns

Medical-bioethical concerns about euthanasia can be grouped into three broad categories: (1) quality of life, (2) how decisions at the end of life are made, and (3) the physician's changing role in end-of-life actions. These concerns generate a broad spectrum of opinion on both sides of the debate.

Quality of Life

Quality of life is a concept that has been defined and redefined over the past 30 years. Today, the perception of quality of life revolves around dignity as determined by the individual; thus, the courts now support an individualistic approach to this issue, rather than imposing a society-wide prescription for what constitutes quality of life. The ability to determine when one's own life has lost meaning or has become too painful to bear underlies our current definition of this concept. Advance directives now allow individuals, should they become incompetent, to express their preferences via proxies.

Extraordinary Measures

For victims of trauma, accidents, and heart attacks, cardiopulmonary resuscitation (CPR) is a lifesaver. An arsenal of expensive, life-saving interventions such as ventilators, feeding tubes, and antibiotics can keep individuals alive who would have died had they suffered from the same medical problems just a few short decades ago. These interventions are also used on terminally ill patients, but they are not always effective in providing patients with a quality of life that is acceptable to them.

Many terminally ill patients are revived by CPR, only to face a protracted death in an intensive care unit (ICU), surrounded by machines instead of family. Often these patients cannot breathe on their own, so they are hooked up to a ventilator that performs this vital function for them. If they are unable to eat or drink, food and water are provided through a tube inserted through their nose or into their stomach. Infections, a common problem in ICUs, are combated with antibiotics.

For years people have been questioning whether these interventions are appropriate. It is argued on the one hand that, although this medical arsenal has saved many lives, it only prolongs the dying process of the terminally ill. People want to have the choice to forego these interventions under certain circumstances. Many medical professionals agree with this point of view. One study published in the *American Journal of Public Health* (January 1993) found that 47 percent of the physicians and 70 percent of the house officers (residents or interns) surveyed had acted against their conscience in providing this kind of care to their terminally ill patients.

In a survey of critical care nurses reported in the *New England Journal of Medicine* in May 1996, 16 percent of the 1,139 nurses who responded indicated that they had assisted patients in euthanasia or assisted suicide. An additional 4 percent had hastened the death of their patients by not following the physician's orders as they were recorded on the charts. In some of these cases, the physician was also complicit in the decision to record a treatment while actually not providing it.

Opponents of euthanasia generally applaud the use of these extraordinary measures, even for terminally ill patients. CPR, they believe, should be administered to all patients because it gives individuals a chance at life and allows doctors to further assess their condition. Opponents feel that, unless we make every attempt to save life, we are going to allow emergency personnel and other health care workers the leeway to make on-the-spot decisions about who to save. Food and water are, in many people's minds, ordinary care that should never be withdrawn or withheld. They believe that it is cruel to starve and dehydrate a patient to death and that these basic needs should always be met. Some believe that we should be trying to save life no matter what the quality of that life will be. There are physicians who support this position as well, believing that it is their duty to save life at all costs.

Nurses represent the largest group of health care professionals in the United States. As the primary sources of delivery of health care services in this country, both the American Nurses Association and the American Association of Critical Care have released position statements indicating that nurses should not participate in assisted suicide. How these positions are actually acted upon has yet to be clearly defined.

Pain

Pain, loss of such functions as the ability to eat, and social interaction, are the most common reasons people ask to die. This is particularly true in contemporary medical settings, where, for example, ventilators cause so much discomfort that many patients need drugs to keep them from gagging or pulling the tubes out. Doctors often are unable to ameliorate the pain and suffering caused by illnesses such as AIDS and cancer. Ceaseless pain can be very frightening.

Several studies, such as "Guidelines on the Termination of Life-Sustaining Treatment and the Care of the Dying" (a report released by the Hastings Center in 1987), have shown that doctors and nurses often assume that patients overreport pain. As a result, they may provide inadequate pain relief. Many health professionals limit pain medications in an effort to minimize the patient's risk of becoming addicted, even though it has been shown that this is a meaningless precaution for the terminally ill patient.

Proponents of euthanasia feel it is cruel to prolong a life so racked with pain that it cannot be lived with dignity or basic comfort. They press for the right to die and the right to refuse treatment because they believe that life-sustaining measures often only cause a patient to suffer a protracted, excruciating, and undignified end. Family members forced to stand by and watch also are traumatized. Proponents point out that the average four-year medical program devotes only four hours to the study of pain relief. The Hastings Center study also revealed that many health care professionals lack the training necessary to provide relief for their dying patients.

People who advocate solutions other than euthanasia believe that providing training in pain relief can bring the profession up to speed with current medical technology and the wide array of choices it affords. They assert that progress is being made in the treatment of pain at the end of life and that we should be expanding upon this progress instead of offering people a quick route to death. They claim that many terminally ill patients would not want to die if their pain were properly managed.

Persistent Vegetative State

Patients who are in a coma or who have suffered irreparable brain damage and are in a persistent vegetative state (PVS) are not considered terminally ill. They can be kept alive for decades. Elaine Esposito, a woman who fell into a coma during routine surgery, survived in a persistent vegetative state for 37 years and 111 days!

In the United States today there are approximately 14,000 patients diagnosed as being in a persistent vegetative state. PVS patients make up 40 percent of all of the right-to-die cases that the courts have heard over the past several decades, and it costs between $1 and $7 billion each year to keep these patients alive, according to a study published by the Multi-Society Task Force on PVS in the 2 June 1994 issue of the *New England Journal of Medicine*.

Because the brain stem of PVS patients is usually intact, they experience sleep/wake cycles, their eyes open and close, and they have muscle spasms. They are not, however, in control of these functions, they do not respond to outside stimulation, and the higher functions of the brain that control intellectual and emotional abilities are lost. This makes their suffering difficult to define. Even if these patients were to recover (which is highly unlikely once they have remained in this state for more than a month), they would be severely disabled and would require constant medical attention for the rest of their lives.

Those who favor euthanasia and physician-assisted suicide feel that doctors, with guidelines and safeguards in place, should be able to offer these patients' families a realistic prognosis based upon the best data available and be allowed to follow their patients' wishes to die without the threat of legal or professional repercussions. It is cruel and wasteful, they say, to keep PVS patients' bodies alive when they have no discernible quality of life.

Those who oppose a hastened death for these patients feel that as long as the patient is alive, there is still hope. They argue that we still do not know enough about these cases to make firm predictions about what kind of quality of life these patients can expect to have. There have been cases in which patients have emerged from vegetative states and gone on living. If we cut short these lives, those who might have recovered some quality of life will lose that opportunity.

This position became more salient after the story of Gary Dockery was reported around the world. Dockery, a policeman who had been diagnosed as being in a form of vegetative state but who miraculously began talking in February of 1996, demonstrated that the criteria for vegetative states will need to be further refined before many people will feel comfortable making the decision to end a loved one's life based on this diagnosis.

People with Disabilities

People with disabilities who favor the legalization of euthanasia or physician-assisted suicide see euthanasia as providing choice in dying. They feel unfairly burdened by a system that glorifies the idea of saving a life but then passes off the burden of dealing with the aftermath to others. In other cases, they say, severely handicapped individuals have been forced to suffer because they were physically unable to commit suicide by themselves. Without physician-assisted death, it is argued, these people face end-of-life discrimination.

Others with disabilities have raised serious concerns about the legalization of euthanasia because they are afraid these laws could be abused by doctors and others who deem their lives not worth living. Studies have shown that physician assessment of patient quality of life is consistently lower than the assessment made by the patients themselves (Pearlman et al. 1986; Pearlman and Uhlmann 1991). Many feel that there is a dangerous potential whereby those whose lives are perceived as less meaningful, including the disabled, the elderly, and babies with serious birth defects such as spina bifida and anacephaly, might be encouraged to die based on the quality of life doctors expect them to have rather than based on their wishes or their proxy's wishes.] Those who argue that euthanasia is a crime feel that every individual should have a chance at life—even if their life is considered less worthy by others. They believe the protection of society is needed to ensure that equal treatment is received.

Incompetent Patients

What if the patient is unable to make a decision on his or her own behalf? Some have prepared advance directives and made their wishes known. But for newborns with serious birth defects and others lacking advance directives there are concerns about who should decide their fate and on what criteria those decisions should be based.)

Those who favor euthanasia assert that doctors often rush in to save the lives of newborns who otherwise would have died, and then walk away from the neonatal ICU without taking any responsibility for the quality of life with which the child and the family are left to cope. They argue that parents should have the opportunity to make decisions on behalf of their own children without interference from medical personnel or the courts.

This can also be true when medical decisions must be made on behalf of incompetent adults. Patients with advanced Alzheimer's disease who have left no living will are a good example. Why should a life that seems to have lost all meaning continue, even when the adult children know that their parent would not have wanted to live in this undignified manner simply because there is no legal mechanism available to allow him or her to die? This is the point at which the family's desire to protect their loved one's quality of life often comes into conflict with the mission of the medical profession, which is charged with safeguarding every patient's life. In the United States this drama is now being played out before ethics committees on a routine basis.

Opponents of euthanasia, including many health care professionals, argue that ending such lives constitutes infanticide and murder. They also worry that severely mentally retarded patients who are unable to understand the ramifications of their illness and its treatment might be killed by the very health care system charged with treating them if the state no longer maintained strict laws that place a high value on their lives. Elderly patients whose children tire of caring for them might choose to have them euthanized and would have the opportunity to do so legally if such laws were passed.

Who Decides?

How decisions are made and who is charged with making them are important aspects of the euthanasia debate. Defining the rights of the individual, the responsibilities of the doctor, and the criteria used in making end-of-life decisions is a complicated task that itself causes much debate.

Those who advocate euthanasia believe that the timing and manner of death should be a personal decision, not one made by a doctor, hospital, or court. Patients, or their families (if the patient is incompetent), should have the final say about when enough is enough. These assertions are based on the belief that a condition that is acceptable to one person may be unbearable for another and that the state cannot create a law that will fulfill everyone's wishes.

Those who argue against the practice of euthanasia worry that seriously ill or terminally ill people are often, by the very nature of their circumstances, depressed. They may choose to end their lives during what, for many, is a temporary, treatable state of depression. Euthanasia opponents believe that the state is charged with the responsibility of making sure that these people's lives are protected. They argue that a doctor's prognosis has never been considered unequivocal and that relying on this inexact science to make life-or-death decisions is very risky. Some patients die just as their physicians predict, while others live, many for periods of time and with a quality of life that initially seemed impossible based upon available data. Opponents feel that, if we begin to follow strict criteria to assess when to give up on a patient, we will be giving up on people who might have regained consciousness or a quality of life that seemed forever lost.

Diagnosis

The unreliability of medical diagnoses is an important issue in end-of-life decision making. The ambiguity leaves ample room for discussion but very little in the way of concrete guidance for those who have to make recommendations and decisions. Ethics committees, ethicists, medical associations, and others are always looking for ways to make a more accurate prognosis, thus providing the patient or family with the most concrete information available to make a decision.

A computerized system called APACHE III (Acute Physiology and Chronic Health Evaluation III) has been developed by Dr. William Knaus of George Washington University Medical Center to track deaths. In use in more than 400 hospitals, it offers a glimpse of the future of bedside decision making. This huge database makes it possible to compare the vital signs of each patient with those of hundreds of thousands of others. After comparing the data, APACHE III provides a numerical assessment of a patient's risk of dying.

Those who favor the use of computerized outcomes analysis and diagnostic tools claim that these will offer both patients and doctors more and better criteria for making decisions. It also promises to relieve some of the psychological burden health professionals face daily.

Those who are against the practice of euthanasia feel that developments such as APACHE III only serve to distance physicians further from their patients. If doctors rely on an impartial computer, their sense of professional responsibility and legal liability in the end-of-life decision-making process may be unacceptably limited. Euthanasia opponents question what would happen if computer-based decision making were used to justify nontreatment in cases deemed hopeless—even if treatment were desired by the patient. There is a risk that patients might be subtly encouraged to give up the fight in the face of undeniable odds spit out by an impartial computer. This may be especially true for those in our society who are, for whatever reason, vulnerable to abuse.

Communication

A crucial aspect of the contemporary debate hinges on the fact that the patient and the doctor must be able to effectively communicate with one another. Questions about whether it is possible to ensure that patients clearly understand the myriad medical options and the possible outcomes of complicated medical treatments arise, as do concerns about the coercive manner in which medical options can be presented.

Those in favor of euthanasia point to studies that show that, even when patients clearly communicate their wishes and needs to medical professionals, these are frequently ignored. A $28 million study, which is believed to be the largest ever done, was carried out by SUPPORT (Study to Understand Prognoses and Preferences for Outcomes and Risks of Treatments) investigators and was published in the *Journal of the American Medical Association* (1995). It found that it is the patient who suffers when doctors neglect to ask about or respect their end-of-life wishes as stated in legal documents. A doctor's aversion to acknowledging death should not force a patient to suffer, proponents argue; doctors must be encouraged to respect their patients' wishes.

Those who stand in opposition to any form of euthanasia point to studies demonstrating that doctor-patient communication is not refined enough to guarantee that patients really understand the full implications of the information presented to them in medical settings (Redelmeier et al. 1993; Redelmeier and Shafir 1995). Sometimes such misunderstandings are due to a combination of stress about the illness and the complexity of the information presented; other times it amounts to negligence. One study of deaf patients found that doctors often neglected to use the services of an interpreter when discussing treatment options (Ebert and Heckerling 1995).

Furthermore, opponents assert, patients are very vulnerable in medical settings and are easily intimidated by the medical personnel who care for them. This creates a power imbalance that some maintain can be very dangerous for the patient if life-and-death decisions are being made.

Subtle ways of addressing issues and the phrases used to describe the chances of living and dying based on percentages have been shown to elicit different responses, depending on how the information is conveyed. There is no way to be certain that patients are not subtly influenced by the wishes of their family members or the biases of hospital personnel. People on both sides of the debate agree that the communication skills required to avoid abuses are not in place.

Physician-Assisted Suicide

When doctors prescribe large doses of pain medication to relieve a patient's suffering, there is a physiological consequence known as the double effect. This means that the quantity of medication needed to eliminate suffering has the secondary (or double) effect of ending the patient's life. Many feel this is an acceptable practice because the doctor's intention is to relieve pain, not to actively end life.

Those who advocate physician-assisted suicide point out that doctors have been quietly performing euthanasia for centuries by such methods as the one just described. They believe that the covert practice of euthanasia is actually more dangerous than legally regulated physician-assisted suicide because it forces doctors to make decisions without the benefit of open discussion with their peers and other interested parties. Instead, they make the choice alone or with the patient, and they bear the burden of that decision alone. Doctors, they assert, should be able to consult openly with ethics committees and other outside sources to responsibly fulfill patient requests to end suffering.

Proponents of assisted suicide claim that doctors sometimes seem blind to the discomfort of their patients. They blame this phenomenon on the lack of training in medical school for the care of incurable patients. Allowing doctors to end their patients' suffering would, some argue, force medical schools to teach doctors about death and dying. This would help them be more sympathetic and empowered in the care of patients.

Even without this specialized training, proponents of physician-assisted suicide maintain that doctors are still the best-trained members of our society to help patients achieve a dignified and peaceful death. Many patients who attempt to take their own lives fail and are left disabled, in pain, or otherwise compromised. Many individuals ask their families to assist them in dying, forcing the families to choose the lesser of two evils: watching loved ones live on in agony, or taking the responsibility for ending their lives. Proponents of physician-assisted suicide claim no untrained individual should ever be asked to do either. A physician's expertise, many argue, would help ensure that a patient's death is peaceful, painless, and effective.

Many argue that it is more humane in some cases to allow doctors to actively bring an end to suffering. Those who favor the use of lethal injection include some handicapped individuals, the parents of some seriously compromised infants, and people who are unable to eat or drink and cannot end their suffering without help.

There is a growing sense that the failure to help those who wish to die but cannot do so without assistance is discriminatory because it denies them the right to die retained by those still capable of taking their own lives.

On the other side of the debate stand many who believe that giving doctors permission to assist in death conflicts with the integrity of a profession dedicated to saving lives. They believe this permission would have a profoundly negative effect on the doctor-patient relationship and that it is inherently wrong for a physician to take on the role of "killer." They argue that no one would ever again be certain that their doctor had their best interests in mind if that doctor were able to prescribe death.

Opponents feel that prescribing a lethal substance of medication is a departure from the doctor's oath to "do no harm." There is nothing passive about filling a syringe with a lethal dose and administering it to stop a patient's heart from beating. Opponents worry that abuses will occur when unethical doctors choose to take lives arbitrarily and that adequate safeguards have not been developed to prevent abuse. They also worry that the medication could fall into the wrong hands or be misused by patients and thus cause even more suffering.

There is a great deal of concern about what kinds of doctors we will have in the future if a "killing curriculum" is implemented in medical schools to teach young physicians how to take lives effectively. Opponents believe that this would create an atmosphere of permissiveness regarding the taking of life that would degrade the profession and, ultimately, society's respect for life. They question whether we really want the withdrawal or withholding of life-sustaining treatment to become psychologically routine for physicians and other medical personnel.

Spiritual-Social-Cultural Concerns

The end-of-life debate involves our most deeply held beliefs and values. It also has economic and cultural implications.

Religion

Religions concern themselves with the core values human beings grapple with over the course of a lifetime. But no single religion can answer a moral question for a group of people who hold vastly different beliefs. The moment of death has a deep spiritual component, and most spiritual traditions take this transition very seriously. Some religions agree that we are not duty-bound to keep all terminally ill patients alive, but beyond this there are a wide range of opinions regarding what is acceptable.

There is also a wide range of interpretation within each spiritual tradition.

On one end of the Judeo-Christian religious spectrum are groups such as the Unitarians, who believe that spiritual decisions about the end of life can be made by the individual. Each person must determine the best way to live and to die. It is typically the more liberal religious traditions that put the needs of the individual ahead of the needs of the group.

At the other end of the spectrum is the Catholic Church, which adamantly opposes euthanasia, and fundamentalist Christians, who share the belief that life and death lie in God's domain and that these decisions are not ours to make. Even sedation is considered unacceptable by some religions because it prevents the individual from consciously preparing for the spiritual passage of death. These groups have stepped forward to condemn euthanasia or physician-assisted suicide as a crime against God. They feel strongly that man should not act like God by deciding when life begins and ends; only God gives life and only God should take it away. Many believe that suffering leads to spiritual growth and that patients and their families should face death courageously as a spiritual challenge.

Culture and Society

Death has become a much less intimate event in contemporary times. The price we pay for medical miracles is often isolation from family, friends, and familiar surroundings in which we can exert some control. This can make dying a much more frightening and less dignified experience.

Fifty years ago, 80 percent of Americans died at home; today, 80 percent die in institutions (Risley 1992). Technology has replaced family members at the bedside. Outside of war-torn countries, random natural disasters, and hospices, death is far removed from our daily lives. Most adults have no idea how to care for someone who is dying, and hospitals keep death hidden behind literal and emotional closed doors. As a society, we tend to be in denial about death. This prevents us from searching for solutions until we are in desperate need of them.

The responsibility of caring for a loved one is also more stressful in our contemporary Western culture because many of the supports that made home care possible in the past have been compromised or no longer exist. Today, youth and vigor are prized, and needing care has become associated with having no dignity or worth. Proponents of euthanasia and assisted suicide point out that many terminally ill patients find that, once they have a way to end their suffering—such as a lethal dose of medication or a person to assist them—they feel more in control of their situation. At this point, many choose to go on living, secure in the knowledge that, if their situation becomes unbearable, they can end it. Many advocates assert that this approach to death allows the terminally ill patient to say good-bye to family members and friends and to spiritually prepare for death with dignity. They believe that we, as a society, are in denial about the degree of suffering that some people are forced to live with against their will due to the intervention of doctors and technology. They believe that the control should always rest with the individual. They also feel that we must provide options for those people who, lacking family or other care options, are forced to die alone under painful conditions. We must begin to face death head on as a society rather than asking individuals to suffer alone because we are afraid to tackle the issue.

Many opponents of euthanasia claim that hospice care eliminates the need for euthanasia. Hospices were developed in London, England, in 1968 by Dame Cicely Saunders to help make the process of dying less frightening and painful. Hospice workers are trained to provide the patient and the family with spiritual and psychological support, as well as relief from physical pain. Some types of hospice care allow patients to die peacefully at home, and hospice facilities are now proliferating in the United States for those who no longer have a home but who wish to die in a homelike setting.

Euthanasia opponents suspect that, if people were given the option of ending their lives, they might get the impression that society would prefer that they do so. Our lack of respect for the elderly creates a climate in which the right to die might be perceived as a duty to die as elderly individuals sense a societal expectation to make way for the needs of the young.

Diversity

The ethnic and spiritual diversity of American culture is not necessarily reflected in the hospital practices or laws currently in place in the United States. Immigrant populations bring with them the spiritual/cultural practices of their country of origin, but these are seldom integrated into the policies of the predominantly Christian ethic found in the United States (Irish et al. 1993).

Difficulties speaking and understanding English exacerbate the cross-cultural confusion that can exist when two cultures collide over medical and spiritual practices. The potential for misunderstandings intensifies when life and death decisions are being made.

Most of these minority populations adapt their traditions to the laws and health care practices of the United States, but this is often done at great cost to their own spiritual traditions. According to Barbara Meyer, M.D., "much has been made in the medical literature . . . of the importance of cultural values to patient compliance and healing" (Irish et al. 1993). Many ethnic populations quickly lose trust in a system that appears to ignore their spiritual/cultural traditions. This can discourage many from these communities from using the health care system at all. In some cases, these gaps in cultural awareness and the decisions they prompt can prove fatal.

There are roughly 950 tribes of Native American/Canadian Indians in the United States and Canada (Irish et al. 1993). Although all of these tribes share the title "Native American" or "Canadian Indian," their beliefs vary widely from tribe to tribe. No single position on euthanasia would accurately reflect the opinions and beliefs of this diverse population. The same holds true for many cultural/spiritual groups in the United States.

For example, in the Lakota tribe, it is terribly important for tribe members to not die alone. The family of a Lakota who dies isolated in a hospital intensive care unit will suffer knowing that a member of their family died alone. This belief can have far-reaching implications if other tribe members avoid using the hospital as a result of hospital policies that ignore their unique needs.

Similarly, followers of Islam desire the presence of a relative while they are dying. A family member provides important spiritual support in the form of prayers and readings during the believer's dying moments. Followers of Islam believe that the dying are more vulnerable to Satan and that even unconscious patients benefit from the prayers and readings of those around them (Irish et al. 1993). The concern is that members of both of these groups may avoid medical care and thus relinquish their access to potential lifesaving therapies in an effort to maintain their spiritual traditions.

A similar pattern has also been established with members of the Jehovah's Witnesses who do not accept the use of any blood products—even during surgery. The medical community has adapted to the needs of this religious group to a degree, but there are still areas in which the two traditions conflict, particularly when the life or death of a child is in the balance.

The Hmong began arriving in the United States from Southeast Asia in large numbers after the Vietnam War. They brought with them a spiritual tradition based on ancestor worship and animism, which varies in practice depending on the region of Southeast Asia from which the individuals come. Other Hmong follow Buddhist teachings. A belief that the Hmong hold in common is that organ removal can prevent reincarnation—just one philosophy of the Hmong religious tradition that can come into direct conflict with the American health care system (Hopfensperger 1989).

Although these spiritual traditions do not directly advocate euthanasia, they are more accepting of the inevitability of death and are less likely to favor heroic measures over spiritual practices. The appropriateness of unwanted medical interventions for these communities should be further explored as life and death choices are being examined by American society. If the needs of these individual traditions are embraced by a more multicultural ethic in the United States, questions of euthanasia among other minority groups may find a more public forum, rather than being drowned out by the spiritual practices of the predominant culture.

Economics

The question of the right to die is more profound in a society faced with hard economic choices. The population of the United States has grown by approximately 2.8 million annually since 1990, when 12.6 percent of the total population was over the age of 65 (U.S. Census Bureau 1990). As individuals live longer in conditions of poor health, more require long-term care. But medical costs in the United States have been skyrocketing, and containing these costs has become a priority. Currently in the United States, one out of every $7 is spent on health care, representing 13.7 percent of the gross national product, or approximately $949.4 billion each year (Office of National Health Statistics 1994). In this climate, fiscal concerns can tip the medical decision-making scales in ways that would be inconceivable in times of plenty. As hard as people try not to address it, there is a fiscal dimension to the contemporary euthanasia debate.

The increase in the aged population is already straining the health care system. The AIDS epidemic has exacerbated this stress as long, painful deaths have become more common among people in their twenties and thirties. Euthanasia proponents point out that approximately 10 percent of the people in the United States account for 75 percent of all medical expenditures (Wachter et al. 1995). Many of these dollars are spent on those who are in the last 30 days of their lives, while others who are expected to live on receive inadequate care due to lack of resources.

The annual cost of nursing-home care in the United States in 1991 was $59.9 billion (Health Care Financing Administration 1996). This long-term care is not adequately covered by most insurance policies, including Medicare. Individuals without family often end up in institutions, unable to pay for the costs of long-term care. Families unable to keep up with the cost of medical and nursing-home care at the end of life can feel trapped by a system that keeps their loved one alive against his or her wishes but still expects the family to pay the financial, physical, and emotional price. Patients suffer, too, when they cannot be isolated from the financial and emotional hardships faced by those they love and terminal care eats up the family savings during a medically prolonged death watch.

Some in favor of euthanasia assert that there simply are not enough resources to provide everyone with the extremely expensive, high-tech medical care that has become available over the past 30 years. They believe that allowing people to die if they so desire will relieve these burdens on the family and on society. In addition, not forcing financial and technological hardships on patients and their families will, they say, allow for a more peaceful and compassionate death.

Those who oppose euthanasia worry that in the current climate of managed care with its focus on profit and a healthy bottom line, patients will be sacrificed to save money. They are concerned that some members of our society will be condemned to an early and unwanted death under the guise of health care rationing or prudent distribution of limited resources. They feel that legalizing euthanasia in the United States could easily create an environment ripe for the Nazi concept of "life unworthy of life" to be reintroduced. They maintain that we must value life at all costs.

Legal-Political Concerns

The search for what is really important at the end of life produces a wide variety of opinions, options, and questions—indeed, more questions than answers. The patient whose religious beliefs allow for the right to die may be cared for by a physician or an institution that philosophically condemns the practice. These types of situations typically end up in the courts, where legal guidance is sought.

There are those who feel that the right to die or to refuse treatment should never have been brought to the courts. These questions, they maintain, should have remained in the medical and spiritual sectors. The courts, however, have provided perhaps the only arena in which diverse groups have been able to come to any type of consensus. In a highly individualistic society, the law is the one thing everyone is expected to respect.

The Courts on the Right To Die

Those who ask the courts to decide for or against the right to die, the right to refuse treatment, and the right to die with assistance want to know if death is a private or a public act. Does our constitutional right to liberty and privacy include the right to end our lives?

Many Americans consider the decision to die a personal one, one to be handled by individuals and their doctors—not by judges and politicians. They believe that families or surrogate guardians should make these decisions in cases in which patients are unable to decide or express their wishes on their own behalf. Polls have shown that there is strong support for this position. The decision in the Cruzan case reflects this support.

Others believe that we have a duty to maintain legally the sanctity of all life or we run the risk of creating a society that no longer values life. Legalizing physician-assisted death would give doctors permission to kill. Opponents fear that an acceptance of euthanasia would allow governments, doctors, family members, and others to eliminate people deemed "expendable."

The legalization of any form of euthanasia or assisted suicide, they assert, will propel our society down the slippery slope exemplified by Nazi Germany. They fear society as a whole will become desensitized to killing and that the safety of the elderly, the disabled, and the mentally infirm will be at risk. Opponents believe that these potential hazards to society as a whole outweigh any benefit to individuals. Once we travel down this slippery slope, they maintain, we will forfeit something that can never be recovered.

The Courts on Physician-Assisted Suicide

In the past, the courts have been very ambivalent in their treatment of doctors who publicly admitted that they have assisted patients to die. Dr. Timothy Quill was not prosecuted for helping his terminally ill patient Patricia Diane Trumbull to die—even though he wrote about his actions in the *New England Journal of Medicine*. Dr. Jack Kevorkian has been taken to court numerous times for his practice of assisted suicide, but he has never been convicted. His actions in assisting people to die have, however, generated protective legislation in many states.

Even some who advocate for physician-assisted suicide question Dr. Kevorkian's actions because they are in direct defiance of the law. Recently he has moved outside the realm of assisting only those who fall under the medical definition of terminally ill. His most avid support comes from individuals who want to request his services for themselves or for someone they love. Kevorkian has kept the issue in the courts and in the news, forcing individuals, health care professionals, ethicists, and politicians to come to terms with physician aid-in-dying.

Opponents of physician-assisted suicide feel that Dr. Quill and Dr. Kevorkian have set a bad example in deciding to ignore the law and assisting people in taking their own lives before society and the courts have decided whether or not it is a good idea. Kevorkian's actions, they say, have provided society with some very ambiguous messages about how laws are altered or enforced. He has been acquitted in three trials involving the question of physician-assisted suicide.

Recent court decisions in the United States have changed the way in which the courts will handle cases involving physician-assisted suicide in the near future. The first case was brought in Washington. It struck down a ban on assisted suicide that had been in effect in that state since 1854, calling it unconstitutional under the Fourteenth Amendment. The decision by the Ninth Circuit Court was handed down on 6 March 1996. This 8–3 decision paves the way for physicians in the nine western states subject to the decisions of the Ninth Circuit Court to legally assist a terminally ill patient to commit suicide by prescribing a lethal dose of medication for the patient to self-administer. The Ninth Circuit encompasses Alaska, Arizona, California, Hawaii, Idaho, Montana, Nevada, Oregon, and Washington. The ban, however, remains in place while appeals are made to request a hearing before the Supreme Court.

The second case, heard by the Second Circuit Court of Appeals in New York, ruled that there is no difference between withdrawing life support and providing patients with a prescription for lethal doses of medication. The rationale behind this decision is that a patient who has no medical interventions to withhold in order to speed death still has an equal right to hasten his or her own death with the assistance of a physician. This decision falls under the Equal Protection Clause of the Fourteenth Amendment of the U.S. Constitution. Patients on respirators, taking medications, or using other interventions that can be withheld already have this right.

These two court decisions are expected to propel the practice of physician-assisted suicide into law by spurring the examination of Oregon's ballot Measure 16, which has been stalled in the courts since it was passed by voters in November 1994.

Legislation in the United States

The right to die cases that have been decided on behalf of individuals in U.S. courts have paved the way for legislation that affects society as a whole. Oregon's Measure 16, introduced in 1994, was designed to allow physicians to provide their terminally ill patients with lethal prescriptions, providing they met certain criteria. The legislation defined a terminal illness as "an incurable and irreversible disease that will produce death within six months." The choice to die must be made voluntarily by a well-informed, competent patient.

The measure was voted into law in November 1994. However, opponents of the law and physician-assisted suicide in general have raised questions, prompting a federal district court to place a restraining order on it. Questions about whether the legislation's language is such that a diabetic or a person with a pacemaker might be considered terminal under the law's broad definition of terminal illness prompted this legal action. The New Hampshire Death with Dignity Bill (HB 339), sponsored by Representative Robert Guest, will go before the full House in 1996. This bill amends some of the language defining a terminal illness that has raised concerns about Oregon's bill.

In response to the Ninth and Second Circuit Court rulings in 1996, Representative Ralph Hall (D-Texas) plans to introduce a bill called the Assisted Suicide Funding Restriction Act of 1996, which would prevent any federal tax funds from being used to "furnish, fund, or support" assisted suicide. Specific programs that would fall under the bill include Medicare, Medicaid, Military Health Care, Indian Health Care Programs, and Federal Employee Benefit Plans, among others. Should the bill be passed, large numbers of people who rely on these programs to cover their health care costs may find that they would not have coverage for the costs associated with assisted suicide.

Euthanasia around the World

The following are brief summaries of attitudes toward euthanasia around the globe.

Africa

Most African cultures accept death and dying more readily than do Western cultures. This does not mean, however, that life is any less revered. For instance, the Akan tribe of Ghana believes that each person has a divine spark, given by God, a unique destiny to fulfill, and a responsibility for their life's path that includes a recognition of self as well as of how to best contribute to society. It is this unique combination that makes life meaningful; when it is not possible to fulfill both components, a person may take his or her own life. A person's intentions in committing suicide determine the reaction of the community to the death. When individuals ask others to assist them in dying, passive euthanasia, such as removal of life support, is allowed. In the Akan tribe, as well as in many other traditional African communities, the terminally ill are cared for by the community, usually family, who are also responsible for decision making, including the decision to allow death if the dying person is unable to make these decisions.

Australia

Natural-death acts, similar to living wills, exist in South Australia. Euthanasia is illegal in all Australian states except the Northern Territory, where, on 1 July 1996, a bill that allows physician-assisted suicide was passed. Physicians may now legally prescribe a lethal substance and either administer the substance themselves or give it to the patient to self-administer. This landmark legislation is known as the Rights of the Terminally Ill Act.

In a survey of Australian nurses, it was shown that 85 percent of those polled had complied with an attending physician's order to "provide euthanasia" for their patients (Khulse and Singer 1993).

Canada

It is against the law to help anyone commit suicide in Canada, but the Canadian House of Commons has been considering measures that would allow physicians to help fulfill a patient's wishes without fear of reproach. The pros and cons are much the same as they are in the United States. There is one difference, however, that could impact choice in dying in Canada.

Canadians do not pay out-of-pocket for medical expenses. Universal health care was introduced in 1966 and is paid for through federal and provincial taxation. In some provinces, employers are responsible for the costs of their employees' health expenses. Doctors' incomes are determined by area of specialization. It is thus not unreasonable to expect it to be possible to test euthanasia policies or physician-assisted suicide in Canada without having to take into consideration the many financial considerations encountered in the United States.

The Canadian system is already so overburdened, however, that it might not accurately reflect what a universal coverage system would be like in the United States. Waiting lists for treatment are the norm, leading some Canadians to travel to the United States for health care services.

France

It is not uncommon for physicians in France to give the terminally ill some form of pharmaceutical to bring about death, but this is done quietly and without legislative sanction. As is the case in the United States, people are afraid to sanction physician-assisted suicide for fear of reducing death to an institutionalized activity. The president of the National Ethical Committee opposes legislated euthanasia because he believes that it will give doctors too much power over life and death.

Germany

Germans still live with the specter of Hitler and are loathe to use the word euthanasia. The country whose Weimar Republic introduced the world to the "slippery slope" by killing thousands of disabled and mentally ill people, defective children, and elderly individuals considers active euthanasia a crime against humanity. Passive euthanasia is accepted quietly as a private matter between doctor and patient. Assisting someone to commit suicide is not against the law in Germany (penal code 216). Catholics in Germany, Italy, and France all hold conservative attitudes toward the sanctity of human life.

Islamic Countries

Death is viewed by the followers of Islam as just one of many stages of existence. Suicide is not condoned, but dying for noble reasons is accepted. Decisions regarding terminal illness are usually made by examining the benefits and burdens to the patient, family, and society as a whole. Life is to be embraced, even when suffering occurs. When there is no hope of recovery, medical treatment may be withdrawn. The Islamic court decides in these cases. This religious faith maintains that a person's moment of death is preordained, so euthanasia can be interpreted as interfering with the divine plan. Individuals and their families are not supposed to pray for deliverance from life.

Israel

In the Jewish culture, many believe that life is not a decision—God gives life, and this life does not fully belong to the person living it. A person who is within three days of dying is called a *gosses* (go-says), meaning "a person at the door of death." The Talmud dictates Jewish law. In the mid-1990s Talmudic laws are interpreted to allow just about any life-sustaining method that works—organ transplants, feeding tubes, etc.

A person expected to die is not considered any less human and is not treated any differently. If anything, a *gosses* is someone whose life must be cherished in the last moments and who should remain undisturbed to avoid any action that might precipitate a premature death. Oral law, or halakah, maintains that it is unacceptable to remove a respirator from a person who is not a gosses. Thus, active euthanasia is prohibited, but Judaism is less clear on the concept of passive euthanasia. Some rabbis believe that a patient should be kept alive as long as possible; others feel that once someone is in the final stages of dying, it is permissible to avoid prolonging the dying process. Most Jewish law is open to the interpretation of individual rabbis and the religious community.

Japan

In Japan, the words *songen-shi* are translated as "death with dignity." Suicide and euthanasia are viewed as different; euthanasia is seen as a way to relieve suffering through a decision arrived at with the support and wisdom of others. Passive euthanasia is accepted, and patients are not forced to accept treatment that prolongs life. Buddhist influence on the culture is apparent in the concept of *sonshi*, meaning "a beautiful death with dignity." The Buddhist tradition places much value on the passage between one life and the next and holds that this passage should be calm and without pain or stress. The Japanese, more than any other industrialized people, tend to believe in the concept of reincarnation, which undoubtedly makes acceptance of death easier. Problems with the concept of euthanasia seem to have developed gradually as the Japanese have become more of an individualistic and technological society—more Westernized. The Japanese have resisted adopting brain death standards because they interfere with Buddist funeral rituals. The Japanese people were shocked when a doctor at Tokai University gave a lethal injection to a patient in April 1991. The doctor acted at the request of the patient's family but did not discuss the case with his colleagues.

The Netherlands

Those interested in right-to-die issues have focused on practices in the Netherlands since the early 1970s. This country has the most liberal euthanasia and physician-assisted death policies in the world. The Dutch penal code clearly states that intentional killing is against the law. Yet since 1973 the Dutch have allowed physicians to end the lives of their patients under certain conditions without fear of legal repercussions.

Article 293 of the Dutch Penal Code states that the intentional taking of life is a crime. Originally drafted in the late nineteenth century, this code was designed to discourage people from assisting others to commit suicide and to help distinguish between murder, manslaughter, and assisted suicide. However, it is now basically a means of codifying exceptions to murder and manslaughter without licensing the indiscriminate taking of life. An explanatory memorandum to the code states that a person who assists someone in voluntarily taking his or her own life deserves considerably less punishment than one who commits murder. Circumstances and methods separate acts of compassion from acts of murder. Extreme circumstances in which a physician might help someone to die are recognized, but respect for life remains the most important consideration of the law. The physician who assists must show that he or she acted out of force majeure, meaning that the patient was in so much pain and suffering that this route was chosen only after careful consideration.

Quietly existing between the law and the actions of physicians is the concept of private space, a legal limbo where the right course of action is defined by an understanding between the physician and the patient and is subsequently reported to the justice system for review. The Dutch like to believe that the decision to end a life is always instigated by the patient, who then requests aid from a physician. This view of the relationship, however, neglects to account for the professional judgment made by the physician, which is the basis for many patients' understanding of their condition and what kind of life or relief they can expect in the future. Family members and physicians are not allowed to make decisions for patients who are no longer competent to make their own health care decisions. However, an interpretation (not a decision, per se) of a person's wishes can be made by a delegate named in the patient's advance directive.

In 1985 lawmakers took serious steps to amend Article 293 so that only conscious, competent patients who were considered terminal would be considered under the "exceptions" guidelines. Two bills were advanced and both were rejected by the Council of State. The Council, a very cautious body, was widely considered to be awaiting more information that would be gleaned by watching and learning from the current practice. Abortion laws in the Netherlands were created using this methodology as well. Attempts to make the practice of euthanasia and the laws that govern this practice more concrete have thus far failed. The courts in the Netherlands have never given express permission for the practice of euthanasia, but have instead addressed the issue retroactively by examining each individual act as reported by physicians. The effectiveness of this method in protecting citizens from abuses has been questioned by scholars and researchers around the world.

The Dutch make no distinction between active and passive euthanasia, and the definition of the word *euthanasia* is vague. A variety of terms such as suicide, assistance with suicide, mercy killing, assistance with death, and medical killing are used interchangeably to describe four distinguishable actions:

> **Termination of pointless treatment**, or ending care that no longer serves the patient.
>
> **Alleviation of pain**, or using medications to ease suffering, which also result in shortening a patient's life (double effect).
>
> **Patient autonomy**, meaning that a patient can refuse any treatment, even lifesaving treatment. The doctor is

not responsible for any outcomes resulting from patient autonomy.

Force majeure, which covers situations in which the physician cannot treat patients who require treatment.

An example of this would be found in a triage situation, in which the doctor's decision to treat one person might result in the death of another. The doctor would not be held responsible for this outcome. Most cases of euthanasia in the Netherlands are the result of overdoses taken orally by those patients who are able to do so, or by injection of a narcotic agent (by the physician), which renders patients unconscious. Then the physician administers a substance such as curare to induce respiratory arrest.

Physicians are protected from legal repercussions if they adhere to the specific guidelines drawn up by the Royal Dutch Society for the Promotion of Medicine (KNMG) in 1984:

1. A voluntary request to die must be made by the patient. It is the job of the physician to be certain that the patient is not being coerced by family members or others into making a hasty or rash decision.
2. A well-informed request to die in which the patient has adequate information must be made. The patient should be made aware of other options before the decision to end life is made.
3. Persistence of intent to die by the patient must be demonstrated. The decision cannot be a transient one due to depression or a temporary condition but needs to be repeatedly asserted over time. Physicians are encouraged to document requests as they are made by the patient. A single request is not considered adequate to satisfy this guideline.
4. Suffering that is considered unacceptable must be present. The physician and the patient are responsible for defining what is unacceptable, and the physician must communicate with the patient sufficiently to understand what that patient considers unacceptable.
5. Consultation with at least one other physician must take place. Psychologists, clergy, and family may also be asked to participate in the decision-making process. No consultation with an impartial third party is required.

It is important to note that, of the approximately 40,000 physicians in the Netherlands, only 25,000 are affiliated with the KNMG (Gomez 1991), and even these physicians are not bound by these guidelines because physicians are not morally obligated to perform euthanasia in the first place. If they are unwilling to participate in ending a patient's life, they may remove themselves from a case. They are required, however, to find a physician for the patient who is willing to assist, and only then may they remove themselves from any further involvement with the patient. They are not allowed to delegate the task of assisting a suicide to anyone other than another physician. Information about the method used must be documented and reported to the prosecutor's office for review. Approximately 54 percent of all Dutch physicians have performed euthanasia at least once (Gomez 1991).

Law in the Netherlands follows the Roman legal tradition, whereas law in the United States follows the Anglo-Saxon legal tradition. In the Roman tradition, individual judges or panels of judges render all decisions. Judges in the Netherlands have lifetime appointments and follow statutory law more rigidly than do judges in the United States, where case law and legal precedent are also important factors considered when rendering a decision. Prosecutors in the Netherlands decide if a criminal case exists and if prosecuting a suspected crime best serves the public. The prosecutor wields a great deal of power and can pursue a case or dismiss it at will; however, they must investigate all cases of euthanasia brought to their attention.

Dutch society values the general social good over individual rights. Doctors are held in high esteem. Roughly two-thirds of the population claims no religion, and the remaining Catholics and Protestants tend to take a more liberal stance than their counterparts in other countries. Differences of opinion on the practice exist throughout the country, however, with coastal towns and Amsterdam holding more liberal views toward euthanasia than areas in the South, where the Catholic Church is prominent, or in the North, where a conservative Protestant ethic makes the practice less accepted.

One study, conducted by the Protestant Christian Elderly Society and reported in the *Canberra Times* on 11 June 1993, indicated that older people are now more afraid of being involuntarily euthanized. About 10 percent of those surveyed expressed concerns, even though the survey itself asked no questions about euthanasia whatsoever. Nursing homes advertise that they do not perform euthanasia in order to help allay these fears. An organization called Sanctuary has developed a document by which individuals can indicate a desire to not have euthanasia performed under any circumstances. This document is similar to the right-to-life directives distributed by the National Right to Life Committee, Inc. in the United States.

A growing concern is that some doctors do not report cases of assistance as they are required to, and that no public records are maintained to help analyze trends in the practice. Estimates of the number of cases per year range from less than 5,000 to as many as 10,000. In a country with a universal health care system that boasts efficient and effective regulatory bodies, many find it surprising and disturbing that accurate records are not being kept and that guidelines are not always enforced. This means that Dutch physicians are really only accountable to themselves, and they control what information is passed to a higher authority for review. Although physicians are also encouraged to discuss requests for euthanasia with the patient's most involved nurse, this also does not happen regularly and possibly represents another gray area in which physicians lack accountability. Doctors may also be protecting nurses from possible criminal prosecution, which can occur in the Netherlands if the nurse is involved in the decision-making process.

The questions that policymakers, physicians, and patients in the United States face today closely resemble those being debated in the Netherlands. Many who propose legislation in the United States point to the Netherlands as an example of how euthanasia can work. But the Dutch themselves have not come to a consensus about whether their methods are effective at avoiding abuses or providing patients with the best care. Their model has merely propelled the debate into a working practice, which they are assessing and refining as they gain more experience with it.

The United Kingdom

There has never been a serious attempt to pass euthanasia legislation in the British House of Commons, but this does not mean that the issue is not discussed among the politicians of this country. The fear of euthanasia has been ebbing, but few legal measures are on the horizon. As in the United States, one of the strongest groups opposing euthanasia is the antiabortion lobby. In general, the British favor euthanasia for patients who suffer from a severe illness, and there is an awareness that doctors sometimes hasten death without the sanction of the law.

Mentally competent individuals are allowed to refuse any kind of medical treatment. In 1985 the Enduring Powers of Attorney Act was passed, allowing proxies to make decisions on behalf of patients unable to act on their own behalf.

Clearly, many countries are grappling with end-of-life issues. We are, as a world community, beginning to look to other societies and share what we are learning about end-of-life decision making. The Netherlands and now Australia and the United States are allowing various forms of physician-assisted suicide, while the rest of the world looks on and wonders what the outcome will·be.

Conclusions

Many forces are bringing about changes in the doctor-patient relationship. Foremost among these is managed care and the bottom-line approach to health care that it has introduced.

Cradle-to-grave doctoring is a thing of the past in the United States. Patients fortunate enough to have insurance often find that policy changes force provider changes. Those who lack insurance often go without a family doctor and rely on hospital emergency rooms for health care services. However, matters of life and death are intimate topics. Discussing them requires a level of trust and a depth of relationship that cannot be achieved on the spot with the doctor who happens to be on duty when such matters arise. Should that same doctor belong to a health maintenance organization that imposes a secrecy clause prohibiting the discussion of treatment options not covered by its plan, can he or she provide patients with the kind of accurate information needed to make life-and-death decisions?

There are currently no safeguards in place to protect patients who may not wish to die but whose health plans limit the alternatives. Those who oppose physician-assisted suicide believe that it is unlikely that well-informed and carefully considered decisions can be made either by the doctor or the patient under these conditions. They are demanding that the system address this lack of safeguards for practices that may soon be common if the Supreme Court upholds the decisions of both the Ninth and Second Circuit Courts (see "The Right to Equal Protection" in this chapter).

The equal protection laws in Washington State and New York are expected to have an impact on the Oregon Death with Dignity Act, which, although passed by voters, has been held up in the courts. Yale Kamisar, a law professor at the University of Michigan, said of the two circuit court rulings, "There's been more movement in this field, for better or for worse, in the last 30 days than there has been in the previous 20 years" (as quoted in *Time* magazine 15 April 1996). Clearly, the idea of physician-assisted suicide is gaining momentum.

The questions that have been asked for the past 30 years have involved the right to self-determination at the end of life, the right to refuse treatment, the right to state one's wishes via advance directives, and the right to choose the manner and timing of one's own death. But more questions are waiting in the wings.

How to provide equal protection to those who cannot ingest a lethal prescription, such as a patient in a persistent vegetative state, needs to be addressed further. Questions involving euthanasia and Alzheimer's patients are likely to become more prominent—unless, of course, a cure is found soon.

People are questioning medical and research establishments, wondering if it is right for vast sums to be spent on developing new ways to hold back death for a select few, despite the fact that everyone (through taxes, higher medical and insurance costs, and fewer services) pays the price for much of this research. Treatment options are being evaluated in terms of their overall benefit to the patient and the patient's quality of life. Resource allocation is an ever more pressing concern as the Baby Boomer generation ages, further straining an already overburdened system. People also question whether we can afford to maintain the lives of compromised newborns and the terminally ill at public expense.

The media is already focusing on the dramas that erupt within individual families over what is best for an incompetent loved one. Families are asking the courts to further delineate which family member is best equipped to decide.

Doctors will come under closer scrutiny if physician-assisted suicide becomes a more common practice. Medical associations are already looking at standards and criteria to provide physicians with guidance in these matters.

Those who lead religious communities and right-to-life organizations have, in some cases, softened their positions toward some aspects of withdrawing or withholding treatment, but most remain strongly opposed to more active forms of death by choice. These groups provide a counterweight to recent developments, forcing individuals and society to examine their choices closely and with appropriate gravity.

Both sides of the debate watch developments in the Netherlands where, after more than 20 years of sanctioned physician-assisted death, some are beginning to question whether the practice is sufficiently monitored to avoid abuses.

The challenge for legislators lies in crafting laws that fulfill society's duty to protect life and simultaneously respect the autonomy and dignity of the individual. Because this is far easier said than done, this debate promises to simmer for many years to come.

References

American Hospital Association. *The Patient's Bill of Rights*. Chicago: American Hospital Association, 1973.

American Nurses Association. *American Nurses Association Position Statement on Assisted Suicide*. Washington, DC: American Nurses Association, 1994.

Asch, David A., M.D. "The Role of Critical Care Nurses in Euthanasia and Assisted Suicide," *New England Journal of Medicine* 334, no. 21 (May 1996): 1374–1379.

Burleigh, Michael. *Death and Deliverance: "Euthanasia" in Germany c. 1900–1945*. Cambridge, England: The Press Syndicate, 1994.

Ebert, David, and Paul S. Heckerling, M.D. "Communication with Deaf Patients· Knowledge, Beliefs and Practices of Physicians," *Journal of the American Medical Association* 273 (18 January 1995): 227–229.

Gomez, Carlos M., M.D. *Regulating Death: Euthanasia and the Case of the Netherlands*. New York: Free Press, 1991.

Hastings Center. "Guidelines on the Termination of Life-Sustaining Treatment and the Care of the Dying," Briarcliff Manor, NY: Hastings Center, 1987.

Health Care Financing Administration, National Center for Health Statistics. Health Care Financing Review 17, no. 03373. Washington, DC: Health Care Financing Administration, Spring 1996.

Hopfensperger, J. "Twin Cities Doctors Work To Bridge Gap with Hmong," *Minneapolis Star Tribune* (25 August 1989): 1A, 12A.

Irish, Donald P., Kathleen F. Lindquist, and Vivian Nelson, eds. *Ethnic Variations in Dying, Death, and Grief*. Washington, DC: Taylor and Francis, 1993.

Khulse, H., and P. Singer. "Voluntary Euthanasia: A Survey of Nurses' Attitudes and Practices," *Australian Nursing Journal* 30 (1993): 311–322.

Lemonick, Michael D. "Defining the Right To Die," *Time* (15 April 1996): 82.

Multi-Society Task Force on Persistent Vegetative State. "Medical Aspects of the Persistent Vegetative State," *New England Journal of Medicine* 330 (22 June 1994): 1572–1579.

Pearlman, R. A., T. J. Starr, and R. F. Uhlmann. "Quality of Life and Resuscitation Decisions in Elderly Patients," *Journal of General Internal Medicine* 1 (1986): 373–379.

Pearlman, R. A., and R. F. Uhlmann. "Perceived Quality of Life and Preferences for Life-Sustaining Treatment in Older Adults," *Arch Internal Medicine* 151 (1991): 494–497.

President's Commission for the Study of Ethical Problems in Medicine and Biomedical and Behavioral Research. "Deciding To Forego Life-Sustaining Treatment." Washington, D.C. & U.S. Government Printing Office, March 1982.

Protestant Christian Elderly Society. "Elderly Dutch Afraid of Euthanasia Policy," *Canberra Times* (11 June 1993).

Redelmeier, Donald A., M.D., Paul Rozin, Ph.D., and Daniel Kahnerman, Ph.D. " Understanding Patients' Decisions: Cognitive and Emotional Perspectives," *Journal of the American Medical Association* 270 (7 July 1993): 72–76.

Redelmeier, Donald A., M.D., and Eldar Shafir, M.D. "Medical Decision Making in Situations That Offer Multiple Alternatives," *Journal of the American Medical Association* 273, no. 4 (25 January 1995): 302–305.

Risley, Robert. "Voluntary Active Euthanasia: The Next Frontier: Impact on the Indigent," *Issues in Law and Medicine* 8 (1992): 361–374.

"Study To Understand Prognoses and Preferences for Outcomes and Risks of Treatments," *Journal of the American Medical Association* 274, no. 20 (1995): 1591.

U.S. Bureau of the Census. Current Population Reports. Washington, DC: U.S. Government, 1990. Series 25, 1045, 1057.

Wachter, Robert M., et al. "Cost and Outcome of Intensive Care for Patients with AIDS, Pneumocystis Carinii Pneumonia, and Severe Respiratory Failure," *Journal of the American Medical Association* 273, no. 3 (18 January 1995): 230–235.

Webster's New Collegiate Dictionary. Springfield, MA: G&C Merriam Webster & Co., 1995.

Chronology 2

Euthanasia is an ancient concept. The degree to which it is accepted or rejected by a culture has a great deal to do with the dominant religious and moral tone of the times. Included here are historical events that helped define the context in which death has been considered throughout the past two millennia.

The rise of modern medicine is also traced within this chronological overview of euthanasia, since advances in the ability to prolong life have further complicated an already complex topic. Key legal decisions on the subject are also included.

1727 B.C.   The Babylonian Code of Hammurabi is created. This is the first known written code in any culture designed to protect patients from the surgical errors of physicians.

850 B.C.   Physicians in ancient Greece are organized as members of a lay craft.

600–   The Greeks coin the word *eu-*
300 B.C.   *thanatos*, which means "good death." Rational philosophy

600– 300 B.C. *cont.*	and scientific medicine develop and healing is no longer perceived to be the result of magic. The Hippocratic Oath is believed to have been written at some point during this period.
500 B.C.	The Pythagorean brotherhood comes into existence. This religious sect believes that the best parts of man's soul are divine and eternal.
497 B.C.	Death of Pythagoras, a Greek philosopher who places the highest value on the soul and believes in immortality.
470– 360 B.C.	Hippocrates is believed to have lived during this period. Many manuscripts written during this time are ascribed to him, but it is not known how many he actually authored.
429– 347 B.C.	Lifetime of Plato, who makes the radical claim that health is the responsibility of the individual and that the brain is the center of thought.
421 B.C.	Some scholars believe the Hippocratic Oath is written this year.
400 B.C.	Roman emperors begin to enact laws to protect infants from infanticide by their parents, a common practice prior to this time. Both healthy and unhealthy infants of both sexes suffer this fate.
383– 322 B.C.	Lifetime of Aristotle, the son of a physician, who maintains that the body and soul are inseparable.
341– 270 B.C.	Lifetime of Epicurus, who writes that death is total oblivion.
A.D. 129	Galen, known as the Father of Medicine, is born. During his lifetime, four medical sects emerge: Dogmatists, Empiricists, Methodists, and Pneumatists. Galen believes that all knowledge of the body can be systematically understood via observation. He is the last prominent Greek physician.

404	High priests in the Christian church begin to expect more rigid adherence to Christian doctrines in Roman society, teaching people that cruelty of any kind is wholly unacceptable except when practiced against enemies of Christ. The monk Telemachus tries to put an end to the battles of the gladiators by standing between two opponents and demanding that they stop in the name of Christ. He is killed by the gladiators. This so shocks the people that the games are first closed and then outlawed by the emperor.
533	The Council of Orleans (France) denies funeral rites to anyone who, when accused of a crime, takes his or her own life.
560s	The Council of Braga (France) expands the Orleans law to include all suicides.
693	The Council of Toledo (Spain) declares that anyone who attempts suicide will be excommunicated.
875–925	Lifetime of Rhases, a Persian who makes use of chemical knowledge to develop medicines.
1100s	Medical practitioners begin to form associations.
1140	State examinations are held in Sicily for persons wishing to practice medicine.
1240	Holy Roman Emperor Frederick II regulates the study and practice of medicine.
1310	Mondino De Luzzi, an Italian anatomist, dissects the human body. This marks the beginning of modern surgery.
1516	Sir Thomas More publishes *Utopia*. This work depicts a society in which voluntary euthanasia is officially sanctioned.
1651	The word *suicide* is first used in English documents. It is taken from the Latin word meaning "to kill one's self."

1770	The practice of defiling the corpses of those who commit suicide is officially abolished in Geneva, Switzerland.
1794	Paradys, a physician, writes *Oratio de Euthanasia,* recommending an "easy death for the patient."
1798	Vaccinations are first introduced by English physician Edward Jenner.
1799	Nitrous oxide, known as laughing gas, is first used as anesthesia by Sir Humphrey Davy, a British chemist.
1803	Frederich Serturner, a German chemist, develops morphine, a narcotic painkiller made from opium.
1824	England's parliament allows for the churchyard burial of persons who have committed suicide, but only between the hours of 9 P.M. and midnight.
1846	Ether is first used in a surgical procedure by William Morton at Massachusetts General Hospital.
	The American Medical Association is founded to promote the art and science of medicine and to advance the state of public health. The first items of business for the organization in 1847 are the creation of standards for medical education and a professional code of ethics for physicians.
1861	French scientist Louis Pasteur develops the germ theory of disease.
1865	Surgeon Joseph Lister develops antiseptic surgery in England.
1869	The word *euthanasia* first appears in the *Oxford English Dictionary.*
1870	The French government forbids discrimination against any person, including those who commit suicide, in the manner of their burial.

1882   The tuberculosis bacteria is isolated.

1895   Wilhelm Röntgen of Germany accidentally discovers X-rays.

1899   German chemist Adolph Bayer's aspirin comes into widespread use.

1905   *Mohr v. Williams* in Minnesota becomes the first cited legal case in which a doctor is taken to task for performing a medical procedure without the patient's consent.

1906   The first bill in the United States dealing with euthanasia is introduced in the Ohio state legislature. It receives almost 25 percent of the vote.

1912   A woman with an incurable disease petitions the New York state court to allow her doctor to put her to death painlessly. This request is denied but causes a sensation.

1917   The Hippocratic Oath is suspended in Russia at the outset of the Russian Revolution, ostensibly to allow doctors to focus on maintaining loyalty to the state rather than to the patient.

1920   Frank Roberts of Michigan helps his ill wife commit suicide by placing arsenic within her reach. *People v. Roberts* is the first recorded prosecution for assisted suicide. Roberts is convicted of murder and dies in jail.

            The concept of *lebensunwerten Leben* (life not worthy of life) surfaces in Germany in a tract published by Karl Binding and Alfred Hoche.

1921   Legislation on euthanasia is discussed and rejected at a medical convention in Germany.

1925   Dr. Harold Blazer is tried in Colorado for killing his daughter, who had been an invalid for 30 years. The case is dismissed because the jury cannot arrive at a verdict.

1929   The stock market crash changes the nature of life insurance policies. Prior to this year, most insurance companies paid in full on suicide claims. However, because there were so many suicides after the crash, many companies insert a noncontestability clause requiring a two-year waiting period before payments are made on claims.

1930s   The words *mercy killing* come into use.

1931   Dr. C. Killick Millard, a physician in England, gives a speech entitled "A Plea for Legalization of Euthanasia" at a meeting of the Society of Officers of Health.

1935   George Bernard Shaw, Harold Laski, Bertrand Russell, and H. G. Wells found the British Euthanasia Society.

1937   Nebraska Senator John Comstock introduces legislation called the Voluntary Euthanasia Act, which calls for the legalization of active euthanasia. It is never voted upon but demonstrates an emerging interest in legislating euthanasia.

                The first blood bank opens in the United States at Cook County Hospital in Chicago. Refrigeration and blood banks make ever more complex surgeries routine.

1938   Charles Potter, a Unitarian minister, founds the Euthanasia Society in New York. The first U.S. euthanasia group and the second organization of its kind in the world, it promotes passive forms of euthanasia.

- 1939   A bill to legalize euthanasia is proposed in New York State.

- 1941   Approximately 100,000 German citizens (non-Jews) are murdered in Nazi Germany because they are handicapped in some way. This mass murder is dubbed "euthanasia" by the Nazis.

1945   The antibiotic streptomycin is developed.

-1946   The Committee of 1776 Physicians for Legalizing Voluntary Euthanasia in New York State comes into existence.

1950s   The sonogram, an offshoot of sonal technology, comes into use, allowing fetuses to be seen in utero.

            Dr. Hermann N. Sanders is prosecuted for first-degree murder for taking the life of a female patient, Abbie Borroto, who suffered from incurable cancer. He notes his actions on the patient's chart.

1951   The General Council of the Presbyterian Church denounces euthanasia as being in direct conflict with the sixth commandment of the Bible ("Thou shalt not kill").

1952   Members of the General Convention of the Protestant Episcopal Church approve a resolution to oppose the legalization of euthanasia under any circumstances.

            The first artificial heart/lung machine is used in a surgical procedure.

1954   Joseph Fletcher's book *Morals and Medicine* is published. It brings the issues of patient autonomy and "good death" to a broader forum.

1955   The first open-heart surgery is performed.

            Scottish bacteriologist Sir Alexander Fleming discovers penicillin in London, England.

. 1957   Pope Pius XII addresses the Seventh International Congress of Doctors in The Hague. He states, "Medical law can never permit the doctor or the patient to practice direct euthanasia," but he concedes that in some cases extraordinary care might be withdrawn.

1959   *The Meaning of Death*, by Herman Feifel, is pub-
        lished. It is considered a seminal work and gener-
        ates contemporary academic interest in the subject
        of death and dying.

1960s   The Euthanasia Society's membership reaches 500.

        Neonatal intensive-care units are created to treat
        infants who would die without specialized care.
        The medical subspecialty neonatology comes into
        existence.

1960   The pacemaker is developed for the human heart.

1961   Suicide and attempted suicide are decriminalized
        in England, but assisted suicide is still a crime.

        The birth-control pill is approved for public use.

1965   The Supreme Court case *Griswold v. Connecticut* (a
        case involving the use of contraceptives) sets a
        precedent for the right to privacy as a constitu-
        tional guarantee. The Supreme Court rules to ex-
        pand the due process clause of the Fourteenth
        Amendment to provide for privacy within the mar-
        ital relationship.

1967   The Euthanasia Society of New York establishes a
        tax-exempt branch called the Euthanasia Education
        Fund to distribute information about dying to the
        general public. The society, in concert with Chicago
        attorney Luis Kutner, develops the first living will.

        The first human heart transplant is performed by
        Christiaan Barnard.

        The Foundation of Thanatology is formed to
        improve care for critically ill patients.

1968   The first modern hospice opens in London, Eng-
        land, founded by Dame Cicely Saunders.

        Dr. Walter Sackett, a Florida physician, introduces
        the country's first living will bill.

1969   Physicians, lawyers, ethicists, theologians, and journalists publish more than four dozen articles and a dozen books on euthanasia, the terminal patient, and laws (or lack of them) which deal with mercy killings.

     On Death and Dying, by Dr. Elisabeth Kübler-Ross, is published. It is the first book to examine the emotional process of dying and bereavement as a series of stages.

     The Hastings Center is founded to explore biomedical ethics and to support research.

     The Euthanasia Education Council is founded. Donald McKinney is the president of this educational group.

     The Voluntary Euthanasia Bill is introduced into the British House of Lords and passes without debate on its first reading. It is then rejected on its second reading.

     The Compassionate Friends, a group for parents whose children have died, is founded in England.

1970   The Euthanasia Society distributes more than 60,000 living wills.

     The Kennedy Institute on Ethics is founded at Georgetown University Medical School.

1971   The word *bioethics* is coined to help refine the concept of medical ethics.

1972   More than 100,000 living wills are distributed in the United States.

     The Senate Special Committee on Aging holds meetings on "Death with Dignity: An Inquiry into Related Public Issues."

     Dr. Vincent Montemaro, a Long Island physician is the second physician to be prosecuted for euthanasia since 1950. The doctor injected his patient,

1972 cont.	Eugene Bauer (59), with potassium chloride. Bauer was terminally ill with throat cancer. Montemaro's actions are verified by the nurse who reported the death.

1973   The National Right to Life Committee is formed. It is a political lobbying group formed by the National Conference of Catholic Bishops.

Roe v. Wade, the Supreme Court case legalizing abortion, provides a precedent for the constitutional right of an individual to outweigh the interests of the state.

Dr. Geertruida Potsma (the Netherlands) receives a one-month suspended sentence and one year of probation for killing her dying mother by lethal injection. This trial is the catalyst for social worker Jaap Sybrandy and his wife, Klazien, to form the Netherlands Society for Voluntary Euthanasia. Their work leads to a case law precedent to allow euthanasia, providing certain guidelines are met.

A Dutch physician from the Leeuwarden district is convicted under Article 293 for killing her mother at the mother's request. The sentence is suspended. The Netherlands Society for Voluntary Euthanasia begins an effort to make euthanasia legal.

The American Hospital Association adopts A Patient's Bill of Rights. Although the document is not legally binding, more than 90 percent of all U.S. hospitals are members of this organization when these guidelines are adopted.

1974   The first American hospice opens in New Haven, Connecticut.

Voluntary Euthanasia Societies are founded in Victoria, Australia, and South Africa.

National Conference Steering Committee of the American Medical Association releases new standards for CPR and emergency cardiac care.

1975   Karen Ann Quinlan consumes a nearly fatal combination of alcohol and sleeping pills and goes into a coma.

British journalist Derek Humphrey assists his wife, Jean, to die, ending her battle with bone cancer.

1976   The Swiss Academy of Medical Sciences publishes guidelines on caring for dying patients. These require the doctor to provide personal support, care, and medical treatment.

Karen Ann Quinlan's respirator is removed by court order. This case establishes that an individual's wishes outweigh the state's duty to preserve life.

In September Governor Jerry Brown signs into law the California Natural Death Act. This is the nation's first right-to-die statute.

1977   A physician in Amsterdam, the Netherlands, is acquitted of giving a patient a lethal overdose.

1978   New York becomes the first state in the United States to make assisted suicide a crime.

The Vatican releases *Declaration on Euthanasia*, which affirms the church's position that dying patients should be free from "burdensome" life support systems.

The President's Commission for the Study of Ethical Problems in Medicine and Biomedical and Behavioral Research is established by an act of Congress (Public Law 95-622) to address the changing public attitude and the law regarding medical care information and decision making.

1979   The Veterans Administration releases guidelines that prohibit doctors from writing do-not-resuscitate (DNR) orders for terminally ill patients.

1979
cont.

Jerry Falwell founds the Moral Majority. Although focused on abortion, this group is also concerned with euthanasia.

1980

Derek Humphrey, Ann Wickett, and Gerald Larue found the Hemlock Society in Santa Monica, California.

The Scottish chapter of EXIT, a right-to-die organization, publishes *How To Die with Dignity*, a booklet by Dr. George B. Mair.

The World Federation of Right-to-Die Societies is founded. Twenty-seven groups in 18 countries join.

1981

AIDS is first diagnosed.

California doctors Neil Barber and Robert Nedjil are charged with murder for taking patient Clarence Herbert (55) off a respirator and discontinuing his IV feedings. The family had requested these steps but a nurse notified authorities, making these doctors the third and fourth U.S. physicians to be prosecuted for euthanasia since 1950.

Derek Humphrey publishes *Let Me Die before I Wake*, a guide to self-deliverance.

The British EXIT group publishes *A Guide to Self-Deliverance*.

A nonphysician is convicted of assisting in a suicide in Rotterdam, the Netherlands. This case establishes guidelines to better determine which cases will be excused from prosecution.

A committee made up of the Los Angeles County Medical Association and the Los Angeles County Bar Association issues formal guidelines for doctors to follow when withdrawing life-support systems from terminal patients without the prior approval of the courts.

1982

Congress passes the Tax Equity and Fiscal Responsibility Act, which classifies illnesses into categories called "diagnostic-related groups." This legislation makes it possible for Medicare to pay only a predetermined amount for services rendered to subscribers. Many believe that this shift causes hospitals to discharge elderly patients prematurely.

The Medical Society of the State of New York issues guidelines for withholding resuscitation from terminally ill patients who have stopped breathing or whose hearts have failed.

The Alkmaar District Court of the Netherlands acquits a physician of practicing euthanasia by assisting a 95-year-old patient to die at her request. This case finds that the patient has a right to self-determination and that her request was an exercise of this right. The physician is found to have followed all due protocols, but the prosecutor appeals the decision.

Queen Beatrix of the Netherlands creates the State Commission on Euthanasia.

Two Parisian journalists publish *Suicide, Mode d'Emploi*, a manual promoting suicide as a revolutionary act that should be used by anyone who chooses it, not just the terminally ill. Nearly 50,000 copies sell in just five months, and the book is linked to ten suicides by individuals who are not terminally ill. The manual causes an uproar in French medical, religious, and political circles, as well as within the French right-to-die society, *Association pour le Droit de Mourir dans la Dignité*. Attempts to ban the publication are unsuccessful.

- 1983   Twenty-three states define death by the action of the heart, while 27 define it by the lack of brain function.

On 11 January 25-year-old Nancy Cruzan has a car accident and is diagnosed as being in a persistent vegetative state. She has no living will. Her parents' legal struggle to provide their daughter with a dignified death initiates another wave of interest in the subject of euthanasia.

1983
cont.

On 7 March the Department of Health and Human Services releases the "Baby Doe" regulations. These require any hospital with federal funding to post in all nurseries, maternity wards, and intensive-care nurseries a notice that reads: "Discriminatory failure to feed and care for handicapped infants in this facility is prohibited by federal law." The new rules are set to go into effect 22 March 1983.

On 18 March the American Academy of Pediatrics and several other national organizations bring a suit against the Department of Health and Human Services and its secretary, Margaret Heckler, to protest the Baby Doe regulations. The judge agrees to review the case quickly.

On 14 April Judge Gerhard Gesell rules that the Baby Doe regulations are in violation of the law and must be amended.

On 8 October the infant Baby Jane Doe is born in New York, suffering from spina bifida, hydrocephaly, and microencephaly. Her parents decide to forego surgery that could allow her to live into her twenties in a severely compromised state. Lawyer Lawrence Washburn petitions the court on behalf of the baby to have the surgery performed against the parents' wishes, claiming the hospital is discriminating against the handicapped infant. The court rules against the parents and the surgery is performed.

The Veterans' Administration issues a ruling that recognizes a patient's right to die. This allows doctors to write orders that explicitly deny lifesaving therapy to critically ill patients. Before issuing do-not-resuscitate orders, the physician must have the permission of the patient or the patient's family in cases in which the patient is unable to make the decision.

- The President's Commission for the Study of Ethical Problems in Medicine and Biomedical and Behavioral Research recommends that patients be allowed to refuse lifesaving treatments if death is imminent. The commission recommends that hospitals create policies regarding the resuscitation of patients whose hearts have stopped.

The case of the physician from Alkmaar, the Netherlands (*see* 1982), is brought to the Amsterdam Court of Appeals, which reverses the prior judgment and convicts the physician under Article 293 of the Dutch Criminal Law regarding euthanasia, but asks for no punishment. The physician appeals the case to the Supreme Court of the Netherlands.

Dr. Pieter Admiraal writes the booklet *Justifiable Euthanasia: A Manual for the Medical Profession*. Its 11 pages offer physicians and pharmacists a summary of drug dosages for effective assistance in hastening death.

1984   The Royal Dutch Society for the Promotion of Medicine sends a letter to the minister of justice of the Netherlands calling for a change in the law to allow euthanasia.

The physician in the Alkmaar case appeals the Amsterdam ruling to the Supreme Court with assistance from the Netherlands Society for Voluntary Euthanasia. In November the Dutch Supreme Court overturns the Amsterdam decision and refers the case to the Court of Appeals in The Hague (*see* 1986).

In October the U.S. Congress passes "Baby Doe" legislation, requiring states that receive grant monies from the federal government for child abuse prevention to adopt rules to prevent the medical neglect of handicapped infants.

1985   Karen Ann Quinlan dies in July after contracting pneumonia.

In August Dr. John Kraii is arrested in New York for giving a lethal injection to his patient Frederick C. Wagner, who is dying from Alzheimer's disease

1985 *cont.*	and gangrene. He is the fifth doctor in the United States to be prosecuted for euthanasia.
	The State Commission of the Netherlands on Euthanasia issues a report that is meant to clarify the issue. It includes legislative reform recommendations for the Queen.
1986	Two lawyers, Michael White and Robert Risely, write the Humane and Dignified Death Act. The initiative fails to get enough signatures to get on the ballot in the state of California.
	Dr. Joseph Hassman, a New Jersey physician, becomes the sixth physician to be prosecuted for euthanasia since 1950.
	The court in The Hague, the Netherlands, dismisses charges against the physician from Alkmaar (*see* 1982) on the basis that there are no norms of medical ethics that forbid his actions.
1987	The trial of Dr. Peter Rosier, charged with murdering his wife, Patti, who suffered from cancer, begins at the end of October in St. Petersburg, Florida. He is acquitted on all counts by a unanimous vote on 1 December.
	All books containing information about how to commit suicide are banned in France.
1988	The group Americans Against Human Suffering sponsors a California initiative, which seeks to legalize euthanasia and physician-assisted death. The initiative fails to get enough signatures to be placed on the ballot.
	On 17 September Gary Dockery, a Tennessee policeman, lapses into a coma after being shot in the head in the line of duty. Doctors feel he has very little hope of ever recovering (*see* February 1996).
1989	Dr. Jack Kevorkian builds a suicide machine that he calls the "mercitron."

Missouri Senator John Danforth introduces the Patient Self-Determination Act (PSDA) in Congress.

The U.S. Supreme Court agrees to hear *Cruzan v. Director, Missouri Department of Health,* the Nancy Cruzan case. This is the first right-to-die case to reach the Court.

The combined membership of Concern for Dying and the Society for the Right to Die is 64,863.

Michigan physician Donald Caraccio becomes the eighth physician to be prosecuted for euthanasia in the United States since 1950. He is sentenced to five years probation with community service.

1990

On 25 June the U.S. Supreme Court rules 5–4 in favor of the Cruzans in *Cruzan v. Director, Missouri Department of Health.* Chief Justice William Rehnquist states that the Fourteenth Amendment of the U.S. Constitution guarantees the right to avoid unwanted medical treatment but leaves the setting of specific guidelines to individual states.

Dr. Richard Schaeffer, a California practitioner, is the ninth U.S. physician to be prosecuted for euthanasia since 1950.

On 4 June Dr. Kevorkian helps Alzheimer's patient Janet Adkins die in his 1968 Volkswagon van.

Dr. Steven Miles publishes findings in *Law, Medicine and Health Care,* which shows that courts are less likely to give weight to women's wishes regarding life support than they are to those of men.

The Patient Self-Determination Act is passed by Congress in November. It requires all centers that receive federal funds to inform patients that they have a right to refuse medical treatment and allows these centers to provide living wills and powers of attorney in advance of any illness or injury. This legislation goes into effect in 1991 and supersedes state living-will legislation.

1990
cont.

On 3 December Dr. Kevorkian is charged with murder in Janet Adkins's death. Criminal charges are dropped on 13 December after Judge Gerald McNally hears a tape made by Janet Adkins before her death.

Nancy Cruzan's feeding tube is removed by court order on 14 December, and she is moved to a hospice care unit. Four days later, 19 right-to-life activists are arrested as they attempt to reconnect Cruzan's feeding tube. They are not successful. She dies on 26 December at 2:47 A.M.

Concern for Dying and the Society for the Right to Die report a combined membership of 143,750.

The Royal Dutch Medical Association, in cooperation with the Ministry of Justice in the Netherlands, agree on a notification procedure that requires physicians to report all cases of patients they assist in dying.

1991

The *New England Journal of Medicine* publishes an article by Dr. Timothy Quill in which he describes helping one of his terminally ill patients, Patricia Diane Trumbull, take her own life. On 26 July, a jury declines to indict Dr. Quill on three charges in Trumbull's death.

Final Exit, by Derek Humphrey, is published and becomes a 1991 nonfiction best-seller. It remains on the *New York Times* best-seller list for 18 weeks.

Dr. Kevorkian's book *Prescription Medicine: The Goodness of Planned Death* is published.

In September the organizations Concern for Dying and the Society for the Right to Die merge and become Choice in Dying, a national council on the right to die.

On 23 October Dr. Kevorkian assists in the suicides of Sherry Miller and Marjorie Wantz in a rented cabin in Michigan.

The Death with Dignity Initiative (#119) fails in Washington State, where 1.3 million voters cast ballots. The failure is attributed to an oppositional media blitz by the American Medical Association and the Catholic Church.

In November the Pennsylvania State House of Representatives votes 186–15 to allow a terminally ill person to forego treatment if the patient has signed a living will while still of sound mind and body. Final passage of this law takes place in April 1992.

On 20 November the Michigan Board of Medicine suspends Dr. Kevorkian's medical license. The decision is unanimous.

The Patient Self-Determination Act goes into effect on 1 December. Right-to-die organizations are flooded with requests for living wills and power-of-attorney forms.

On 18 December Michigan Prosecutor Richard Thompson issues a homicide ruling against Dr. Kevorkian in the deaths of Miller and Wantz.

Nancy Cruzan's parents establish the Cruzan Foundation to assist other families in similar circumstances.

Brenda Young of Flint, Michigan, is admitted to the emergency room of St. Joseph Hospital suffering from a seizure. Her mother tells physicians that her daughter does not want life support. The hospital puts her on a ventilator anyway.

1992   Dr. Kevorkian is indicted for murder in the cases of Miller and Wantz (*Michigan v. Kevorkian*) on 5 February.

HB #1481, known as the Feeding Tube Bill, passes in Washington State by an 82–14 vote on 13 February. It allows a patient in an irreversible coma to be

1992
cont.

taken off of life support if he or she has so requested in a living will.

The California Death with Dignity Act (Proposition #161) obtains enough signatures to be placed on the ballot.

Governor Lawton Chiles signs the Health Care Advance Directives Act into law in Florida on 10 April.

In May Derek Humphrey resigns as director of the Hemlock Society.

Dr. Kevorkian assists Susan Williams to commit suicide on 15 May in Clawson, Michigan.

Final Exit is banned in New Zealand, Australia, and France.

On 5 June the Oakland County (Michigan) deputy chief medical examiner declares Dr. Kevorkian's actions in the death of Susan Williams a homicide.

On 11 June the Washington state attorney general files a lawsuit against the #119 Vote No! Committee for circulating a flyer that states initiative 119 "would let doctors end patients' lives without benefits of safeguards." He asks for $10,000 in penalties.

On 21 July Kevorkian is cleared on two charges of first degree murder in the October 1991 deaths of Sherry Miller and Marjorie Wantz. Judge Breck rules that the *Roberts* opinion (*see* 1920), which made assisting a suicide the same as murder, was too limited in scope to apply to this case.

Initiative #161, the Death with Dignity Act, is defeated in California 54 to 46 percent.

The ban on *Final Exit* is repealed in Australia and New Zealand in August.

Dr. Kevorkian helps Lois Hawes to end her life on 26 September in Michigan. On 23 November he assists in the suicide of Catherine Andreyev, a Pennsylvania woman suffering from cancer.

The Danish Parliament passes legislation (L 1992-05-14, no. 351) that provides for a standard format for advance directives. Up until this time, legal advance directives did not exist.

On 24 November the Michigan House of Representatives votes 72 to 29 to make assisted suicide a felony punishable by four years in prison. The measure is to become effective on 30 March 1993.

On 15 December Kevorkian assists in the suicides of Marguerite Tate and Marcella Lawrence.

1993   Dr. Kevorkian assists in the suicide of Jack Miller on 20 January, of Stanley Ball and Mary Biernat on 4 February, of Elaine Goldblum on 8 February, of Hugo Gale on 15 February, and of Jonathan Grenz and Martha Ruwart on 17 February.

The Select Committee on Medical Ethics, representing all parties of the British House of Lords, agrees in February that there should be no change in the law to permit euthanasia.

On 9 February the Dutch Parliament passes the first modern euthanasia law in the world. It guarantees doctors will be safe from prosecution providing they follow the guidelines established.

On 25 February the Michigan Senate bans assisted suicide by passing a special measure that goes into effect immediately rather than on 30 March, as originally intended. It is signed into law by Governor Engler.

On 1 March the American Civil Liberties Union challenges Michigan's assisted-suicide ban in court.

1993
cont.

Dr. Kevorkian assists in the suicide of Ronald Mansur on 15 May, of Thomas Hyde on 4 August, and of Donald O'Keefe on 9 September.

1994

On 24 January *Compassion et al. v. Washington State* is brought to the U.S. District Court for western Washington by the organization Compassion in Dying. The complainants, three terminally ill patients and four physicians, claim that Washington state law intrudes on the constitutional rights of liberty and equal protection under the Fourteenth Amendment. On 3 May federal Judge Barbara Rothstein rules that it is unconstitutional to forbid physician aid-in-dying for a terminally ill, competent adult in the state of Washington.

On 12 February Canadian Sue Rodriguez dies with the assistance of an anonymous physician. Svend Robinson, a personal friend and member of Parliament, confirms that a doctor did assist her in dying.

In June the Council on Ethical and Judicial Affairs of the American Medical Association issues an opinion that organs may be removed from anencephalic (having no functioning cerebral hemispheres) infants while they are still alive.

On 29 July *Quill et al. v. New York* is filed in the U.S. District Court by three doctors and three terminally ill patients to test New York's ban on suicide.

Death upon Request, a Dutch-produced documentary about the mercy killing of Cees van Wendel de Joode, a 63-year-old man who suffered from amyotrophic lateral sclerosis (ALS), is shown on television in the Netherlands in October.

The World Health Organization's director general calls for "Teaching medical ethics ... to ensure that physicians are sensitive to ethical issues in all their decisions throughout their professional lifetime" on 14 October in his closing address to the Consultation on the Teaching of Medical Ethics, held in Geneva, Switzerland. Medical ethics are not compulsory in many medical schools worldwide.

Michigan's ban on assisted suicide expires in November.

On 8 November the world's first assisted-suicide law (The Dutch Criminal Code does not explicitly allow assisted suicide), Oregon's Death with Dignity Act, or Measure 16, is passed by voters 52 to 48 percent. It is to take effect one month later.

On 17 November bishops representing the 1,200 Catholic hospitals in the United States release a statement that forbids physician-assisted suicide in any of their facilities.

On 7 December District Judge Michael Hogan issues a temporary restraining order to prevent Oregon's Death with Dignity Act from going into effect the following day.

On 7 December the Michigan Senate votes 26 to 9 to ban assisted suicide permanently. On 13 December the Michigan House passes a similar bill on a 67 to 35 vote, but adds a requirement for a statewide referendum in November 1996. The Michigan State Supreme Court rules that there is no constitutional right to assisted suicide and thus the state's ban is constitutional.

On 15 December Judge Thomas P. Griesa of the U.S. District Court in New York City rules in *Quill et al. v. New York* to uphold the law making assisted suicide illegal. The plaintiffs appeal the case to the Second Circuit Court of Appeals.

On 27 December District Judge Michael Hogan rules to postpone the implementation of Oregon's Death with Dignity Act indefinitely until constitutional concerns can be heard and analyzed.

1995   The Washington state legislature introduces a bill on 26 January to allow physician-assisted suicide.

On 9 March the U.S. Ninth Circuit Court of Appeals overturns Judge Barbara Rothstein's ruling in the case of *Compassion et al. v. Washington State* by a 2–1 vote (*see* January 1994).

The trial of Dr. Henk Prins begins on 13 April in Alkmaar, the Netherlands. The court charges that the doctor took the life of a three-day-old baby born in 1993 with hydroencephaly, spina bifida, and leg deformities without the clear consent of the child's parents.

Dr. Kevorkian assists in the suicide of Rev. John Evans on 8 May and in that of Nicholas Loving on 12 May.

On 6 June, after 16 months of deliberation, the Canadian Senate Special Committee on Euthanasia and Assisted Suicide recommends that assisted suicide remain a criminal offense, but that it should have a less severe penalty. Prime Minister Jean Chretien wants the issue of assisted suicide put to a vote in Parliament.

Dr. Kevorkian assists in the suicides of Erika Garcellano on 26 June and of Esther Cohan, who suffers from multiple sclerosis, on 21 August.

On 4 July New York editor George Delury assists his wife to die by mixing a lethal drug concoction for her in their Manhattan apartment. His wife, Myrna Lebov, is 52 at the time of death and suffering from multiple sclerosis.

On 25 August the Royal Dutch Medical Association releases a revised policy on euthanasia, which says it would be better for patients to take their own lives whenever possible rather than having a physician assist them.

On 1 September oral arguments are heard by three judges of the Second Circuit Court of Appeals in *Quill et al. v. New York* (*see* July and December 1994).

In October an *en banc* hearing is held in the case of *Compassion in Dying v. Washington State*. This type of hearing, which involves all judges (all those qualified to sit on a hearing in a given circuit) in the case, is reserved for cases of much import (*see* March 1996).

On 30 October Kevorkian forms a group with five doctors and a psychologist to write medical guidelines for physicians who choose to assist their terminally ill patients in committing suicide. The group is called Physicians for Mercy.

Dr. Kevorkian assists in the suicide of Patricia Cashman on 8 November.

1996 A Michigan probate judge gives Dr. Gerald "Chip" Klooster II permanent custody of his father, Gerald Klooster, a retired physician who has Alzheimer's disease. The son believes that other members of his family want his father killed based on written communications with Dr. Kevorkian

On 4 January House Bill 339, the New Hampshire Death with Dignity Bill, is defeated 256 to 90 by the House of Representatives. The bill, sponsored by Robert Guest (Democrat), is the third such bill in the past five years in New Hampshire.

Also on this day, a licensed practical nurse, Janice Mercinko, is fined $1,000 in a Maine court after she pleads guilty to tampering with a patient's file and endangering the welfare of an innocent person. Mercinko had administered a fatal narcotic dose to Glenice Stearns, a 67-year-old woman who was dying. Licensed practical nurses are not allowed to administer prescription drugs and Mercinko forged a registered nurse's initials on the patient's chart.

1996
cont.

On 29 January 200 delegates attending the annual Convention of the Episcopal Diocese of Newark approve a resolution allowing suicide for the terminally ill. Bishop John Shelby Spong, leader of the 40,000-member diocese, tells delegates that the time has arrived to redefine what "life" means in a religious faith.

On 9 February Dr. Jack Kevorkian files a $10 million lawsuit in Wayne County Circuit Court against the American Medical Association and the Michigan State Medical Society. Kevorkian claims that these groups have slandered him by calling him a killer.

In early February 42-year-old policeman Gary Dockery emerges from a seven-and-a-half-year vegetative state able to clearly communicate with his family. He successfully undergoes surgery to treat pneumonia on 15 February and is once again able to speak on 21 February. A great deal of debate regarding the accuracy of diagnosis in cases involving coma and brain function ensues.

On 16 February a Michigan jury awards approximately $16 million to Brenda Young (38), who sued the Genesys Health System for keeping her on life support against her wishes.

On 20 February opening arguments are heard in the assisted-suicide trial of Dr. Kevorkian for the 1993 deaths of Dr. Ali Khalili of Oakbrook, Illinois, and Merian Frederick of Ann Arbor, Michigan. He is the eleventh physician to be prosecuted for euthanasia in the United States since 1950.

On 1 March the Roman Catholic archbishop of New York, Cardinal John O'Connor, helps to transfer a brain-dead infant from a Queens hospital to a Catholic facility. This happens because physicians at Long Island Jewish Medical Center are unwilling to continue life support for the baby, who they had pronounced dead a week earlier.

On 6 March the Ninth U.S. Circuit Court of Appeals strikes down the ban on physician-assisted suicide in an 8–3 decision in the case brought by Compassion in Dying.

On 7 March a jury of six men and six women begins deliberations in the Kevorkian case. Attorneys for Oregon's Measure 16 file an emergency motion with the Ninth Circuit Court of Appeals to lift Judge Hogan's ban in light of the court's decision striking down Washington's ban on assisted suicide on 6 March.

On 8 March Dr. Kevorkian is found not guilty in the deaths of Dr. Ali Khalili and Merian Frederick.

On 1 April Kevorkian goes on trial for assisting in the 1991 suicides of Marjorie Wantz and Sherry Miller.

On 2 April the Second Circuit Court of Appeals rules in *Quill et al. v. Vacca* to strike down the New York state law prohibiting assisted suicide. The New York attorney general says he will appeal the Quill case to the Supreme Court. On 11 April the court rules further that there is no difference between removing artificial life support and prescribing lethal doses of medications for terminally ill patients.

On 6 May Dr. Jack Kevorkian assists Austin Bastable, a 53-year-old Canadian man suffering from multiple sclerosis, to commit suicide. Bastable is the first non-American assisted by Dr. Kevorkian. Bastable was a right-to die activist in Canada who used the Internet to garner support for his decision to die. His is the twenty-eighth suicide assisted by Dr. Kevorkian.

On 11 May closing arguments are heard in Dr. Jack Kevorkian's third trial in Oakland County Circuit Court to determine if he broke the December 1994 Michigan Supreme Court ruling that banned

1996
cont.

assisted suicide. On 14 May Kevorkian is found not guilty.

On 17 May George Delury, a 72-year-old editor, is sentenced to six months in jail by Manhattan (New York) Supreme Court Judge Herbert Altman for assisting his wife, Myrna Lebov, who was 52, to die.

On 29 May Supreme Court Justice Sandra Day O'Connor orders the ban on physician-assisted suicide to remain in effect in Washington State while opponents of the Ninth Circuit Court decision file their arguments with the court.

On 9 June Dr. Jack Kevorkian assists Ruth Neuman, a 69-year-old Columbus, New Jersey, woman, to commit suicide. She had suffered from multiple strokes. This is the twenty-ninth suicide assisted by Kevorkian.

On 18 June Dr. Jack Kevorkian attends the death of 58-year-old Lona Jones of Virginia. She was suffering from a malignant brain tumor. Jones is the thirtieth person Kevorkian assists to commit suicide.

On 20 June Dr. Jack Kevorkian attends his thirty-first suicide. Sixty-seven-year-old Bette Lou Hamilton from Ohio was suffering from a disease called sryingomyelia, in which the spinal cord is destroyed. On this same day in Canada, 49-year-old Dr. Maurice Genereaux is charged with assisting in the 10 April suicide of his 31-year-old patient Aaron McGinn. McGinn had been diagnosed as HIV-positive. Genereaux is the first Canadian doctor to be charged with "aiding a suicide."

On 25 June the American Medical Association publicly reaffirms its long-standing policy against physician-assisted suicide.

On 1 July the Rights of the Terminally Ill Act goes into effect in the Northern Territory of Australia.

On 4 July Shirley Cline, a 63-year-old California woman suffering from cancer, becomes the thirty-second person to commit suicide with assistance from Dr. Jack Kevorkian.

On 9 July Rebecca Badger, a 39-year-old California woman is the thirty-third person to be assisted by Dr. Jack Kevorkian and the fifth since his acquittal in May. She was suffering from multiple sclerosis at the time of her death. On this same day, Cardinal Adam Maida of the Roman Catholic Archdiocese of Detroit announces a 24-hour hotline called "Project Life" to offer people alternatives to assisted suicide and abortion. Simultaneously, a panel of three judges from the Ninth Circuit Court of Appeals meets in Portland, Oregon, to hear arguments regarding the constitutionality of Measure 16, the Oregon law allowing physician-assisted suicide that passed in November 1994.

On 21 July press reports indicate that an Oregon physician, Dr. James D. Gallant, is being investigated for administering a lethal injection to his 78-year-old patient, Clarietta Day, who died on 22 March. The State Board of Medical Examiners had voted 10–0 to pursue disciplinary action.

On 24 July Dr. Jack Kevorkian files a petition requesting that the United States Supreme Court rule on the question of assisted suicide. Kevorkian specifically wants the court to determine whether or not he can use his "mercitron" to assist people in suicide. The machine is known to have been used in the death of Janet Adkins in 1990.

On 29 July Dr. Ljubisa Dragovic, a Detroit county medical examiner, accuses Dr. Jack Kevorkian of murder in the deaths of Rebecca Badger and Shirley Cline. Dragovic's report indicates that both women were injected with potassium chloride, that neither death was self-inflicted, and that neither woman had been diagnosed as terminally ill. His report indicates that both women were unconscious at the

1996
cont.

time of death, and traces of several sedatives were reported found in their bloodstreams. On this same day, Dr. Georges Rene Reding, a Michigan psychiatrist who has attended the five previous suicides assisted by Dr. Kevorkian, makes a public statement in support of Dr. Kevorkian's actions.

On 6 August Dr. Jack Kevorkian assists 59-year-old Elizabeth Mertz to commit suicide. The Cincinnati woman was suffering from Lou Gehrig's disease at the time of her death. She is the thirty-fourth person to die with the assistance of Dr. Kevorkian since 1990.

On 15 August Dr. Jack Kevorkian assists 42-year-old Judith Curren of Massachusetts to commit suicide. At the time of her death, Curren was diagnosed as having chronic fatigue and immune system dysfunction and fibromyalgia. Neither of these conditions is terminal. She is the thirty-fifth person assisted by Kevorkian.

On 20 August Dr. Jack Kevorkian assists 76-year-old Louise Siebens of Texas, who was suffering from Lou Gehrig's disease, to commit suicide. She is the thirty-seventh person he has assisted since 1990.

On 22 August Dr. Jack Kevorkian assists a woman, 40-year-old Patricia Smith, with multiple sclerosis in committing suicide in the presence of her husband and father and takes her body to Pontiac Osteopathic Hospital (Michigan). Eight hours later, Kevorkian takes the body of 66-year-old Pat DiGangi to the same hospital. DiGangi was also suffering from multiple sclerosis when he died. Kevorkian is arrested at that hospital on charges of disorderly conduct.

Biographical Sketches   3

The following individuals are representative of the many who have been involved in the right-to-die issue. Some lived long ago, while others are alive today and still participating in the debate. Patients, their physicians, psychologists, ethicists, religious leaders, legislators, judges, and academics—all are represented here.

Dying touches everybody at one time or another; this is not an issue limited by profession or station in life. The following individuals are notable either because they represent an important aspect of the historical development of the euthanasia issue or because they directly affect the debate today. All are listed alphabetically by last name.

Janet Adkins (1936–1990)

Janet Adkins's death on 4 June 1990 at the age of 54 brought the issue of physician-assisted suicide to the front pages of newspapers around the world. She was the first person to make use of Dr. Jack Kevorkian's "suicide machine." Her death set off a renewed public interest in developing legislation to regulate or prohibit physician aid-in-dying.

Adkins was a schoolteacher. She lived with her husband in Portland, Oregon, and the couple had three adult sons. A year before her death she was diagnosed as having Alzheimer's and was told that she would soon be unable to care for herself. This did not qualify her as terminally ill, but her mental abilities were rapidly deteriorating. A vibrant and active woman, Adkins did not want to be completely incapacitated. She underwent psychological counseling, which helped her sort through her desire to die. She then tried to obtain help-in-dying from three different Oregon doctors. They were unwilling to assist her. She heard about Dr. Kevorkian through the media and contacted him in 1989. He reviewed her medical records and agreed to help her. In early June 1990 Janet and her husband flew to Michigan.

Adkins's death took place in Kevorkian's 1968 Volkswagon van at a campsite called Grovelands, just outside Royal Oak, Michigan. The process did not go smoothly. Dr. Kevorkian had forgotten several tools for his suicide machine and spilled some drugs while attempting to repair it. Adkins waited several hours while Kevorkian ran errands to remedy the situation. When death finally came, it was by Adkins's own hand. She flipped a switch that released thiopental, a sleep-inducing drug. A timer, set to switch the solution to potassium chloride a minute later, then stopped her heart. On the day that Janet Adkins died, some of the major players in the nascent right-to-die movement were attending a conference on euthanasia in the Netherlands.

Dr. Kevorkian was charged with murder in the death of Janet Adkins but was later acquitted.

Pieter Admiraal (1929–)

A retired Dutch anesthesiologist, Dr. Pieter Admiraal is among the most experienced physicians in the world in the actual practice of physician-assisted suicide. He has actively promoted euthanasia in the Netherlands since 1973 and is considered one of the leaders of the euthanasia movement in his country.

Before his retirement in 1995, Admiraal was on staff at Reinier de Graf Hospital in Delft for 30 years. In 1977 he compiled the first table of lethal drug dosages ever published. In 1987 he established the lethal-dosage guidelines for the Royal Dutch Society for the Advancement of Pharmacy. He believes euthanasia should be an option made available to patients as a way of respecting patient autonomy. He feels that doctors who do not mention this option deny patients alternatives when making health care decisions.

Admiraal has written extensively on the subject of effective physician-assisted suicide methodologies, including an 11-page booklet called *Justifiable Euthanasia: A Manual for the Medical Profession*, which includes information about lethal drug dosages. This pamphlet was distributed to doctors and pharmacists throughout the Netherlands in 1983. He speaks internationally on the subject of physician-assisted death.

Daniel Callahan (1930–)

Daniel Callahan's study of bioethics began in earnest in 1962, marking the beginning of this important field of inquiry. His numerous reports, essays, and articles have covered topics ranging from population and aging to abortion, from religion to euthanasia and physician-assisted suicide. This work has served to educate legislators, health care professionals, educators, and individuals around the world, and he is considered the foremost expert on medical ethics in the United States.

A cofounder of the Hastings Center (formerly the Institute of Society, Ethics, and the Life Sciences) in 1969, Dr. Callahan still serves as president of this respected organization. He holds a Ph.D. in philosophy from Harvard (1965), a master's degree from Georgetown University (1957), and an undergraduate degree in English and psychology from Yale University (1952).

Dr. Callahan has served as special consultant to the Presidential Commission on Population Growth and the American Future (1970–1971), sits on the Advisory Board for the Center for Philosophy and Public Policy (1976–present), acts as consultant to the Medical Ethics Committee of the American College of Physicians (1983–present), serves on the Biomedical Ethics Committee of the National Foundation of the March of Dimes (1983–present), and was a member of the advisory committee to the director of the U.S. Centers for Disease Control and Prevention, U.S. Department of Health and Human Services (1995).

He currently sits on the editorial advisory boards of 16 publications, including *Ethics in Science and Medicine, Science, Technology and Human Values, Bioethics*, and the *Journal of Medicine, Ethics and Law* (Canada). He has authored, coauthored, and edited more than 30 books, including *A World Growing Old* (1995) with Ruud ter Meulen and Eva Topinková; *The Troubled Dream of Life: In Search of a Peaceful Death* (1994); *What Kind of Life: The Limits of Medical Progress* (1990); and *Setting Limits: Medical Goals in an Aging Society* (1987), which was one of three finalists for the 1988 Pulitzer Prize for nonfiction.

Nancy Cruzan (1957–1990)

Nancy Cruzan's tragic car accident in 1983 marked the beginning of a long journey her family would take on her behalf to allow her to die. It culminated in the creation of a new legal landscape for the terminally ill.

Cruzan's active life was cut short at the age of 25 when an automobile accident left her in a persistent vegetative state (PVS). Her family waited four years for her to regain consciousness, thinking that this was possible. Then one day her father read about PVS and realized that this was the state in which his daughter would permanently exist. When the doctors confirmed this, the family realized that Nancy would not have wanted to be kept alive in this condition.

The Cruzan family's fight to have Nancy's feeding and hydration tube removed took the right-to-die issue all the way to the U.S. Supreme Court. This battle prompted Republican Senator John Danforth of Missouri to introduce the Patient Self-Determination Act (PSDA) of 1991. Passed by Congress in November 1990, the PSDA required all health care centers receiving federal aid to inform patients of their right to refuse medical treatment and to make their wishes known through advance directives, living wills, and health care powers of attorney.

Nancy Cruzan's surgically implanted feeding tube was removed on 14 December 1990, and she died 11 days later.

Baby Doe (1982)

Baby Doe was born in 1982 with Down's syndrome and a malformed esophagus. His parents made a decision to withhold surgery to repair his esophagus and also to withhold artificial feeding and hydration. This was intended to cause death by starvation.

The hospital went to court, where it was decided that the parents could make these decisions on behalf of their child. Further legal wrangling involved allegations that this decision constituted parental neglect. Baby Doe died at the age of six days in April 1982.

The subsequent outcry spurred the Reagan administration to direct the Department of Health and Human Services (under Secretary Margaret Heckler) to issue the Baby Doe Directive in May 1982. It forbade medical discrimination against handicapped infants. The department threatened to cut federal funding to any hospital that discriminated by withholding nutrition, hydration, medication, or surgery because of a handicap that, although it might diminish quality of life, was not considered fatal.

After many court battles questioning this directive, the U.S. Supreme Court decided in *Bowen v. American Hospital Association et al.* that parents do have the right to make treatment decisions on behalf of their children in cases such as these.

Baby Jane Doe (1983–)

Born on 8 October 1983, Baby Jane Doe suffered from a number of birth defects including spina bifida, excessive water in her brain, and an abnormally small brain. Her parents were told that, unless she had surgery, she would die within two years, and that after undergoing surgery she would be severely mentally retarded, in pain, and physically disabled. Her parents elected not to have surgery performed.

Right-to-life groups became involved and petitioned the courts to order surgery. Instead, the federal government enacted the Baby Doe regulations sooner than anticipated, stating that no child should be refused treatment based on an anticipated mental or physical handicap. Although struck down in May 1984, the regulations effectively stopped Baby Jane Doe's parents from making health care decisions on her behalf. Although still listed in critical condition at the age of two months, Baby Jane Doe survived and flourished, even as a heated legal debate addressed the complex issues she had inadvertently raised, such as medical neglect and the right of parents to make medical decisions on behalf of their children.

In 1996 Keri Lynn (Baby Jane) was a 12-year-old who attended school and enjoyed a far better quality of life than was initially expected.

Geoffrey Nels Fieger (1950–)

Geoffrey Nels Fieger is Dr. Jack Kevorkian's lead attorney. His defense of Dr. Kevorkian has provided a platform for his personal and professional opinions on end-of-life issues. He has successfully defended Kevorkian in the three trials (1995–1996) that questioned Kevorkian's actions in assisting people to end their lives. Kevorkian was acquitted in all three trials. Fieger's work on behalf of Kevorkian has set legal precedent for physician-assisted suicide in the state of Michigan and could heavily influence the future of the debate, both in and out of the courtroom.

Fieger received his B.A. in theater from the University of Michigan in 1974; an M.A. in speech from the same institution in 1976, and his law degree from Detroit College of Law in 1979. He is a member of the bar in three states: Michigan, Florida, and Arizona, and he heads the law firm of Fieger, Fieger, and Schwartz, P.C., located in Michigan. His legal speciality is personal injury and medical malpractice. He has the highest profile of any other attorney in the world working in the field of physician-assisted suicide due to his work for Dr. Kevorkian. He has won 27 jury verdicts in excess of $1 million covering a wide range of medical issues for his other clients.

Between 1985–1988, Mr. Fieger hosted a weekly television series called *Legalities*, and he has been a guest on numerous television programs in the United States, such as *Frontline, Face the Nation, 20/20*, and many others. He has also appeared in programs taped in Australia, Great Britain, France, Spain, and Portugal. He was a commentator for local and national news organizations with regard to the O.J. Simpson case and often speaks to medical, legal, and public interest groups on various issues related to the Kevorkian cases he has won. His most recent publications include: "Michigan Tort Reform: An Exercise in Futility," *Detroit College Law Review* (1987), Issue 4, and "Medical Malpractice Tort Reform: An Analysis and Comparison of Existing Acts," *Michigan Bar Journal* 66: 3 (1987).

Joseph Fletcher (1905–1991)

Dr. Joseph Fletcher was one of the first non-Catholics to write about the religious ethics of end-of-life issues. He addressed thorny topics such as patient self-determination and what constitutes a good death. An Episcopal minister, he served as president of the Society for the Right to Die (now known as Choice in Dying) from 1974 to 1976. In a paper he presented to a euthanasia conference in 1974, he offered eight perspectives on and analyses of human actions that can be chosen at the end of life. These generated much debate on the process of end-of-life decision making. He felt there was no real difference between active and passive euthanasia because a deliberate decision is made to act in one way or the other. His books and articles have been very influential in generating greater acceptance of euthanasia in the United States.

A professor of theological ethics at the Episcopal Theological Seminary in Cambridge, Massachusetts, Dr. Fletcher wrote "The

Patient's Right To Die," published in *Harpers* magazine, as well as several books on medicine and active euthanasia, including *Morals and Medicine* (1954) and *Humanhood: Essays in Biomedical Ethics* (1979).

Carlos F. Gomez (1958–)

While Carlos Gomez was completing a Ph.D. in public policy at the University of Chicago, his study of euthanasia took him to the Netherlands. There he uncovered information he thought would be meaningful to those interested in legalizing physician-assisted suicide in the United States. His research culminated in the book *Regulating Death: Euthanasia and the Case of the Netherlands.*

This is one of the few books available that focuses on the actual practice of euthanasia, and it thoroughly examines numerous possible abuses that stem from its quasi-legal standing in the Netherlands. Dr. Gomez consulted with both jurists and physicians, looking at the question of euthanasia from a public policy point of view. His book demonstrates that, despite the best of intentions, in practice euthanasia is virtually unregulated in the Netherlands. He questions whether it could ever be properly regulated anywhere.

Dr. Gomez also coauthored *Protocols for the Elective Use of Life-Sustaining Treatments* (1989) and contributed to a study carried out by the Office of Technology Assessment to prepare recommendations for medical personnel about the use or withholding of life-sustaining treatments for patients.

Hippocrates (ca. 470–360 B.C.)

The Greek physician Hippocrates, to whom authorship of the Hippocratic Oath is attributed, is said to have been born on the island of Cos. To the modern mind, Hippocrates is a symbol of a long and noble medical tradition that swears to "first do no harm."

The works attributed to Hippocrates are the earliest recorded medical documents known to originate from ancient Greece. These include the Hippocratic Laws, which delineate the qualities a person should possess to become a physician and be educated in: "those things which are sacred [medical arts]...." Many scholars debate the authorship of the Oath, as well as many other works from this period. The Hippocratic Oath has been modified many times over the centuries. A modernized version is still in use today.

Alfred Hoche (1856–1944)

A professor of psychiatry at Freiburg University (Germany), Hoche introduced the concept of *balance-sheet suicide*, or *Bilanz-Selbstmord*, which argued that competent individuals could weigh the pros and cons of their lives and make valid decisions about whether to live or die.

Two years later, along with jurist Karl Binding (1841–1920), Hoche introduced the related concept of life not worthy of life *(lebensunwertes Leben)*, and the two later published *Permission for the Destruction of Life Unworthy of Life* (1920). This tract was extremely influential in its time and promoted ideas that eventually formed the theoretical foundation of the Nazi Euthanasia Programme, under which thousands of handicapped, retarded, and mentally disturbed patients were systematically murdered.

These two men, through this single work, created a negative historical connotation for both the word and the practice of euthanasia that, for many, still exists today.

Derek Humphrey (1930–)

Derek Humphrey may qualify as the most active spokesperson, advisor, and advocate for the dying and their families in the United States today.

Born in Bath, England, Humphrey was abandoned by his parents and raised by relatives. He left school for the world of work at the age of 15, starting as a messenger for the *Yorkshire Post* and rapidly becoming a reporter for *The Bristol Evening World*. Drafted at the age of 18, he served as an infantryman from 1948 to 1950 in the British Army. He then continued his career, working as a reporter at the *Manchester Evening News* and *The London Daily Mail*. By the age of 33 he was an editor. In 1971 he published his first book, *Because They're Black*, which won a Martin Luther King Jr. Memorial Prize. More books followed, including a biography of Malcolm X.

In 1975 Humphrey helped his wife, Jean, who had inoperable bone cancer, commit suicide. He remarried, and he and his second wife, Ann Wickett, moved to the United States, where Humphrey took a job as a reporter at the *Los Angeles Times* in 1978. He also published *Jean's Way* in March 1978, describing Jean's life and his role in her death. The book caused an international uproar and, for a time, Humphrey thought he would be prosecuted for murder. After a six-month investigation, the London director of public prosecutions decided not to press charges.

Humphrey found he was frequently approached by strangers looking for help in dying. It was these requests that propelled Humphrey, Wickett, Gerald A. Larue, and Richard S. Scott to found the Hemlock Society in 1980 in Santa Monica, California. Royalties from *Jean's Way* provided the initial funding for the organization.

In 1981 Humphrey published *Let Me Die before I Wake*, the first book to spell out detailed, accurate suicide methodologies. The royalties from this book provided additional funding for the Hemlock Society. *The Right To Die* (1986), a reference book, was coauthored by Wickett, who was soon thereafter diagnosed as having breast cancer. The couple moved the Hemlock Society to Oregon, and Humphrey served as president and executive director from 1988 to 1990. Humphrey and Wickett divorced in 1989, and Humphrey married Gretchen Crocker in 1991. Later that same year, as her battle with cancer heightened, Ann Wickett committed suicide.

Final Exit: The Practicalities of Self-Deliverance and Assisted Suicide was published in 1991. It describes methods of suicide even beyond the scope of those contained in *Let Me Die before I Wake*. It caused a stir from the moment it hit the stands and has become known in some circles as a "suicide manual." Several countries attempted to ban the book. Although most failed, it remains banned in France. Nearly a million copies have been sold.

In 1992 Humphrey left the Hemlock Society. A year later he formed the Euthanasia Research and Guidance Organization (ERGO), a small nonprofit organization. He has also written two additional books: *Dying with Dignity: Understanding Euthanasia* (1993) and *Lawful Exit: The Limits of Freedom for Help in Dying* (1994).

Pope John Paul II (1920–)

Pope John Paul II was born Karol Wojtyla in Cracow, Poland. Before ascending to the papacy on 16 October 1978 he held numerous jobs ranging from working in a quarry to serving as a professor of philosophy and ethics. He is the first Slavic pope in history. Pope John Paul II has also traveled more extensively than any other pope, sharing his message around the globe. A very significant part of this message has been the sacredness of life, from the womb to the grave.

In his 1980 Papal Encyclical, the pope eloquently condemned euthanasia in any form, explaining the spiritual value of suffering and affirming life and death as God's domain for all Roman Catholics. The euthanasia debate has accelerated rapidly during his papacy, and he has become an influential spokesperson on this and related right-to-life issues.

Jack Kevorkian (1928–)

For many in the United States, Dr. Jack Kevorkian is the personification of euthanasia. By openly assisting in the deaths of at least 38 people, ostentatiously flaunting laws passed to prevent him from proceeding, he has forced society to think about physician-assisted suicide. He has been repeatedly tried and acquitted on murder charges for these actions.

Born on 28 May 1928 in Pontiac, Michigan, Jack Kevorkian was the oldest of three children. He graduated from the University of Michigan Medical School in 1952 and decided to specialize in pathology while doing his internship at the Henry Ford Hospital in Detroit. In 1953 Kevorkian served in Korea as an army medical officer. Three residencies he held upon his return focused primarily on the history of autopsies. His father died of a heart attack. His mother died of cancer after a long and painful illness.

His nickname, "Dr. Death," predates by decades his advocacy of physician-assisted suicide. He earned it during his years at Detroit Receiving Hospital, where he took photographs of patients' corneas before, during, and after their deaths as part of his search for new ways to determine the precise moment of death.

In 1956 Kevorkian visited the Ohio State Penitentiary to interview two death-row inmates about having medical experiments performed on them during their executions. Although the inmates were willing, the courts would not allow Kevorkian to proceed. He lost his job at Michigan Medical Center when he continued to pursue this idea after it had been rejected. At Pontiac General Hospital he performed experiments on cadavers. His résumé began filling up with papers on topics such as how to use cadavers as blood donors, which tended to frighten prospective employers.

He took up oil painting in the 1960s. His works were an extension of his interest in death, dealing with cannibalism, skulls, and other body parts. He changed jobs several times and finally opened his own Checkup Diagnostic Center. In 1970 he was employed by Saratoga General Hospital as chief pathologist. He continued to write books and articles.

Between 1976 and 1981 Kevorkian moved back and forth between Michigan and California several times, and he changed jobs frequently. He wrote up various experiments he performed on executed people for several issues of the *Journal of the National Medical Association* during this period and also expanded his organ-harvesting concept to include patients who choose euthanasia by lethal injection.

In Michigan during the mid-1980s Kevorkian developed the concept of building "obitoria," or places where people could go to be euthanized. Unable to find a job in a hospital, he continued his controversial writing. In 1987 he flew to Amsterdam but was not welcomed by the medical profession there. He began to explore ways to help terminal patients commit suicide. He ran a classified ad that read: "Death Counseling. Is someone in your family terminally ill? Does he or she wish to die—and with dignity? Call Physician Consultant."

Unable to work in the medical profession, Kevorkian took a job as a salesman for a short time. When he began to explore the legal implications of opening an obitoria, he found no laws in Michigan that addressed the concept. On the basis of these inquiries, however, he was reported to the Michigan State Medical Board, which concluded that he was trying to change the law but was not acting on his ideas.

Kevorkian then began to develop a device he called a "thanatron," or death machine, which he later renamed "mercitron." This device brought him significant media exposure. The mercitron is very simple. Kevorkian starts an IV line in a patient and injects a simple saline solution. When the patient is ready, he or she simply presses a switch that shuts off the saline and begins a flow of thiopental, a sleep-inducing drug. A built-in timer then automatically initiates a flow of potassium chloride, which stops the heart, causing the patient to die.

The individuals Dr. Kevorkian has helped to commit suicide are not people he knew well; he did not have a long-term care relationship with any of them. Among many right-to-die or physician-assisted death groups, Kevorkian is viewed as having caused fear and confusion regarding end-of-life issues. More than a few feel he has set the movement back, rather than promoting the right-to-die agenda, through his dramatic actions. All admit he has succeeded in focusing attention on the issue.

Kevorkian's name is inextricably linked with the concept of physician-assisted suicide in the public mind.

Charles Everett Koop (1916–)

Former U.S. surgeon general during the Reagan and Bush administrations, Koop is quoted as asking, "Once any group of human beings is considered fair game in the arena of the right to life, where does it stop?" Dr. Koop first became famous for his surgery separating siamese twins and for other corrective surgical procedures he performed to improve the quality of life for birth-defective children.

Koop was a significant player in the Baby Doe regulations. His support of the decision to facilitate the Baby Doe Directive in May 1982 saved the life of Baby Jane Doe by forbidding discrimination against handicapped infants. Although the Supreme Court has since made decisions that countermand this directive (such as *Bowen v. American Hospital Association et al.*), Koop remains an outspoken and influential opponent of legalized physician-assisted death and most other forms of euthanasia.

His treatise on the case of Karen Ann Quinlan, published in *Euthanasia: The Moral Issues* (1989), eloquently urges that life-and-death decisions remain a function of the doctor-patient relationship. In it he states, "It is unthinkable that the law could direct this decision making on the part of the physician, because to do so would undermine the fundamental principles in all the great world of health care."

Elisabeth Kübler-Ross (1926–)

This Swiss psychologist was one of the first individuals to observe that the terminally ill pass through several psychological stages before they die. These stages have come to represent a road map of sorts for the dying. The five stages are: denial, anger, bargaining, grieving, and acceptance.

Born in Zurich, Kübler-Ross moved to the United States in 1958 and became a naturalized citizen in 1961. She received her medical degree from the University of Zurich in 1957.

In her classic book *On Death and Dying*, Kübler-Ross wrote that it is important to give dying people an opportunity to share their concerns during each of the stages until they finally arrive at an acceptance of their mortality. Her work spawned a much wider acceptance and understanding of the process of dying, even though it is now considered unscientific and critics assert that not all dying patients experience all five stages.

Kübler-Ross also has contributed to a greater understanding of the interaction between patients and their caregivers. She has demonstrated, for instance, that hospital staff avoid discussions of death and speak defensively when referring to patients who have died.

Books by Elisabeth Kübler-Ross include *On Death and Dying* (1969), *Questions and Answers on Death and Dying* (1974), *Death — The Final Stages of Growth* (1975), *To Live Until We Say Goodbye* (1978), *Working It Through* (1981), *Living with Death and Dying* (1981), *Remember the Secret* (1981), *On Children and Death* (1985), *AIDS: The Ultimate Challenge* (1988), and *On Life after Death* (1991).

Luis Kutner (1908–1993)

Luis Kutner was the Chicago lawyer who first proposed a living-will document. The publication of his paper "Due Process of Euthanasia: The Living Will, A Proposal" (*Indiana Law Review*, 1969) is considered by many to have been the most significant contribution to the discussion of euthanasia in the 1960s.

In mercy-killing cases, he asserted, neither the defendant nor the victim was well protected by the law, and terminally ill persons who wished to die were not legally allowed to do so. He proposed the creation of a document that a mentally competent, healthy adult could use to make known his or her wishes regarding type of treatment in the event of an illness or incapacitation.

"Where the patient is incapable of giving consent, such as when he is in a coma, a constructive consent is presumed, and the doctor is required to exercise reasonable care in applying ordinary means to preserve the patient's life. However, he is not allowed to resort to extraordinary care, especially where the patient is not expected to recover from the comatose state."

Living-will legislation has since been passed by many states, and the term coined by Kutner is now part of everyday speech.

Richard A. McCormick (1922–)

Notre Dame University's John A. O'Brien Professor of Christian Ethics Richard McCormick wrote the landmark book *Moral Dilemmas since Vatican II* (1990). From 1965 through 1984 McCormick wrote the column "Notes on Moral Theology," which appeared regularly in *Theological Studies*. These learned treatises have made him an authoritative Catholic voice speaking on end-of-life issues.

McCormick has also written about physicians and AIDS, pointing to doctor-patient relationships in AIDS cases as a move away from what he calls the "service-oriented roots of medicine." He opposes assisted suicide but acknowledges that the right-to-life movement's insistence that life be prolonged under all circumstances may ultimately prove to be counterproductive to the goal of preventing the legalization of physician-assisted suicide.

He is a prominent moderate pro-lifer who stands in firm opposition to assisted suicide.

Rita Marker (1940–)

Rita Marker has served as executive director of the International Anti-Euthanasia Task Force since its inception in 1987.

Formerly an adjunct professor of political science and ethics at the University of Steubenville, Ohio, Marker was one of the first people to be profiled in a series on "people making news in an era of dramatic change in medicine," published in the American Medical Association's *AMA News*. In addition to lecturing around the world on human rights, bioethics, and family relationships, Marker has also appeared on numerous television programs and radio shows.

Her book *Deadly Compassion* (1993) presents both the public and the personal sides of the euthanasia debate. She has authored numerous articles, including "Euthanasia: An Historical Overview" for the *Maryland Journal of Contemporary Legal Issues* (1991).

Ralph Mero (1937–)

A retired Unitarian Universalist Minister, Ralph Mero is the executive director and founder of the nonprofit organization Compassion in Dying. This group's mission is to help the terminally ill decide for themselves how and when their lives should end. It offers information and counseling and works to change laws to make assisted suicide illegal. As of January 1995 Mero had personally helped a dozen terminally ill patients end their lives.

Ralph Mero's father died of emphysema and heart disease in 1988 after a nine-year battle. Although his father did not request any assistance in dying, his suffering helped Mero see the agony with which many terminal patients must live. This solidified his commitment to seeing that others have options should they find themselves in similar circumstances.

Mero helped cofound the Hemlock Society of Washington State. In 1991 he helped draft the landmark Washington State Initiative #119. Although the measure lost, it remains significant as the first legislation introduced in the United States designed to decriminalize physician-assisted suicide.

In January 1994 Mero joined with four other physicians and three terminally ill patients to legally challenge the Washington State statute that makes assisted suicide a criminal act *(Compassion et al. v. Washington State)*. Mero is also involved in reversing the statute in New York State. He is a calm and reasoned spokesperson for those who favor choice-in-dying.

Edmund Pellegrino (1920–)

Along with three of his colleagues, Dr. Pellegrino was one of the first and most notable voices of protest heard when the *Journal of the American Medical Association (JAMA)* chose to publish an anonymous letter from an intern relating the tale of how he assisted in the death of a terminally ill patient ("It's Over, Debbie," *JAMA*, 8 January 1988).

Pellegrino, a renowned Georgetown University Medical Center professor, is a vocal opponent of all forms of euthanasia and physician-assisted suicide. "Now is the time for the medical profession to rally in defense of its fundamental moral principles, to repudiate any and all acts of direct and intentional killing by physicians and their agents," he wrote in *JAMA* in his April 1988 response to the "It's Over, Debbie" letter. He leads the charge of those in the medical profession who do not want euthanasia to be legalized.

Charles Francis Potter (1885–1962)

Dr. Charles Potter, a humanist and clergyman, was instrumental in bringing the euthanasia debate to a highly public forum during a time when the subject was taboo.

Potter began his theological career as a Baptist minister, but his liberal doctrinal views soon led him to the Unitarian faith. He founded the First Humanist Society of New York City in 1929 and served as biblical expert in the *Scopes* trial (in which the courts were asked to decide whether teachers should be allowed to teach the concept of evolution to students). He believed that man should base his faith in man and rely on mankind to make the world a better place. In 1938 he founded the Euthanasia Society, the first euthanasia group in the United States. Later called the Society for the Right to Die, this group advanced the concept that the American people have a right to engage in debate regarding life-and-death issues and should not be expected to unquestioningly accept the teachings of any church. He served as president and director of this organization, working to legalize some form of euthanasia until his death in 1962.

Timothy Quill (1950–)

Dr. Timothy Quill, an internal medicine specialist from Rochester, New York, single-handedly forced the medical profession to confront publicly the many complex ethical issues raised by physician-assisted suicide. His 7 March 1991 article in the *New England Journal of Medicine* describes the process he went through when deciding to help a terminally ill patient die. He provided "Diane" with a lethal prescription, which she later used to take her life. The article and its heated aftermath suggested that physicians had been covertly assisting in suicide for many years and raised questions about whether lethal prescriptions should be legally sanctioned. The letter provided pro-euthanasia groups with concrete evidence that the practice already occurs but remains covert. Anti-euthanasia groups used the letter to demonstrate an even greater need for laws to prevent these kinds of actions on the part of physicians.

Dr. Quill was investigated by the New York State Health Department for his role in Diane's death. It was ultimately determined that, since he had not directly participated in her death and had no way of knowing how she would use the prescription, there was no professional misconduct involved.

In a second *New England Journal of Medicine* article, Quill went on to propose that physicians be allowed to assist their patients in dying. He maintained that physicians should not be forced to abandon patients during their last months because of a lack of further ability to help them. He suggested instead that doctors should be able to refer patients to "palliative care" specialists, who would help assess the needs of individual patients and do everything possible to relieve their symptoms. These specialists would also be required to review all cases in which euthanasia is requested and to work with the patient and physician to provide for every need. If nothing further could be done, this specialist, in concert with a review committee, would authorize the physician to aid in the patient's death.

His book *Death with Dignity* calmly presents perspectives on the many difficult issues surrounding the role of medical professionals in helping meet the needs of terminally ill patients.

Karen Ann Quinlan (1954–1985)

Karen Ann Quinlan provided the American public with a heart-breaking, real-life drama showing what it is like to lie suspended between life and death. Images of her emaciated, 70-pound body lying in an irreversible coma drew public attention to the right-to-die cause and prompted tens of thousands of Americans to sign advance directives and durable powers of attorney.

Quinlan, then 21, had been drinking and using drugs at a party on 15 April 1975. She stopped breathing but was resuscitated by paramedics. Although she had suffered severe brain damage, there was still some brain activity. Quinlan was able to breathe via a respirator and was fed artificially. After three months her parents decided to remove all life support, but the physician and the hospital disagreed.

The legal battles that followed ended in a New Jersey Supreme Court ruling that declared that keeping her alive in this manner was a violation of her constitutionally guaranteed right to privacy. After the court's decision, Karen was taken off the respirator on 17 May 1976, but she did not die because she had been weaned off of it by her Catholic nurse prior to the Court's decision. Instead, she remained in a coma and was fed artificially. She died ten years later, in 1985.

Dame Cicely Saunders (1919–)

Founder of the modern Hospice Movement, Dame Saunders worked to make the process of dying as humane and personalized as possible.

Her work began in England in the 1960s. She opened St. Christopher's, the first modern hospice in the world, in suburban London in 1967. The hospice concept originated in the Middle Ages, when the term was used to describe a way station where weary travelers could stop for food and rest. It had nothing to do with medical care and terminal illness, but Dame Saunders presumably used the term intentionally to imply a place of rest and relief, and to characterize the process of death as a journey. Dame Saunders also toured the United States giving lectures on comfort care for the terminally ill.

The hospice concept embraces a philosophy that values spiritual care for the patient and the family, as well as modern medical care. Saunders was once quoted as saying in a discussion about the right to die, "If you had an illness which made you fairly dependent on other people, and somebody gave you the possibility to have a quick way out, would you really feel you could go on asking for that care?" Hospice care, however, with its focus on comfort care and pain relief, is intended to provide death with dignity and compassion without resorting to any form of euthanasia.

Saunders has had a profound impact on the end-of-life debate. She did pioneering medical research in pain treatment. She was made a dame in England in 1980 for her work in the area of hospice, and she is best known for devising this type of care, which provides some terminally ill patients with a humane and dignified alternative to hastening death.

Joni Eareckson Tada (1950–)

An accident on 30 July 1967 left Joni Eareckson a quadriplegic at the age of 17. Her story, one of courage and faith in the face of incredible odds, raises questions about whether we give up too soon on ourselves and others.

Her close-knit family offered Joni much-needed support during her ordeal, setting an example of the kind of loving care absent in many hospital rooms. Her account of her accident and subsequent recovery was originally published as *Joni* (1976), and more recently as *When Is It Right To Die: Suicide, Euthanasia, Suffering, Mercy* (1992). Her message is one of compassion that comes not through easy solutions, but through the hard work needed to maintain hope in the face of terrible odds.

Tada does not advocate prolonging life when it is no longer a meaningful experience, but she strongly advocates other solutions, particularly for people with disabilities who, she believes, can still find meaning in their lives. She is the founder and president of JAF Ministries, a group working to promote Christian ministry in the disability community. She has also served as a presidential appointee to the National Council on Disability under Presidents Reagan and Bush.

Facts, Documents, and Quotations

4

This chapter illustrates the end-of-life debate by providing key statistics, the text of landmark documents, and the words spoken or written by individuals who have influenced opinion on this controversial issue.

The material is divided into three sections: "Facts and Data" contains numerical data and charts and tables; "Documents" provides the full text or excerpts from key publications and legislation; and "Quotations" includes a broad cross section of quotations that add meaning to the raw statistics and text that precede them.

Each of these sections is divided into the three broad subtopics established in chapter 1: Medical-Bioethical, Spiritual-Social-Cultural, and Legal-Political.

Facts and Data

Medical-Bioethical

The medical-bioethical facet of the debate has progressed rapidly since the late 1960s, when a new definition of death was devised. "Brain death" made it possible to preserve vital organs for eventual transplantation. Today, the debate revolves around how to devise criteria to allow physicians to assist terminal patients to end their lives. The facts and data in this "Medical-Bioethical" section attempt to follow the progression of this debate and are thus organized into three subsections: Factors Influencing Determination of Death, Factors Influencing Requests for Euthanasia, and Physician-Assisted Suicide.

Factors Influencing Determination of Death

In 1968 a group of Harvard scholars formed the Ad Hoc Committee to Examine the Definition of Brain Death. The need to do this arose because physicians, with the help of technological advances, were finally able to maintain the functions of the body nearly indefinitely. The committee consisted of doctors, lawyers, theologians, and philosophers. Their purpose was to establish criteria for the moment of death. This would, in turn, make it possible for a person to be declared dead but still be maintained on life support until their organs could be transplanted. The group established four points that doctors still use as the medical definition of brain death. Dr. Christiaan Barnard, who performed the first heart transplant and pioneered in this area, summarizes these criteria as follows:

1. *Unreceptivity and lack of responsiveness.* Total unawareness of externally applied stimuli and inner need, and complete unresponsiveness—irreversible coma. Even the most painful stimuli evoke no vocal or other response, not even a groan, withdrawal of a limb, or quickening of respiration.
2. *No movement or breathing.* Observation by physicians, covering a period of at least one hour, is adequate to satisfy the criteria of no spontaneous muscular movements, no spontaneous respiration, and no response to stimuli such as pain, touch, sound, or light.
3. *No reflexes.* Irreversible coma with abolition of central nervous system activity is evidenced in part by the absence of elicitable reflexes. The pupil will be fixed and dilated and will not respond to a direct source of bright light.
4. *Flat encephalogram.* Of great confirmatory value is the flat or isoelectric EEG. We must assume that the electrodes have been properly applied, that the apparatus is functioning normally, and that the staff in charge is competent (Barnard 1980, 31–32).

In the United States today, more than 40,000 patients are currently waiting for an organ transplant. Approximately 2,000

Figure 1 Comparison of Organ Transplant Recipients to Those on Waiting List

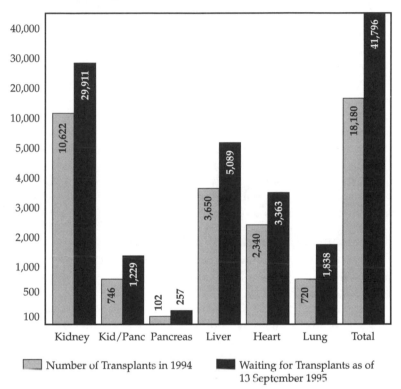

Source: Adapted from data provided by the United Network for Organ Sharing, Richmond, Virginia, 13 September 1995.

new patients are added to the waiting list by the United Network for Organ Sharing (Richmond, Virginia) each month. Every day, eight to nine people die while waiting for the transplant of a vital organ. Figure 1 indicates the number of organs transplanted in 1994, as well as the number of individuals still on the national waiting list as of 13 September 1995. This need for organs caused ethical questions to arise regarding the timing of death in the late 1960s. Today, there are concerns that the disparity between available organs and those in need of them could precipitate involuntary euthanasia of terminally ill patients.

Once brain death became the standard for deciding the moment of death, choices and questions about the end of life expanded dramatically. Families suddenly needed to make difficult decisions about the timing of a loved one's death. By 1990 the American Hospital Association estimated that 70 percent of the 6,000 deaths that occurred in the United States each day were already somehow timed or negotiated; i.e., medical technology was either not applied at all or was withdrawn at the request of family members. For instance, every year some 12,000 of the 80,000 patients on artificial kidney machines voluntarily quit, thus ensuring a self-determined death through passive euthanasia within two weeks (Cox 1993, 211).

Between 1985 and 1995, withholding cardiopulmonary resuscitation became a well-accepted practice. This action is codified into hospital policy as "No CPR," "Do Not Resuscitate (DNR)," or "Do Not Attempt Resuscitation (DNAR)" orders. DNAR orders are written for 3 to 4 percent of patients who receive medical services while in a hospital. In the ICU, the frequency of DNAR orders ranges from 0.4 to 14 percent (Curtis et al. 1995).

Factors Influencing Requests for Euthanasia

Clearly, many people were ready for their doctors to take a more active role in helping them to die. This trend in patient requests stemmed from the heightened perception that some heroic measures such as CPR were futile, and to some extent, by an increase in people's exposure to excruciatingly painful deaths from cancer and AIDS over the past two decades. The diminishing quality of life experienced by patients with Alzheimer's disease, Lou Gehrig's disease, and persons in persistent vegetative states also helped focus attention on our increasing ability to keep people's bodies alive but our still limited ability to make the life "saved" livable.

In a study reported in the *Journal of the American Medical Association* in 1988, 31 percent of patients 70 years of age or older who experienced cardiac arrests were revived through CPR. Of these, 92 percent were still alive 24 hours later. However, none of these patients lived to be discharged from the hospital (Taffet and Taffet 1988).

The *Journal of the American Medical Association* published in November 1995 the results of a study in which researchers found that only 47 percent of doctors were aware that their patients did not want CPR to be performed. Of these individuals, 49 percent did not have "DNR" written on their charts. Forty-six percent of all DNR orders were found to have been written within 48 hours of death, and 38 percent of the patients who died in the hospital spent at least ten days in the ICU prior to death. Half of the patients who were conscious and who died in the hospital reported that they experienced moderate to severe pain (Support Principal Investigators 1995).

In a 1987 study published in *Pain*, 78 percent of 454 randomly selected patients in a midwestern academic hospital reported having pain during hospitalization. Of these, 45 percent recall experiencing excruciating pain (Donovan et al. 1987). In a survey of medical professionals to determine views on end-of-life treatment and decision making that was carried out in five hospitals and reported in the *American Journal of Public Health*, 89 percent of the professionals polled felt that "sometimes it is appropriate to give pain medication to relieve suffering, even if it may hasten a patient's death"; 41 percent indicated that "clinicians give inadequate pain medication most often out of fear of hastening a patient's death"; 81 percent felt that "the most common form of narcotic abuse in the care of the dying is undertreatment of pain" (Solomon et al. 1993).

There have been sharp increases in the rates of cancer and AIDS. Cancer deaths are historically documented in Table 1 (page 106). Figure 2 (page 106) illustrates the rate of new cases of cancer diagnosed in 1996 by state, and the incidence of AIDS cases and deaths over nearly a decade is shown in Figure 3 (page 107). These two particularly painful conditions have contributed to an escalating incidence of requests for euthanasia.

In addition to excruciating pain, severe declines in quality of life can also lead to requests for euthanasia. These conditions head the list: Alzheimer's disease, amyotrophic lateral sclerosis (ALS), also known as Lou Gehrig's disease, and persistent vegetative state (PVS), which can be caused by brain injury, stroke, or a variety of other medical trauma.

According to the Alzheimer's Association of America, approximately 4 million Americans have Alzheimer's disease, and 14 million Americans will suffer from this progressive, degenerative illness by the next century unless a cure or prevention method is discovered. It attacks the brain and results in impaired memory, thinking, and behavior. It is the fourth leading cause of death in adults. The rate of progression of dementia varies from 3 to 20 years, the average being 8. When vital body functions cease to be controlled by the brain or the patient becomes ill, the patient finally dies (Alzheimer's Disease and Related Disorders Association, Inc. 1994).

About 20,000 people in the United States have ALS, and there are approximately 5,000 new cases each year. It has no known cause or cure. People with ALS may live seven to ten years. In the middle to late stages of the disease, victims cannot

Table 1 U.S. Trends in Cancer Death Rates, 1960–1962 and 1990–1992

Sex	1960–1962	1990–1992	Percent Change	Number of Deaths (1962)	Number of Deaths (1992)
Male	185.3	220.0	19	150,009	274,838
Female	135.4	141.9	5	128,553	245,740

Note: Death rate per 100,000 people. Rates reflect the age distribution of the 1970 U.S. Census population.

Source: American Cancer Society. *Cancer Facts and Figures, 1996: 30-Year Trends in Cancer Death Rates per 100,000 Population, 1960–1962 to 1990–1992*, 1996.

Figure 2 New Cancer Cases Diagnosed in 1996

Source: American Cancer Society. *Cancer Facts & Figures.* 1996. Cover.

move their arms and legs or speak. However, the sense of touch and complete mental capacity are retained. ALS attacks motor neurons, is progressive, and prevents patients from chewing or swallowing. At this point, a feeding tube must be inserted to maintain life. Fewer than 15 percent of ALS patients indicated

Figure 3 The Incidence of AIDS Cases and AIDS Deaths in the United States, 1985–1994

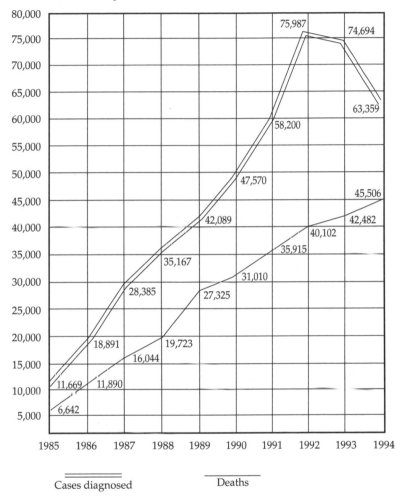

Cases diagnosed   Deaths

Source: Adapted from data published by the National Center for Health Statistics in *HIV/AIDS Surveillance Report* 7, 2 (1995): 19.

they would wish to be placed on a respirator, the majority hoping to die in their sleep when their diaphragm fails to function (Kinella 1995).

There are no hard statistics on the number of individuals in the United States who are currently in a persistent vegetative state. A PVS diagnosis means that the patient has lost the neurophysiological basis for consciousness. Although these patients may have sleep/wake cycles and sometimes make sounds, they have no awareness.

The President's Commission found that two-thirds of patients who are kept alive on a ventilator during a coma that has lasted for at least six hours die within 30 days. Another 6 percent remain in a persistent vegetative state. Roughly 12 percent of those who fall into a comatose state due to drug intoxication recover, while another 12 percent are left with serious disabilities (President's Commission 1983a, 172–173).

The traumatic Coma Data Bank study reported that 6 of 93 adult patients in a vegetative state recovered consciousness within one to three years following the injury. Four of these patients had a severe disability, one was moderately disabled, and the status of the last patient could not be determined. Recovery of consciousness after 12 months is unlikely in adults and children who have suffered traumatic injuries, and the likelihood of recovery decreases with age. PVS patients may be medically maintained in this state indefinitely via the use of respirators and feeding tubes. When these artificial means are withdrawn, it takes between 10 and 14 days for death to occur from dehydration and electrolyte imbalance. During this time, patients do not experience thirst or hunger (Multi-Society Task Force on PVS 1994).

Those who disagree with negotiated deaths, euthanasia and assisted suicide assert that, while quality of life and pain are important factors, not all people die painful deaths and many, in fact, are able to enjoy a reasonable quality of life without pain until they die.

A study of 1,227 people in Fairfield County, Connecticut, who were known to be dying was conducted by the National Institute on Aging. The results, published in *Aging Magazine* in 1992, revealed that more than half of these individuals died in their sleep. Sixty-one percent were pain-free the day before they died; 13 percent were still able to walk; 28 percent could still feed themselves; 43 percent could still see and hear; and 51 percent knew who and where they were (Jones 1992).

Physician-Assisted Suicide

Increases in the number of seriously debilitating, painful, terminal illnesses for which no cure has been found have led patients and their families around the world to seek a physician's assistance in dying. Because the Netherlands is the only country in which assisted suicide has been openly practiced, *official* statistics on the incidence of euthanasia are available only from this country.

The first official government study of euthanasia in the Netherlands is known as the Remmelink report. It was undertaken by the Committee to Study the Medical Practice Concerning Euthanasia and was based on interviews with 405 physicians from a variety of disciplines. The report stated that in 1990, 2,300 people died as the result of physicians killing them on request and 400 people died as a result of physician-assisted suicide in which physicians provided them with the means of killing themselves. Moreover, 1,040 people died from involuntary euthanasia (without their consent or knowledge). Of these, 14 percent were fully competent, 72 percent had not indicated that they would want their lives terminated, and 8 percent were euthanized when their physician knew other options were available. In addition, 8,100 patients died from overdoses from pain medication administered by a physician with the intention of hastening death. In 61 percent of these cases, there was no patient consent. The reasons most frequently cited by physicians for euthanizing patients without their consent or knowledge were: "low quality of life," "no prospect for improvement," and "the family couldn't take it anymore" (Committee to Study the Medical Practice Concerning Euthanasia 1991).

More than half (54 percent) of the Dutch physicians polled by researchers in 1992 reported having performed euthanasia or assisted suicide in the past. Thirty-four percent had not done so, but felt they could under certain conditions. Eight percent said they could not, but would refer requests to other physicians, and four percent were utterly opposed to the practice (Van Der Maas et al. 1992).

More than 2,000 Australian physicians in Victoria were surveyed in 1988 by the Center for Human Bioethics at Monash University in Melbourne. Almost half (869) supported voluntary euthanasia. One-third had been involved in the practice on at least one occasion. Almost half said they would practice voluntary euthanasia were it legal (Warden 1992).

Although no official figures are available from government sources in the United States, a 1992 survey conducted by the American Society of Internal Medicine found that one in five U.S. physicians said they had deliberately taken action to cause a patient's death (Famighetti 1994, 709).

In 1993, 837 Boston area physicians who treat the dying responded to a survey conducted by the *Boston Globe* in cooperation with the Massachusetts Medical Society. Fully 53 percent said that, were it legal, they would provide their terminally ill patients with a lethal dose of medicine under certain circumstances and if it were requested by the patient; 30 percent said they would not do so, while 15 percent did not know. Twenty-one percent said they had patients who had requested a lethal prescription, and 19 percent had already fulfilled such a request. Twenty percent had been asked for a lethal injection; 13 percent had administered one. The final question on the survey asked respondents: "What if you found yourself suffering from a terminal illness? Would you be likely to take steps so that you had the option to administer a lethal dose to yourself?" Forty percent responded "Yes," while 29 percent said "No," and 30 percent did not know (Lear 1993).

In 1995 the Center for Ethics and Health Care at Oregon Health Sciences University polled 2,761 Oregon physicians for their views on physician-assisted suicide. The voters of this state had passed an assisted-suicide law the previous year. Seventy-three percent of physicians agreed that a competent, terminally ill patient has the right to commit suicide; 66 percent believed that physician-assisted suicide would be ethical in some cases; 60 percent thought the practice should be legal under certain conditions; but fully 33 percent felt that assisting a patient to die by providing a lethal prescription would be "immoral" (Lee et al. 1996).

A survey of 852 critical care nurses was conducted in 1995 by David Asche, M.D. through *Nursing* magazine. A total of 141 nurses (17 percent) reported receiving requests to engage in euthanasia or assisted suicide. Of these, 108 were requests from patients and 101 were from family members or surrogates. On average, each nurse complied with 8 percent of the requests from patients and 12 percent of the requests from surrogates. A total of 129 nurses reported having participated in active euthanasia or assisted suicide at least once in their careers, 65 percent reported doing so 3 or fewer times, while 5 percent reported doing so more than 20 times. Fully 59 percent of the nurses reported having only pretended to carry out a physician's order or engaged in some other clandestine practice in order to hasten a patient's death. Ninety-one percent reported that the most important reason they did not perform euthanasia or assisted suicide was a fear of getting caught, while 83 percent were concerned that the practice might be illegal, and 80 percent felt the patient's preferences were not fully understood (Asche 1996).

In May 1995 Jesse Vivian, a pharmacist and professor of law at Wayne State University, surveyed 600 fellow Michigan state pharmacists. The results were published in the *Michigan Pharmacists Association Journal*. Fifty percent of all pharmacists indicated that they felt assisted suicide is not acceptable and that pharmacists should not be dispensing medication that would be used to assist in a suicide (Susman 1995).

A survey published in 1993 in the *American Journal of Public Health* found that professionals who are most intimately involved in end-of-life decisions—for instance, the decision to stop treating and instead begin to help a patient die a peaceful and dignified death—are questioning the value of saving life at any cost. Percentages represent respondents who "strongly agreed" with statements.

Almost half of the providers (47 percent) reported they had acted against their conscience in providing care to the terminally ill. About seven of ten interns and residents, five in ten nurses, and between three and four attending physicians reported acting against their conscience. Fifty-five percent felt that sometimes the treatments they offered patients were overly burdensome; 12 percent felt they had given up on patients too soon.

The same survey also reported concerns about the inappropriate use of specific treatments for critically and terminally ill patients. Sixty-seven percent felt that mechanical ventilation was most likely to be inappropriately used, followed by CPR (64 percent), artificial nutrition and hydration (54 percent), dialysis (51 percent), antibiotics (42 percent), and pain medication (35 percent) (Solomon et al. 1993).

Spiritual-Social-Cultural

Population and Longevity

The sheer number of people making demands on limited health care resources is a growing issue throughout the world. Many argue that we cannot even provide basic health care for children around the world and question why we are using precious resources to keep people alive who would prefer to die. For example: "It took hundreds of thousands of years for our species to reach a population level of 10 million, only 10,000 years ago. This number grew to 100 million about 2,000 years ago and to

Figure 4 Projections of the United States Elderly Population, 1995–2050

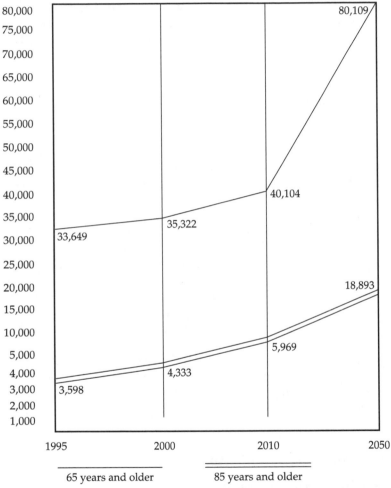

Source: Adapted from data provided by the Bureau of the Census, U.S. Department of Commerce. Based on July 1992 population estimate consistent with the 1990 decennial census.

2,500 million by 1950. Within less than the span of a single life-time, it has more than doubled to 5,500 million in 1993" (Mehra 1994). According to the U.S. Census, the number of people in the United States over the age of 65 nearly tripled between 1950 and 1990, increasing from 12 million to 30 million. In the

Netherlands, 1,905,000 people were over the age of 65 in 1990 (CBS 1994).

Overall, the world's population grew at a rate of 1.7 percent between 1990 and 1995, but the population over age 65 is increasing by some 2.7 percent annually. In 1993 the world total of people over 65 was 355 million. Although Europe, Japan, and the United States currently have the "oldest" populations, the most rapid aging is seen in the developing world, with predicted increases in some countries of up to 400 percent during the next 30 years (World Health Organization 1995). Not only is the U.S. population increasing, but the average life span has increased by eight years since 1950, when life expectancy in the United States was 68. In 1995 the average American could expect to live for 76 years. According to the U.S. Census Bureau, the world's population reached 5.6 billion in 1994 and is expected to reach 7.9 billion by the year 2020.

More and more people are approaching the end of life and must decide how to pay for the cost of any care that might be needed. But not only the elderly die. At least 50 million people die every year throughout the world ("Death" 1993).

At the other end of life's spectrum, medical advances are increasingly allowing doctors to keep at-risk newborns alive. The debate about whether newborns with serious illnesses or deformities should be kept alive began in earnest in the 1970s. The rate of neonatal mortality in the United States declined by 57 percent between 1930 and 1970. In just one decade, 1970–1980, this rate dropped by another 24 percent. Between 1980 and 1990 the rate dropped again to just 9.2 deaths for every 1,000 births (Wegman 1981, 1993).

Changes in the Way We Die

Advances in medical technology have altered not only how we die but where we die. These changes have had an enormous impact on end-of-life decision making. Comparisons are often drawn between the United States and the Netherlands to advance acceptance of physician-assisted suicide in the United States. But the social, legal, and health care systems in these two nations are so very different that caution must be exercised when attempting to draw parallels. For instance, in the Netherlands, most individuals have a long-term relationship with their physician and consider this person a trusted advocate. Also, there is little or no medical malpractice litigation in the Netherlands. In the United States, an escalating number of malpractice suits have encouraged physicians to overtreat to avoid potential legal consequences. "Forty percent of all deaths in Holland occur at home, especially patients with cancer (48 percent)...euthanasia occurs at home in one of about 25 deaths, in hospitals in one out of 75, and in nursing homes in one out of 800" (Dillman 1994).

In 1949 just half of all deaths in the United States took place in institutions such as hospitals and nursing homes. By 1958 this figure had risen to 61 percent, and by 1977 more than 70 percent of all Americans died in institutions (Zimmerman 1983, 17). By the 1990s more than 85 percent of all Americans died in institutional settings. Fewer than 15 percent died at home (Bristow 1994).

The impact of life-threatening illnesses is not limited to Americans in poor health. Fully 31 percent of Americans report that they or a member of their immediate family have had a life-threatening illness or medical condition. Although life-threatening illnesses are more common among those who are in poor health, 27 percent of these individuals were in excellent health and 32 percent of those in good health reported a life-threatening illness in their family. Of these, 6 percent of those in excellent health and 8 percent of those in good health said they have experienced a life-threatening condition (President's Commission 1983b, 56).

It is estimated that 15 percent of the adults in the United States are currently providing care for a sick or disabled relative. There are 12.8 million Americans across all age groups who require assistance to carry out everyday activities such as eating, dressing, and bathing. Eighty-five percent of the care they need is provided for by family and friends. Eleven percent of caregivers are providing constant care for a family member, while 36 percent spend an average of 21 hours per week providing assistance. Twenty-eight percent provide care for less than 8 hours per week, while the remainder average at least 12 hours per week. Seventy-two percent of all caregivers are female and the average time these women can expect to spend caring for an elderly or disabled parent is 18 years. In addition to time commitments, 51 percent of caregivers report a loss of leisure time. Taking a vacation is not possible for 28 percent of caregivers, and 34 percent sacrifice time with other family members and attention to their own health in order to provide care for a loved one. Those who care for patients with Alzheimer's disease report that they suffer from personal health impacts to a higher degree than do the caregivers of cancer patients. In addition to suffering from ill health themselves, Alzheimer's caregivers report a higher use of antianxiety drugs and lower life satisfaction. Sixty percent of caregivers who are also employed outside of the home report physical strain as a consequence of caring for a relative or friend. Eighty percent report emotional strain from their caregiving responsibilities and 10 percent report a great deal of emotional strain associated with their caregiving responsibilities (Family Caregiver Allliance 1996, 1–5).

Many believe that our emphasis on youth and work leaves elderly people—particularly men—feeling useless at the end of life. Others suggest that we should be focusing our attention on better care for pain and depression rather than contributing to a sense of worthlessness by offering death as a treatment option to a depressed elderly population. Moreover, attitudes about intentional death can have a negative effect on other susceptible populations, such as teenagers.

Costly treatments that are often painful or ineffective can contribute to depression, which, in turn, can play a major role in end-of-life decisions. Approximately 15 percent of independent older adults, 20 percent of older patients who are hospitalized, and at least 25 percent of nursing home residents suffer from depression. Of these, 60 percent are not treated for this illness. Yet, according to the National Institute of Mental Health (NIMH), the majority of people who suffer from clinical depression can be successfully treated (Schmall and Stiehl 1993, 52). The National Center for Health Statistics reported that in 1993 suicide ranked ninth among the ten leading causes of death in the United States. And as the population has grown in numbers and increased in median age, other disturbing trends have become apparent. Between 1980 and 1990 suicide rates increased by more than 32 percent among elderly white men over the age of 75. This brought the actual number up to 60 to 70 deaths for every 100,000 men in this age group. In 1990 this rate was nine times higher than that for women of the same age. During the period 1985–1990, the number of deaths by firearms among white males between the ages of 75 and 84 was more than twice that of black males. This was due to an increase in suicide by firearms (National Center for Health Statistics 1993, 4).

Figure 5 (page 116) shows the number of people who took their own lives, divided by age group and gender.

Economic Influences

Skyrocketing health care costs have had an enormous impact on the health care delivery system, the health insurance system, and how taxpayer dollars are spent in the United States. The

Figure 5 Suicides in the United States by Age, Race, and Sex, 1993

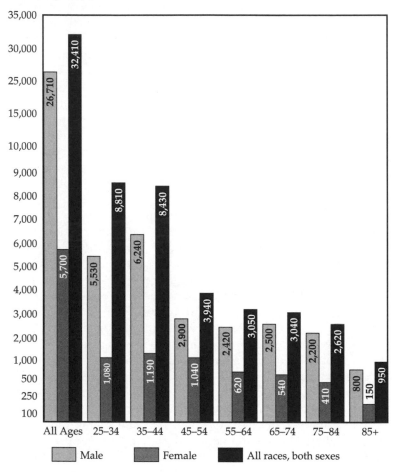

Note: Data are provisional, estimated from a 10 percent sample of deaths.
Source: National Center for Health Statistics, U.S. Department of Health and Human Services. *Monthly Vital Statistics Report* 43, no. 13 (23 October 1995): 18.

impact of these changes on patients, families, and taxpayers are still being assessed. Questionable practices by managed care companies, insurers, and insurance brokers, for instance, generate concerns that economics could soon play a pivotal role in end-of-life decisions. Moreover, the rising number of people in the United States who are uninsured and thus have little or no access to health care may be subject to de facto, involuntary

Figure 6 Increase in National Health Care Expenditures in Billions of Dollars in the United States, 1960–1994

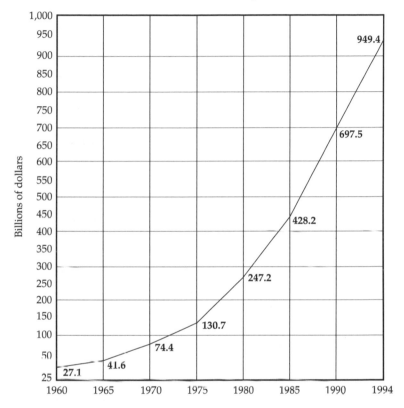

Source: Adapted from data published by the National Center for Health Statistics in *Health, United States, 1995.* Hyattsville, MD: Public Health Service, 239.

euthanasia through neglect. Figure 6 illustrates the dramatic rise in health care expenditures over a 34-year period in the United States.

"In all [U.S.] state budgets, Medicaid is the second largest budget item after education. Persons over 85, in fact, use four times as much money to cover a hospitalization than those under 85. There will be fewer individuals 'in the middle' to bear the burden of caring for the young and the elderly. Already the phenomenon of the elderly (75 to 85 years of age) caring for the 'old old' (those over 85) has begun" (Humber et al. 1994, 116).

Many question whether the vast resources spent on the care of critically ill patients is a wise use of health care funds.

Figure 7 U.S. Long-Term Care Cost Projections, 1988–2048

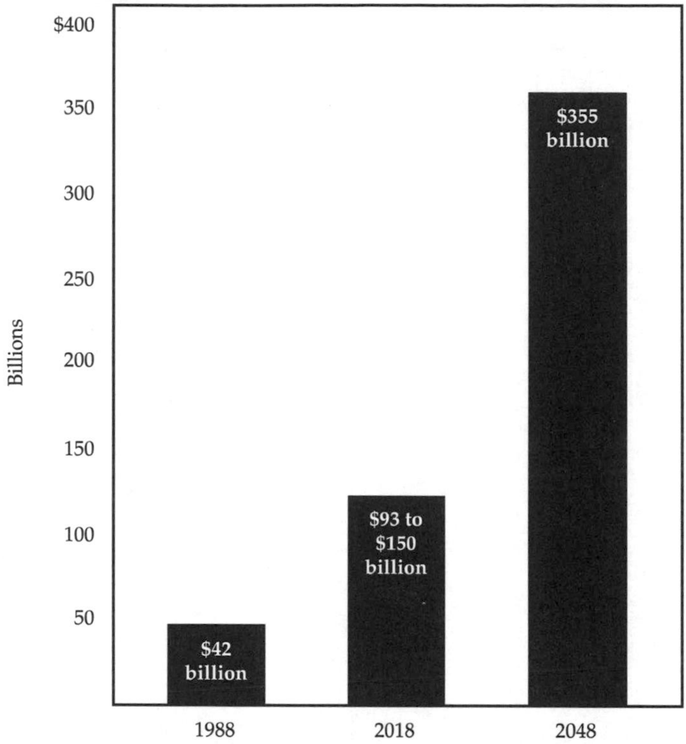

Source: Fowles, Donald G. "Projections of Long-Term Care Needs." *Aging Magazine* 363–364 (1992): 76.

Figure 7 illustrates that the cost of providing long-term care for those who need it is expected to surpass $100 billion by 2018 and then double or triple yet again by the middle of the next century. The Health Care Financing Administration (HCFA) found that 28 percent of the Medicare budget, or about $30 billion annually, is spent on care during the last year of life, and primarily during the final 30 days (Hoefler 1994, 58). The high costs of health care may not, however, be directly tied to the age of the population. Currently, the United States spends more money than any other country on health care (14 percent of the gross national product) even though the percentage of elderly in the population is relatively low (12.6 percent). In Sweden, health care costs account for 7.5 percent of the country's gross national product even though 17.8 percent of the population is elderly (Marwick 1995, 1320).

Figure 8 Comparison of Selected Monthly Hospital vs. Home Care Costs

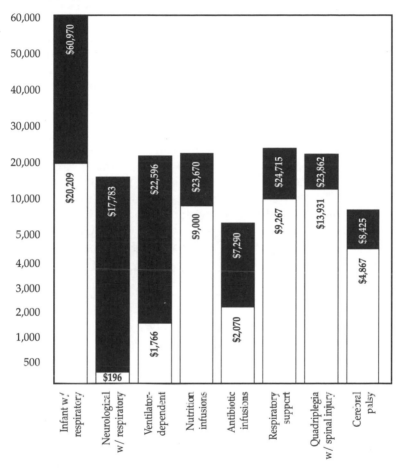

Source: Adapted from Inlander, Charles B. *The Consumer's Medical Desk Reference.* New York: Hyperion, 1995, 287.

The costs associated with intensive care units in the United States in 1995 accounted for almost 1 percent of the U.S. gross national product (Oye and Bellamy 1991, 685–689). Figure 8 illustrates the cost differences found between treating specific types of illnesses on an outpatient basis using home care services.

Although the impact on society may decrease when patients needing care are brought home, the financial costs are great for those who care for them. Forty percent of caregivers report that they incur additional expenses related to the care they provide;

26 percent spend up to 10 percent of their monthly income on caregiving; 31 percent report travel-related expenses tied to their caregiving; 24 percent report additional spending to meet dietary requirements; and 25 percent incurred additional telephone and utility charges (Family Caregiver Alliance 1996, 1–5). Medicare-covered home health care has become a growth industry, increasing from 26 persons served per 1,000 Medicare enrollees in 1980, to an estimated 89 persons per 1,000 enrollees in 1994 (Arras 1995, 1690–1691).

A handful of high profile, high impact terminal illnesses have captured both media headlines and a significant share of the total dollars spent on end-of-life care. Not only do these illnesses cost a great deal, Alzheimer's disease, cancer, AIDS, and persistent vegetative state also generate the lion's share of patient/family requests for euthanasia. Scarce dollars may be spent to treat those who do not wish to continue living.

In 1993, 84 percent of hospice patients in the United States had cancer, 4 percent had AIDS, and the remaining 12 percent had a variety of other terminal illnesses (Beresford 1993, xviii). "Alzheimer's Disease costs U.S. society $80 to $100 billion per year. Neither Medicare nor private health insurance covers the long-term type of care most patients need. Half of all nursing home patients suffer from Alzheimer's Disease or a related disorder. The average cost for a patient's care in a nursing home is $42,000 per year, but can exceed $70,000 per year in some areas of the country. The average lifetime cost per patient is $174,000. It is the third most expensive disease in the United States, after heart disease and cancer" (Alzheimer's Disease and Related Disorders Association, Inc. 1994).

The financial costs of cancer are great for both the individual and for society as a whole. The National Cancer Institute estimates overall costs for cancer at $104 billion: $35 billion for direct medical costs, $12 billion for morbidity costs (cost of lost productivity), and $57 billion for mortality costs (American Cancer Society 1996, 5).

The costs associated with each additional year of life that can be achieved through intensive medical interventions to treat Pneumocystis carinii pneumonia (PCP) and respiratory failure as complications of AIDS have skyrocketed. Between 1986 and 1988 the cost associated with keeping one individual alive for one year with these conditions was $94,528. During 1989–1991 this cost more than doubled, reaching $215,233 (Wachter et al. 1995, 230–235).

The cost of just the first three months of care for a person in a persistent vegetative state is estimated to be $149,200. The estimated cost of long-term care in a skilled nursing facility ranges from $350 to $500 per day, or $126,000 to $180,000 per year. A rough estimate of the total cost of caring for the adults and children in the United States who have been diagnosed as being in a persistent vegetative state is between $1 billion and $7 billion per year (Multi-Society Task Force on PVS 1994, 1576).

The way in which health care costs are paid for has changed dramatically in the United States over the past 15 years. Among the countries in the forefront of the assisted-suicide debate (the Netherlands, the United States, and Australia), the United States is the only country that does not provide universal health coverage for its citizens.

"[In the Netherlands] almost all patients (99.4 percent) have health care insurance, and 100 percent of the population is insured for the cost of protracted illness. There are no financial incentives for hospitals, physicians, or family members to stop the care of patients. Moreover, the legal right of patients to health care on the basis of their insurance will override budget and other financial agreements" (Dillman 1994, 1346). In 1992, 38.6 million Americans were uninsured. According to the American Cancer Society, by 1996 more than 41 million Americans did not have health insurance.

A 1993 poll found that 34 percent of uninsured Americans reported that during the previous 12 months they had needed medical care but did not receive it, and 71 percent reported that they had postponed seeking necessary medical care because they could not get it (Henry J. Kaiser Family Foundation et al. 1993).

A survey reported in 1994 revealed that 84 percent of employers who offer health insurance to their employees offer only one plan. Thus, those who do have access to health insurance frequently have access to only one type of coverage (Henry J. Kaiser Family Foundation and KAPMG Peat Marwick 1994).

The trend toward managed care has developed in response to the increasing costs associated with health care services. Insurance companies and federal health care programs have been sorely strained by the costs of providing expensive, high-tech interventions and the long-term care to which this often leads. Figure 9 illustrates the sharp rise in HMO enrollment, particularly between 1980 and 1990.

In 1991 more than 25 percent of all Medicaid payments were made to nursing facilities, and 10 percent of the Department of

Figure 9 Increases in Health Maintenance Organization Enrollment, 1976–1992

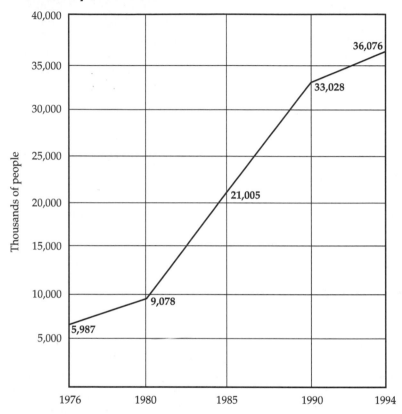

Source: Adapted from data published by the National Center for Health Statistics in *Health, United States, 1995*. Hyattsville, MD: Public Health Service, 1996, 184.

Veterans' Affairs $12.4 billion budget for health care was paid for nursing home care. Medicaid payments for the elderly, blind, and disabled accounted for 70 percent of all expenditures, covering 26 percent of those participating in the program (National Center for Health Statistics 1993, 7).

A June 1994 CBS News poll showed that more than half of all Americans (51 percent) are willing to pay higher taxes in order to achieve universal health coverage in the United States.

A May 1996 poll conducted by Wirthlin Worldwide asked "Should tax dollars be spent to pay for the cost of assisting suicide and euthanasia?" More than 80 percent (83 percent) answered "No."

In the United States, independent brokers can legally buy
out life insurance policies. Terminally ill patients, particularly
those suffering from AIDS, have been forced to sell their policies
to pay for medical expenses not covered by health insurance or
government programs. The broker pays 50 to 80 percent of the
policy's face value and collects a profit when the patient dies.
The sooner the patient dies, the greater the profit realized by the
broker (Lane 1995, B1).

Spiritual/Social/Cultural Viewpoints

Just as those in the health care professions hold a variety of opinions regarding euthanasia, so does society at large. These are
formed to some extent by people's perceptions of the words used
to define actions taken at the end of life. Table 2 traces public
opinion regarding the legalization of physician aid-in-dying
from 1947 to 1991. Respondents were asked, "When a person has
a disease that cannot be cured, do you think doctors should be
allowed by law to end the patient's life by some painless means
if the patient and (his or her) family request it?" Acceptance
reached an all-time low in 1950 following World War II. Table 3

Table 2   Public Opinion of Physician Aid-in-Dying, 1947–1991

Year	Organization	Results Yes	No	No Opinion/ Unsure/ Not Sure
1947	Gallup	37%	54%	9%
1950	Gallup	36%	64% (No or no opinion)	
1973	Gallup	53%	40%	7%
1982	National Opinion Research Center	61%	34%	5%
1982	Louis Harris	53%	38%	8%
1986	National Opinion Research Center	66%	31%	4%
1987	Louis Harris	62%	34%	4%
1991	Associated Press	60%	24%	7–8%
1991	KRC Communications	63%	28%	9%
1991	National Opinion Research Center	70%	25%	5%

Source: © Roper Center for Public Opinion Research, University of
Connecticut, Storrs, 1992. Reprinted by permission.

Table 3 Public Perceptions of the Term *Euthanasia* in Washington State, 1991

Positive	20%
Negative	18%
Mercy killing	12%
Helping someone to end their life	9%
Right to live or die by choice	8%
Death not by choice/killing/murder	8%
Not sure of exact meaning	8%
Ending life	6%
Putting someone to sleep	6%

Source: A Washington State poll of 600 registered voters, April 1991. The poll was carried out prior to Initiative 119.

reveals public opinion approximately half a year prior to the appearance of Initiative 119 on the ballot in Washington State. Participants in a Washington State poll were asked, "What does the term *euthanasia* mean to you?" and "Does it seem like a positive or negative term to you?"

According to the Remmelink report, 25,000 patients in the Netherlands asked their physician to assist them in dying if their suffering became too great. Of these, 8,900 requests were explicit and involved actions to be taken in the near future (Fenigsen 1991).

The Remmelink report estimated that 2.1 percent of the country's deaths in 1991 were the result of euthanasia or assisted suicide. Figures released by the government show a steady increase in the number of reported assisted suicides or euthanasia deaths, but there is some question as to whether this increase represents a growing number of cases of euthanasia or simply an increase in the number of cases that are reported by physicians. Reported deaths in 1991 totaled 591; in 1992, 1,323; in 1993, 1,350; and in 1994, 1,436 (Waxma 1995, B1).

A 1990 Gallup poll found that 75 percent of Americans agree that a terminally ill patient has the right to have treatment withheld to allow death to occur. Eighty-four percent indicated that they themselves would want to have treatment withheld if they were terminally ill. Three-quarters said they would like to have a living will, but only 20 percent had actually prepared one (Allen 1995, 1).

Once a significant segment of the U.S. population had accepted passive euthanasia, a growing number of people began to ask for more active assistance in dying. This was due, in part, to a recognition that some people are unable to take their own lives or have no artificial life supports to withdraw that would permit passive euthanasia to occur. In the 1991 Roper Poll of the West Coast reported in *Hemlock Quarterly* (1991), three important questions of a cross section of Americans were asked:

> 1. *Should doctors be allowed to prescribe lethal drugs to terminally ill patients who request them so that patients can end their own lives, if and when they decide to?*
>
>   60%—Yes   32%—No
>
> 2. *If the patient had signed a power of attorney while still fully competent, giving a family member or friend the power to make the decision as to whether and when lethal drugs are to be given, do you think that should be allowed or not?*
>
>   68%—Yes   26%—No
>
> 3. *Should doctors be allowed to give patients lethal injections in cases in which patients wish to die but are unable to take the lethal drugs themselves?*
>
>   54%—Yes   36%—No

By 1993 a Harris poll taken in November reported that 73 percent of Americans favored legalizing the practice of physician-assisted suicide (Canella 1995, A9).

In 1993 the editors of *Choices* (formerly *Choice in Dying News*) published a survey asking their readers: "Is assisting a suicide ever morally acceptable?" A total of 8,468 readers responded (7,677 of whom were members of Choice in Dying) representing 12 percent of that organization's total membership. Of the respondents, 7 percent responded in the negative; 16 percent responded affirmatively. Sixty-four percent responded "yes," qualifying their answer by saying only if the person is dying or in severe pain; 44 percent indicated "yes" if the person is physically unable to commit suicide without help.

Outside of their duties as healers, physicians are also individuals. Their religious affiliations influence their personal opinions regarding physician-assisted suicide. Table 4 illustrates the results of a 1995 survey of physicians in Oregon who might be willing to participate in physician-assisted suicide if it were legal. Physician responses were broken down by religious affiliation.

Table 4 Survey of Oregon Physicians' Attitudes Regarding Physician-Assisted Suicide by Religious Affiliation

Religious Affiliation	Might Participate	Would Not Participate
Protestant	41%	59%
Catholic	23%	77%
Jewish	67%	43%
No affiliation	66%	34%

Note: Forty-six percent of those who responded that they might participate had cared for a terminally ill patient in the past year; 50 percent had not.

Source: Lee, Melinda A., et al. "Legalizing Assisted-Suicide: Views of Physicians in Oregon," *New England Journal of Medicine* 334, no. 5 (1 February 1996): 314.

Legal-Political

Shifting Attitudes—Suicide and Death

Attitudes about death and dying have shifted significantly over the past 30 to 40 years. Suicide was banned in England until 1961, when it was decriminalized by the Suicide Act of 1961.

The taboos that have traditionally surrounded intentional death have lifted somewhat, particularly for those who suffer from a terminal illness. Legal tools, known as advance directives, have been developed to give people some degree of control over end-of-life decisions. However, not enough people make use of these documents. According to Thomas Cavalieri, director of the Center for Aging at the University of Medicine and Dentistry of New Jersey in Stratford, only 20 percent of all Americans have any type of advance directive, even though the vast majority of older Americans believe they should have one. Many receive an advance directive but never take the time to fill it out. The Choice in Dying organization sent out more than 150,000 state-specific living wills and forms for health care proxies in 1994 alone (Anthony 1995, 58, 61).

The only way advance directives will be of any help is if people learn how to fill them out and make an effort to keep them available in the event of an emergency. Choice in Dying maintains an up-to-date collection of the advance directives for each state. The following four maps (reprinted by permission of Choice in Dying, 200 Varick Street, New York, NY 10014, 212-366-5540) illustrate four possible health care decisions and the states in which they are legal. Figure 10 indicates which states

Figure 10 State Statutes Governing Nonhospital Do-Not-Resuscitate Orders (June 1996)

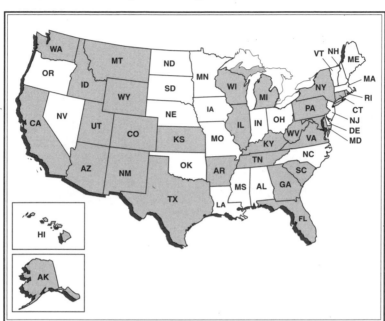

■ States with statutes authorizing nonhospital DNR orders (29 states: Alaska, Arizona, Arkansas, California, Colorado, Connecticut, Florida, Georgia, Hawaii, Idaho, Illinois, Kansas, Kentucky, Maryland, Michigan, Montana, New Mexico, New York, Pennsylvania, Rhode Island, South Carolina, Tennessee, Texas, Utah, Virginia, Washington, West Virginia, Wisconsin, and Wyoming).

□ Jurisdictions without statutes authorizing nonhospital DNR orders (the District of Columbia and 21 states: Alabama, Delaware, Indiana, Iowa, Louisiana, Maine, Massachusetts, Minnesota, Mississippi, Missouri, Nebraska, Nevada, New Hampshire, New Jersey, North Carolina, North Dakota, Ohio, Oklahoma, Oregon, South Dakota, and Vermont.)

Note: This map refers to statutes that address DNR orders in the nonhospital setting only. Some of these statutes explicitly apply also to inpatient situations. However, most hospitals already have institutional policies regarding DNR orders, in compliance with the accreditation standards of the Joint Commission on Accreditation of Health Care Organizations. Thus, we have not provided any information in this publication concerning DNR orders within health care institutions. For information about specific state laws, please contact Choice in Dying.

In addition, states that have not enacted nonhospital DNR statutes may have local or state-wide protocols adopted by government agencies or by private, professional organizations that regulate nonhospital DNR orders.

Figure 11 State Statutes Governing Surrogate Decision Making (June 1996)

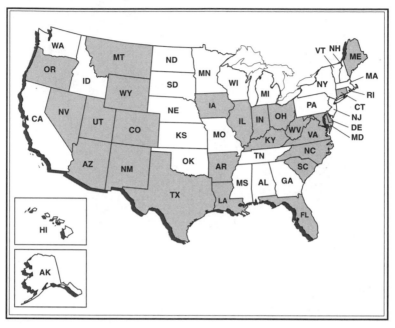

Jurisdictions with statutes authorizing surrogate decision making in the absence of advance directives (the District of Columbia and 25 states: Arizona, Arkansas, Colorado, Connecticut, Delaware, Florida, Illinois, Indiana, Iowa, Kentucky, Louisiana, Maine, Maryland, Montana, Nevada, New Mexico, North Carolina, Ohio, Oregon, South Carolina, Texas, Utah, Virginia, West Virginia, and Wyoming).

States without statutes authorizing surrogate decision making (25 states: Alabama, Alaska, California, Georgia, Hawaii, Idaho, Kansas, Massachusetts, Michigan, Minnesota, Mississippi, Missouri, Nebraska, New Hampshire, New Jersey, New York, North Dakota, Oklahoma, Pennsylvania, Rhode Island, South Dakota, Tennessee, Vermont, Washington, and Wisconsin).

currently have statutes governing nonhospital do-not-resuscitate (DNR) orders. These are orders that would be followed by paramedics in emergency and other nonhospital situations. Figure 11 clarifies state statutes governing surrogate decision making when no advance directive has been completed. Figure 12 indicates the various forms of state law addressing minors and end-of-life decision making. Figure 13 (page 130) illustrates the current state of assisted-suicide laws in the United States.

Although the Patient Self-Determination Act made it possible for all patients to have a say in end-of-life decisions, it is still in the hands of each individual state to determine what choices

Figure 12 State Law Addressing Minors and End-of-Life Decision Making

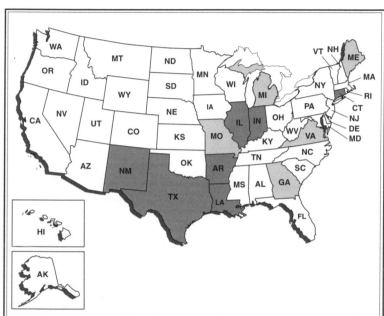

■ States with advance directive or surrogate decision-making statutes that permit parents and other related adults to authorize the withholding or withdrawal of life-sustaining medical treatments from minors, either indirectly by executing a living will on the minor's behalf or directly by oral direction (7 states: Arkansas, Connecticut, Illinois, Indiana, Louisiana, New Mexico, and Texas).

▨ States with appellate-level court decisions permitting the withholding or withdrawal of life-sustaining treatment from minors (5 states: Georgia, Maine, Michigan, Missouri, and Virginia).

□ Jurisdiction whose advance directive and surrogate decision-making statutes do not specifically address end-of-life decision making for minors (the District of Columbia and 38 states: Alabama, Alaska, Arizona, California, Colorado, Delaware, Florida, Hawaii, Idaho, Iowa, Kansas, Kentucky, Maryland, Massachusetts, Minnesota, Mississippi, Montana, Nebraska, Nevada, New Hampshire, New Jersey, New York, North Carolina, North Dakota, Ohio, Oklahoma, Oregon, Pennsylvania, Rhode Island, South Carolina, South Dakota, Tennessee, Utah, Vermont, Washington, West Virginia, Wisconsin, and Wyoming).

can be made in that state's directives. Currently, states are deciding whether to allow physician assistance in dying. As with other legislation, cases that pass at the state level and remain unchallenged will probably be adopted by other states to avoid forum shopping. This seems to be the case with states that are watching the progress of the assisted-suicide bill in Oregon.

Figure 13 Assisted-Suicide Laws in the United States (September 1996)

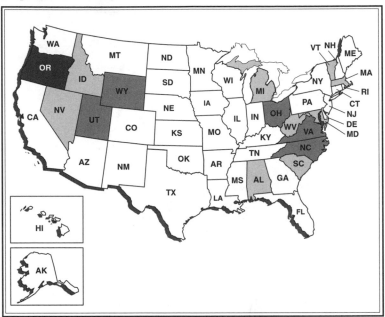

States with statutes that explicitly criminalize assisted suicide (35 states: Alaska, Arizona, Arkansas, California, Colorado, Connecticut, Delaware, Florida, Georgia, Hawaii, Illinois, Indiana, Iowa, Kansas, Kentucky, Louisiana,[1] Maine, Minnesota, Mississippi, Missouri, Montana, Nebraska, New Hampshire, New Jersey, New Mexico, New York,[2] North Dakota, Oklahoma, Pennsylvania, Rhode Island, South Dakota, Tennessee, Texas, Washington,[3] and Wisconsin).

Jurisdictions that criminalize assisted suicide through the common law (the District of Columbia and 9 states: Alabama, Idaho, Maryland, Massachusetts, Michigan, Nevada, South Carolina, Vermont, and West Virginia).

States in which the law is unclear concerning the legality of assisted suicide (5 states: North Carolina,[5] Ohio,[6] Utah,[5] Virginia,[4] and Wyoming[5]).

States with laws permitting physician-assisted suicide in limited circumstances (1 state: Oregon[7]).

---

[1] Also, the Louisiana constitution stipulates that "no law shall subject any person to euthanasia."

[2] A federal circuit court ruled the New York statute criminalizing assisted suicide unconstitutional.

[3] A federal circuit court ruled the Washington statute criminalizing assisted suicide unconstitutional.

[4] Case law in Virginia may be applicable to assisted suicide.

[5] These states have abolished the common law of crimes and therefore do not explicitly prohibit assisted suicide.

[6] The Ohio Supreme Court ruled that assisted suicide is not a crime.

[7] The Oregon law that permits doctors to prescribe medications for use by terminally ill patients to commit suicide was found unconstitutional by a federal district court and is not in effect. The matter is now under appeal.

Advance directives allow individuals to name someone to make decisions for them in the event that they are unable to do so themselves. The President's Commission for the Study of Ethical Problems in Medicine and Biomedical and Behavioral Research (1983a, 128) recommended that, whenever possible, a family member should act as a surrogate decisionmaker in cases in which the patient is deemed incapacitated. This policy is based on the following reasoning:

- The family is generally most concerned about the good of the patient.
- The family is also usually the most knowledgeable about the patient's goals, preferences, and values.
- The family deserves recognition as an important social unit that ought to be treated, within limits, as a responsible decisionmaker in matters that intimately affect its members.
- Participation in a family is often an important dimension of personal fulfillment, especially in a society in which many other traditional forms of community have eroded.
- Since a protected sphere of privacy and autonomy is required for the flourishing of this interpersonal union, institutions and the state should be reluctant to intrude, particularly regarding matters that are personal and on which there is a wide range of opinion in society.

In the case of minors, U.S. law requires that special precautions be taken by physicians and hospitals to ensure that decisions are made in the best interests of minor patients. A parent or legal guardian must consent before a DNR order can be written for a minor. If there is another parent who shares custody, it is the responsibility of the attending physician to make a reasonable attempt to gain that parent's consent as well. If no parents are available to give their consent, the courts must appoint a guardian to make decisions regarding DNR orders for minor patients.

At least one of several criteria must be met before DNR orders can be written for a minor. These are as follows:

1. The patient must have a terminal condition, or
2. The patient is permanently unconscious, or
3. Resuscitation would be medically futile, or

4. Resuscitation would impose an extraordinary burden on the patient in light of the patient's medical condition and the expected outcome of resuscitation (Goldfluss 1994, 94–95).

In 1994 Choice in Dying recorded at least 15 states that had introduced bills to allow physicians to prescribe medications that can be used for suicide. These are: California, Colorado, Connecticut, Maine, Maryland, Massachusetts, Michigan, New Hampshire, New Mexico, New York, Rhode Island, Vermont, Virginia, Washington, and Wisconsin (Davol 1995, 7).

Six months before the Michigan ban on assisted suicide expired (Spring of 1994), a group of Michigan physicians and social researchers from the Survey Research Center (Institute for Social Research at the University of Michigan) surveyed over a thousand Michigan physicians. A second questionnaire was mailed to more than 600 Michigan physicians in the spring of 1995. A total of 1,119 surveys were analyzed. Survey authors noted, "Assisted suicide has [also] been the focus of legislative and judicial action in Michigan during the past several years, prompted by the actions of Dr. Jack Kevorkian." During the survey period, Kevorkian assisted with four suicides, one of which took place in a former hardware store, which Kevorkian had opened as an "obitoria."

The first survey asked: "Suppose that the Michigan legislature were deciding between just two choices: (1) enacting a law banning all physician-assisted suicide, and (2) enacting a plan for physician-assisted suicide. Which do you think would be the better choice for the legislature?" Responses were as follows:

- Definitely / probably ban all physician-assisted suicide: 37%

- Definitely / probably enact a plan for physician-assisted suicide: 56%

- Uncertain about banning all physician-assisted suicide: 8%

The second survey provided physicians with a wider range of choices and produced the following responses:

- Pass a law prohibiting physician-assisted suicide: 17.2%

- Legalize physician-assisted suicide: 38.9%

- Enact "No Law" regarding physician-assisted
  suicide: 37%

These "No Law" responses were broken down as follows:

- Leave it to the doctor/patient relationship: 16.1%

- Medical profession provides regulations/
  guidelines: 16.6%

- Uncertain: 4.8%

When doctors were provided with a wider range of choices regarding potential legislation, support for a total ban dropped by nearly half. Support for legislation specifically allowing physician-assisted suicide also dropped (Bachman et al. 1996, 303–309).

Legal Decisions That Have Shaped the Debate

Since 1960 advances in medical technology, combined with a growing demand for personal autonomy in the United States, have prompted serious debate regarding the right to die. Much of this discussion has taken place in the courts, since politicians in the United States have been reluctant to pass legislation without first gauging public sentiment. Many doctors, hospitals, and individuals have taken personal and professional risks to promote a thorough examination of this issue.

The concept of the right to die has been defined and redefined by case law in the United States over the past 30 years. Each case has raised new questions about such issues as guardianship, withdrawing treatments, and providing equal protection in treatment options. New questions have inevitably emerged as each court decision has been handed down. As these questions, in turn, have been addressed and clarified by the courts, legislation has taken form. Thus, our interpretation in the United States of the right to die is by no means static.

This summary attempts to outline some of the cases that have helped define the debate in the U.S. courts over the past 20 years.

The right to have control over one's own body—Union Pacific Railroad v. Botsford (141 U.S. 250, 251: 1891).

The concept of informed consent was recognized as long ago as 1891, when the U.S. Supreme Court ruled that a person should not be forced to submit to a physical examination against his or her own will. This right was further expanded to include the concept of informed consent in the later case *Schloendorff v. Society of New York Hospital* (211 N.Y. 125, 105 N.E. 92: 1914), in which Justice Benjamin Cardozo stated that, "every human being of adult years and sound mind has the right to determine what shall be done with his body." This case recognized that surgery performed without a patient's consent is a form of assault.

The right to privacy, providing it does not interfere with the best interests of society at large. Two cases advanced this concept. The first was *Griswold v. Connecticut* (381 U.S. 479: 1965), which overruled state legislation making it illegal to use or dispense information about contraceptives to married adults. The case rested on the concept that the Bill of Rights is implicit in its guarantee that "zones of privacy" be honored— that what makes privacy meaningful is being able to exercise it. This decision left the question of privacy open to interpretation, and it has been decided one case at a time. Since 1965 the courts have followed this ruling without clarifying whether the right to die impinges on the best interests of society at large. Eight years after this case was heard, privacy rights were further reinforced in the case of *Roe v. Wade* (410 U.S. 113: 1973), which struck down the Texas law that had, until that time, made abortion a criminal act.

The substituted judgment standard—*In re Quinlan* (70 N.J. 10, 355 A.2d 647, 670: 1976, cert. denied, 429 U.S. 922: 1976). Seventeen-year-old Karen Ann Quinlan was brought to a New Jersey hospital in a coma. Her doctors agreed after several months that she had suffered irreversible brain damage and was in a persistent vegetative state. Her parents wished to remove the respirator (extraordinary means) that kept her alive. Removing food and hydration (then considered ordinary means) was not considered an option.

The Quinlan case was heard in the New Jersey Supreme Court in 1976, which determined that, in the case of an incompetent patient, the right to refuse lifesaving treatment could be exercised by a surrogate if the individual were unable to act on his/her own behalf. This is now known as the substituted judgment standard. Karen Ann Quinlan remained in a persistent vegetative state for eight years after artificial respiration was discontinued.

The right to refuse medical treatment and the best-interests standard—*Superintendent of Belchertown State School v. Saikewicz* (373 Mass. 728, 370 N.E.2d

417, 426 n.11: 1977). The Massachusetts Supreme Court considered the attempt of 67-year-old Joseph Saikewicz, who had been legally incompetent his entire life, to discontinue chemotherapy treatments for his leukemia. Saikewicz was unable to understand the treatment, its side effects, or the prognosis, and he was therefore represented by a court-appointed, or *ad litem*, guardian.

The court stated unanimously that everyone has the right to refuse treatment. This case differs from the Quinlan case in that Saikewicz had never been competent, so a guardian was unable to make a "substituted judgment" on his behalf. The decision had to rest on more objective criteria, such as his age, long-term prognosis, and his ability to follow through on necessary therapy to keep him alive. By looking at a broader range of criteria in making a decision, the court conceived the best-interests standard, which was further clarified in 1985 (*see Conroy* below).

The right of a mentally competent, terminally ill adult to refuse treatment—Satz v. Perlmutter (379 So. 2d 359, Fla.: 1980). Abe Perlmutter, a 73-year-old man suffering from amyotrophic lateral sclerosis (ALS), petitioned the court to approve his decision to discontinue treatment when he was close to death and no longer able to breathe without a respirator. Although he was in extreme pain, he was deemed competent to make this decision. He was fully aware that discontinuing the respirator would render him dead in less than one hour. His physician was concerned that discontinuing treatment would be considered a criminal act and refused Mr. Perlmutter's request.

The Fourth District Court of Appeals determined that Perlmutter had the right to refuse treatment. (*Perlmutter v. Florida Medical Center*, 47 Fla. Supp. 194, Broward County Cir. Ct. 1978). A year later the Florida Supreme Court upheld this decision in a 6–0 ruling allowing a mentally competent, terminally ill adult with no minor dependents to refuse extraordinary medical treatment, providing all family members agreed with this decision. This case put the right to privacy and self-determination ahead of the state's interest in preserving life, preventing suicide, and protecting others from the adverse effects of a decision that will result in death, while still maintaining the ethical integrity of the medical profession.

Circumstances that justify ending life-sustaining treatment of elderly patients with limited life expectancy and severe physical and mental impairments—In re Conroy (188 N.J. Super. 523, Ch. Div.: 1983); and In

re Conroy **(No. A-108 Slip op. at 62, N.J.: 17 January 1985).** Mrs. Claire Conroy was an 85-year-old nursing home resident with multiple illnesses that severely limited her life expectancy. Her nephew was named her guardian and asked the court to remove the feeding tube that kept her alive. An *ad litem* attorney was appointed and opposed the removal of the tube. The court granted permission, but the case was appealed by the court-appointed lawyer. Before the case could be heard, Mrs. Conroy died with the nasogastric tube still in place. The court proceeded and reversed the earlier decision, asserting that the right to refuse life-sustaining treatment is limited to the terminally ill, the permanently comatose, and those who would gain nothing from additional treatment. Removal of Mrs. Conroy's feeding tube, on the other hand, would have hastened her death rather than allowing it to take its natural course.

The New Jersey Supreme Court then heard an appeal and ruled that incompetent patients have a right to refuse treatment, but that this right is not absolute, as it is in the case of a competent patient. Instead, the state's duty to preserve life, prevent suicide, protect third parties, and maintain the integrity of the medical profession (*see Satz v. Perlmutter* 1980) can take precedence over the individual's right to refuse treatment. The court also established three conditions to be met before treatment can be terminated: (1) a clear understanding of whether the patient would have refused the treatment; (2) a surrogate to weigh the pros and cons of maintaining or withdrawing treatment, focusing on the degree of pain suffered by the patient; and (3) a state representative to oversee the decision-making process and prevent abuse.

Withdrawing or withholding artificial nutrition and hydration (ANH)—*Barber v. Superior Court* (147 Cal. App. 3d 1006, 195 Cal. Rptr. 484: 1983). The family of Clarence Herbert, who had suffered a heart attack after having intestinal surgery and had been rendered comatose, requested that artificial feeding be discontinued. Doctors Robert Nedjil and Neil Barber complied with the family's written request when it became clear that his condition was irreversible. When Herbert died six days later, the doctors were charged with murder by the Los Angeles district attorney. The charges were at first dismissed and then reinstated on 5 May 1983. The case was heard by the California Superior Court. The California Court of Appeals dismissed the charges against the two physicians. Important aspects of the decision include:

- Since ordinary treatment should offer some hope of benefit to the patient without undue discomfort or expense,
  artificial nutrition and hydration are extraordinary treatments that can be withheld or withdrawn. This moved
  the courts away from the position of the Catholic Church,
  which has held that artificial nutrition and hydration are
  ordinary treatments.
- Since no distinction was made between withdrawing
  food and removing a respirator or other type of artificial
  life support, this shifted the responsibility for decision
  making to the patient when possible or to the family and
  the physician, and away from the courts.
- "Ineffective treatment" was defined as any treatment that
  would fail to alter a patient's chances of recovery.
- This case established a patient's right in the state of
  California to refuse medical treatment even if death will
  result.

**Nonterminal patients' right to refuse treatment when
death will result—*Bouvia v. Superior Court* (179 Cal.
App. 3d 1127, 225 Cal. Rptr. 297: 1986).** Elisabeth
Bouvia, a 28-year-old quadriplegic with cerebral palsy, was in
severe pain, able to move only her fingers. A nasogastric feeding
tube was inserted to provide adequate nutrition. Bouvia asked
the courts for permission to reject this treatment and to be
allowed to die of starvation in the hospital. The California Court
of Appeals granted Bouvia's request and forbade the hospital
staff to replace the tubes against her wishes. Article 4 of the U.S.
Constitution guarantees the right of people to be secure in their
persons, an aspect of this case that was applied when hospital
personnel force-fed Bouvia.

**Clear and convincing evidence standard—the Cruzan
case.** On 25 June 1990 the U.S. Supreme Court in *Cruzan v.
Director, Missouri Health Department* (497 U.S. _____, 111 L. Ed.
2d 224, 110 S. Ct. _____: 1990) recognized the right to die as a
constitutionally protected liberty interest. This assumes that the
right to refuse treatment, including tube feeding, is guaranteed
in the liberty clause of the U.S. Constitution, but the evidence
indicating a patient's wishes must be clear and convincing.

**Forum shopping to facilitate the right to die—*In re
Busalacchi* (Mo. App. LEXIS 315: 1991).** In May 1987
high school junior Christine Busalacchi was in a car accident in
suburban Missouri. After neurosurgery to save her life, she was

fed through a tube inserted in her stomach. Her condition deteriorated until she had very limited chances of recovery. Her father
asked that the feeding and hydration tube be removed, but doctors refused to comply with this request. Mr. Busalacchi then
tried to have his daughter moved to a facility in Minnesota, a
state that allows families greater decision-making power. The
hospital refused to release Christine to her father and went to
court to ensure that she would not be moved. A ten-day restraining order was issued in December 1990, allowing the hospital to
retain custody of Christine. The hospital's attorney claimed that
Christine's chances of recovery were better than her father indicated, and the judge was concerned that if he allowed the father
to have custody, it would set a precedent for forum shopping,
motivating families to move individuals to states with lenient
laws.

In January 1991 the case was moved to St. Louis. Another
temporary restraining order was issued, lifted, and immediately
appealed. Two days later the court decided that Christine could
not be moved until the case had been reviewed by a hospital
panel. In February the Missouri Department of Health took Peter
Busalacchi to court. At the same time and without her father's
consent, they released a 13-minute video of Christine in the hospital to the press to show that Christine was alert and responsive.
This inserted a "right-to-privacy" question into the case.

In April the Missouri State Supreme Court agreed to hear
the case. The Health Department stated that Christine was
recovering and that with intensive therapy she could improve.
In November 1991 Judge Louis Kohn (who sat on the St. Louis
court case) wrote to the Missouri Supreme Court recommending
that it rule in Mr. Busalacchi's favor. The case remained stalled
for more than a year until January 1993, when newly elected
Attorney General Jay Nixon asked the court to dismiss it without issuing an opinion. Elizabeth W. McDonald, a member of
Missouri Right to Life, then petitioned the court to allow her to
become Christine's legal guardian, but it was decided that
McDonald had no legal standing to involve herself in the case.
Christine Busalacchi died within a few weeks of this decision.

This case highlighted the disparity among states regarding
right-to-die laws and brought the term *forum shopping* to the
right-to-die debate. The videotape released by Christine's doctor
increased public awareness of the loss of dignity and privacy
imposed on patients unable to protect themselves. Most impor-
tantly, it created a sense that people should have the right to
make their own life-and-death decisions.

Developments in Physician Aid-in-Dying

Prior to contemporary times, the euthanasia debate revolved around individuals, the decisions made by and for them, and the actions taken by them or by others on their behalf. The legal questions that have surfaced during the last decade of the twentieth century, however, have revolved around the physician's role in end-of-life decisions and actions. This section documents the increasing legal and legislative efforts to involve physicians in aid-in-dying.

Although mass communications have created the perception of a world community, not all legal systems operate in the same way. Thus, legal actions in one nation can spur debate in another, but cannot be directly translated into another legal environment or culture. Developments in physician aid-in-dying that have occurred in the Netherlands, the United States, and Australia should be viewed within the context of the different system that each uses to evaluate the practice. In the Netherlands, physician aid-in-dying is being evaluated in actual practice.

In 1981 a district court in Rotterdam (the Netherlands) issued the following guidelines after passing sentence on a lay-person who had assisted a suicide. This represented the first time the Dutch courts had explicitly stated which acts of euthanasia would be most likely to escape prosecution under Dutch Penal Code 293 (1886). This established euthanasia as an acceptable medical practice in the Netherlands.

1. There must be unbearable suffering on the part of the patient
2. The desire to die must emanate from a conscious person
3. The request for euthanasia must be voluntary
4. The patient must have been given alternatives and been given time to consider them
5. There must be no other reasonable solutions to the patient's problem
6. The death does not inflict unnecessary suffering on others
7. More than one person must be involved in the decision
8. Only a physician may actually euthanize the patient
9. Great care must be exercised in making this decision (Takken 1987, 4)

These guidelines, which had governed the practices of physicians since 1984, were codified by the Dutch Parliament on 9 February 1993. In an opinion poll taken in the Netherlands in

January 1993, 78 percent of those asked supported the right of the terminally ill to request euthanasia, while only 10 percent said they were opposed (Simons 1993, 1–9). It is significant that these opinions were expressed after 20 years of sanctioned physician aid-in-dying in the Netherlands.

Unlike that used in the Netherlands, the process in the United States tends to avoid the hands-on medical arena, turning instead to the courts to evaluate the practice.

In order to protect themselves from being charged with murder for assisting in a patient's death, U.S. physicians are forced to either watch their patients suffer or to quietly and anonymously assist them without the benefit of outside review.

A number of doctors have been prosecuted for their role in assisting a patient to die. These physicians and their legal battles have prompted greater discussion of the right-to-die debate. But no physician has provoked as much controversy as Dr. Jack Kevorkian. He has helped more than 38 terminally ill people commit suicide and his actions have spurred state legislatures across the nation to create laws that either regulate assisted death or make it illegal. Whatever his motives, Kevorkian has moved the debate over physician-assisted suicide out of the shadows and kept it firmly and consistently in the limelight. Table 5 provides a chronological overview of Kevorkian's physician-assisted suicide activities and the legal and legislative fallout they have precipitated. Several key events that help place these activities in context are listed in bold.

Political activity related to physician aid-in-dying has also accelerated. Legislatures and parliaments worldwide have been pressed by the medical community and the public for more guidance.

On 8 November 1994 the world's first explicit assisted-suicide law was passed by Oregon voters by a margin of 52 to 48 percent. Measure 16, known as the Death with Dignity Act, permits physicians to prescribe a lethal dose of medication but not to administer it. This law remains tied up in the courts as the U.S. judicial system further reviews it.

The Northern Territory Rights of the Terminally Ill Act (Australia) is the second key piece of physician aid-in-dying legislation to be passed in the world. This law will apply only to the Northern Territory of Australia; physician aid-dying remains illegal in all other Australian states and territories. The Northern Territory is about twice the size of Texas and has a population of 170,000, a quarter of which is indigenous (Aborigines and Torres

Table 5 People Who Have Committed Suicide with Dr. Kevorkian's Assistance

	Name	Age	Date	Residence	Illness	Location
1.	Janet Adkins	54	4 June 1991	Oregon	Alzheimer's disease	Kevorkian's van
2.	Marjorie Wantz	58	23 October 1991	Michigan	Chronic pain	Rented cabin
3.	Sherry Miller	43	23 October 1991	Michigan	Multiple sclerosis	Rented cabin

On 20 November 1991 the Michigan Board of Medicine votes 8–0 to suspend Jack Kevorkian's license. He no longer can prescribe medications, so he uses carbon monoxide gas to assist individuals to commit suicide.

	Name	Age	Date	Residence	Illness	Location
4.	Susan Williams	52	15 May 1992	Michigan	Multiple sclerosis	At own home

On 5 June 1992 Oakland County Medical Examiner Dr. Kanu Virani declares Kevorkian's assistance in Miller's death a homicide.

In July 1992 Circuit Court Judge David Breck dismisses murder charges against Kevorkian in the cases of Miller and Wantz. In August Kevorkian appeals the suspension of his medical license, but his appeal is denied.

	Name	Age	Date	Residence	Illness	Location
5.	Lois Hawes	52	26 September 1992	Michigan	Lung cancer	Private home
6.	Catherine Andreyev	45	23 November 1992	Pennsylvania	Breast/lung cancer	Private home

A bill passed (72–29) on the last day (November 24) of the Michigan House 1992 session makes assisted suicide a felony during a 21-month period during which a study of the issue will be undertaken. This measure will go into effect on 30 March 1993 and is intended to stop Kevorkian from continuing to assist individuals to die.

	Name	Age	Date	Residence	Illness	Location
7.	Marguerite Tate	70	15 December 1992	Michigan	ALS	At own home
8.	Marcella Lawrence	67	15 December 1992	Michigan	Multiple illness	Tate's home
9.	Jack Miller	53	20 January 1993	Michigan	Bone cancer	At own home

Doctors are reassured that they will not be prosecuted for providing large doses of pain medication to their patients under the new law passed to stop Kevorkian.

Table continued on next page

Table 5 People Who Have Committed Suicide with Dr. Kevorkian's Assistance (continued)

	Name	Age	Date	Residence	Illness	Location
10.	Stanley Ball	82	4 February 1993	Michigan	Pancreatic cancer	At own home
11.	Mary Biermat	73	4 February 1993	Indiana	Breast cancer	At Ball's home
12.	Elaine Goldblum	47	8 February 1993	Michigan	Multiple sclerosis	At own home

On 9 February 1993 the Dutch Parliament passes a law that guarantees immunity from prosecution for doctors who perform euthanasia according to established guidelines.

13.	Hugo Gale	70	15 February 1993	Michigan	Emphysema	At own home
14.	Jonathan Grenz	44	17 February 1993	California	Throat cancer	Private home
15.	Martha Ruwart	40	17 February 1993	California	Cancer	Private home

The Michigan Senate puts an immediate ban on assisted suicide on 25 February 1993. The House passes the bill (92–10) as does the Senate (28–6). The action is intended to stop people from being assisted by Kevorkian by making assisted suicide a felony.

On 1 March 1993 the American Civil Liberties Union challenges in court Michigan's ban on assisted suicide.

16.	Ronald Mansur	54	15 May 1993	Michigan	Cancer	Real estate office
17.	Thomas Hyde	30	4 August 1993	Michigan	ALS	Van
18.	Donald O'Keefe	73	9 September 1993	Michigan	Bone cancer	At own home
19.	Merian Frederick	72	22 October 1993	Michigan	ALS	Apartment rented by Kevorkian
20.	Dr. Ali Khalili	61	22 November 1993	Illinois	Bone cancer	Apartment rented by Kevorkian
21.	Margaret Garrish	72	26 November 1994	Michigan	Rheumatoid arthritis	Location not known

The ban on assisted suicide in Michigan expires in November 1994.

Table 5 People Who Have Committed Suicide with Dr. Kevorkian's Assistance (continued)

Name	Age	Date	Residence	Illness	Location
In December 1994 the Michigan State Supreme Court rules that there is no constitutional right to assisted suicide and that the practice is illegal under common law. This ruling makes it possible for Kevorkian to be prosecuted for assisted suicide.					
22. Rev. John Evans	78	8 May 1995	Michigan	Lung disease	At own home
23. Nicholas Loving	27	12 May 1995	Arizona	ALS	Private home
Dr. Kevorkian rents a former hardware store 40 miles north of Detroit in Springfield Township and opens an "obitoria," which he names the Margo Janus Mercy Clinic, after his late sister. It is intended to provide a place for him to assist people to commit suicide.					
24. Erika Garcellano	60	26 June 1995	Missouri	ALS	Margo Janus Mercy Clinic
The Margo Janus Mercy Clinic is shut down days after Garcellano's death.					
25. Esther Cohen	46	21 August 1995	Illinois	Multiple sclerosis	Found in car
Also on August 21 Senator Jim Berryman, a Democratic senator from Michigan, files a bill to regulate assisted suicide. If approved by voters, it will appear on the November 1996 ballot.					
On 14 September 1995 Dr. Kevorkian is ordered to stand trial for the deaths of Wantz and Miller (1981). He has been acquitted on murder charges and will now be tried for assisted suicide. The trial is set for 1 April 1996.					
26. Patricia Cashman	58	8 November 1995	California	Breast cancer	Found in car
27. Linda Henslee	48	29 January 1996	Wisconsin	Multiple sclerosis	Kevorkian's van

Table continued on next page

Table 5 People Who Have Committed Suicide with Dr. Kevorkian's Assistance (continued)

	Name	Age	Date	Residence	Illness	Location

On 9 February 1996 Dr. Kevorkian files a $10 million lawsuit against the Michigan State Medical Society and the American Medical Association. He accuses these organizations of slander for saying, "the deliberate killing of our patients [by Kevorkian] must end."

On 20 February 1996 opening arguments are heard in the Kevorkian trial for the deaths of Ali Khalili and Merian Frederick in 1993.

On 6 March 1996 the United States Ninth Circuit Court strikes down a ban on physician-assisted suicide.

On 8 March 1996 Kevorkian is acquitted in the deaths of Frederick and Khalili.

On 1 April 1996 Kevorkian is set to go on trial for assisting in the suicides of Miller and Wantz.

On 2 April 1996 the United States Second Circuit Court of Appeals rules in *Quill et al. v. Vacca* to strike down the New York State law that prohibits physician-assisted suicide.

On 6 May 1996 Kevorkian testifies on his own behalf in the trial to determine if he is guilty in assisting in the deaths of Wantz and Miller.

| 28. | Austin Bastable | 53 | 6 May 1996 | Canada | Multiple sclerosis | Location of death not reported |

On 14 May 1996 Kevorkian is acquitted of assisting Wantz and Miller to commit suicide.

29.	Ruth Neuman	69	9 June 1996	New Jersey	Multiple strokes	Location of death not reported
30.	Lona Jones	58	18 June 1996	Virginia	Malignant brain tumor	Location of death not reported
31.	Bette Lou Hamilton	67	20 June 1996	Ohio	Sryingomyelia	Location of death not reported

Table 5   People Who Have Committed Suicide with Dr. Kevorkian's Assistance (continued)

	Name	Age	Date	Residence	Illness	Location
	On 25 June the American Medical Association publicly reaffirms its long-standing policy against physician-assisted suicide.					
32.	Shirley Cline	63	4 July 1996	California	Cancer	Location of death not reported
33.	Rebecca Badger	39	9 July 1996	California	Multiple sclerosis	Location of death not reported
	Dr. Georges Rene Reding, a Michigan psychiatrist who has attended the five previous suicides assisted by Dr. Kevorkian, makes a public statement in support of Dr. Kevorkian's actions.					
34.	Elizabeth Mertz	59	6 August 1996	Ohio	ALS	Location of death not reported
35.	Judith Curren	42	15 August 1996	Massachusetts	Chronic fatigue and immune system dysfunction, fibromyalgia	Location of death not reported
36.	Louise Siebens	76	20 August 1996	Texas	ALS	Location of death not reported
37.	Patricia Smith	40	22 August 1996	Missouri	Multiple sclerosis	Location of death not reported
38.	Pat DiGangi	66	22 August 1996	New York	Multiple sclerosis	Location of death not reported

Source: Compiled by C. Roberts from press reports: "Transitions," *Newsweek* (18 March 1996): 73; Betzold, Michael. *Appointment with Dr. Death.* Troy, MI: Momentum Books, 1993.

Strait Islanders). There is universal health coverage for all citizens. The Northern Territory Law is more permissive than the Oregon assisted-suicide law. It not only allows physicians to assist patients who choose to die by prescribing medication, it also allows them to administer lethal injections. Any physician who assists a patient must have at least five years of postgraduate experience and be registered to practice in the Northern Territory. The law recognizes that there is no way for a physician to predict exactly when a patient will die, and thus does not explicitly define a time frame for a terminal diagnosis (the Oregon Law, for example, defines terminal as having six months to live). A concern has been raised that this lack of definition may leave room for abuses to occur.

The Northern Territory Rights of the Terminally Ill Act, which was passed by the Northern Territories Parliament on 25 May 1995, has not yet gone into effect. Lawmakers in this territory have chosen to delay enactment until public education and adequate palliative care services are in place.

In the United States, court cases have helped define the concept of physician-assisted suicide. The first of these cases occurred in Washington State. In 1994 the U.S. Ninth Circuit Court in Washington State addressed physician-assisted suicide by questioning a ban that had been enacted in 1854. The issue being decided was whether a mentally competent, terminally ill adult has the right to end his or her suffering with a lethal prescription provided by a physician. Organizations on both sides of the debate filed amicus (friend of the court) briefs. The list of organizations that filed these briefs paints an interesting picture of the polarization of the debate in the United States.

Among those who supported the ban on assisted suicide were: International Anti-Euthanasia Task Force, National Legal Center for the Medically Dependent and Disabled, the United States Catholic Conference, Americans United for Life, Washington State Hospital Association, Catholic Health Association of the United States, and the American Medical Association.

Opposed to the ban were: Euthanasia Research and Guidance Organization, the American Civil Liberties Union of Washington, Northwest Women's Law Center, Lambda Legal Defense and Education Fund, the Grey Panthers, Older Women's League, the Seattle Chapter of NOW, the American Humanist Association, National Lawyer's Guild, Temple DeHirsch Sinai, Unitarian Universalist Association, and the Pacific Northwest District Council of the Japanese-American Citizens League.

In 1995 new guidelines were developed to reflect the changing practice of euthanasia in the Netherlands. These guidelines were drafted by a group of physicians, lawyers, and ethicists and distributed to all 24,000 physician-members of the Royal Dutch Medical Society. This group represents 60 percent of all the doctors in the Netherlands. The new guidelines included the following refinements:

- Encouraging patients to administer a fatal drug to themselves rather than having the physician provide a lethal injection in cases in which this is possible. This change was made in recognition of the fact that assisting in a patient's death can be very stressful for physicians and should only be done when absolutely necessary.
- Requiring that the consulting physician who provides a second opinion have no professional or family relationship to the patient or the physician.
- Not requiring physicians to perform euthanasia, but encouraging all physicians to make their ethical position known to their patients and helping them find a physician willing to assist if they themselves are unwilling to do so (Simons 1995).

These three countries are employing different methods to accomplish the same end: careful examination of a controversial practice in which so much is at stake.

Documents

The end-of-life debate, including the changing relationships between doctors, patients, and institutions, has been shaped by a number of landmark documents produced over the course of more than 20 centuries. Full text or pertinent excerpts of the most influential of these are included in this section.

Medical-Bioethical

Health Care Professional Ethics

For centuries doctors have been asked or required to declare an oath to uphold a standard of care and ethics developed primarily for the benefit of the patient. Many scholars believe the original Hippocratic Oath was written circa 421 B.C. Alternative oaths have been developed by various organizations over the years to keep pace with changing medical practices and mores.

The Hippocratic Oath

I swear by Apollo the physician, by Aesculapius, Hygeia and Panacea, and I take to witness all the gods, all the goddesses, to keep according to my ability and my judgment the following oath:

To consider dear to me as my parents him who taught me this art; to live in common with him and if necessary to share my goods with him; to look upon his children as my own brothers, to teach them this art if they so desire without fee or written promise; to impart to my sons and the sons of the master who taught me and the disciples who have enrolled themselves and have agreed to rules of the profession, but to these alone, the precepts and the instruction. I will prescribe regiment for the good of my patients according to my ability and my judgment and never to harm anyone. To please no one will I prescribe a deadly drug, nor give advice which may cause his death. Nor will I give a woman a pessary to procure abortion. But I will preserve the purity of my life and my art. I will not cut for stone, even for patients in whom the disease is manifest; I will leave this operation to be performed by practitioners (specialists in this art). In every house where I come I will enter only for the good of my patients, keeping myself far from all intentional ill-doing and all seduction, and especially from the pleasures of love or with women or men, be they free or slaves. All that may come to my knowledge in the exercise of my profession or outside of my profession or in daily commerce with men, which ought not to be spread abroad, I will keep secret and will never reveal. If I keep this oath faithfully, may I enjoy my life and practice of my art, respected by all men and in all times; but if I swerve from it or violate it, may the reverse be my lot.

Source: Hensyl, William R., ed. *Stedman's Concise Medical Dictionary* (New York: Prentice Hall, 1987), 343.

By the early 1900s the medical profession had already moved away from many of the precepts of the original Hippocratic Oath, which forbade surgery. Physicians around the world have not consistently been asked to swear to the Hippocratic Oath, but have more often subscribed to more modern ethical guidelines developed by professional organizations.

International Code of Medical Ethics.

Adopted by the World Medical Association in 1949, amended in 1968, 1983, and 1994.

DUTIES OF PHYSICIANS IN GENERAL

ALL PHYSICIANS SHALL always maintain the highest standards of professional conduct.

ALL PHYSICIANS SHALL not permit motives of profit to influence the free and independent exercise of professional judgment on behalf of patients.

ALL PHYSICIANS SHALL, in all types of medical practice, be dedicated to providing competent medical service in full technical and moral independence, with compassion and respect for human dignity.

ALL PHYSICIANS SHALL deal honestly with patients and colleagues, and strive to expose those physicians deficient in character or competence, or who engage in fraud or deception.

The following practices are deemed to be unethical conduct:

a) self-advertising by physicians, unless permitted by the laws of the country and the Code of Ethics of the national medical association.

b) Paying or receiving any fee or any other consideration solely to procure the referral of a patient or for prescribing or referring a patient to any source.

A PHYSICIAN SHALL respect the rights of patients, colleagues, and of other health professionals, and shall safeguard patient confidences.

A PHYSICIAN SHALL act only in the patient's interest when providing medical care which might have the effect of weakening the physical and mental condition of the patient.

A PHYSICIAN SHALL use great caution in divulging discoveries or new techniques or treatment through non-professional channels.

A PHYSICIAN SHALL certify only that which he has personally verified.

DUTIES OF THE PHYSICIAN TO THE SICK

A PHYSICIAN SHALL always bear in mind the obligation of preserving human life.

A PHYSICIAN SHALL owe his patients complete loyalty and all the resources of his science. Whenever an examination or treatment is beyond the physician's capacity, he should summon another physician who has the necessary ability.

A PHYSICIAN SHALL preserve absolute confidentiality on all he knows about his patient, even after the patient has died.

A PHYSICIAN SHALL give emergency care as a humanitarian duty unless he is assured that others are willing and able to give such care.

DUTIES OF THE PHYSICIAN TO EACH OTHER

A PHYSICIAN SHALL behave toward his colleagues as he would have them behave toward him.

A PHYSICIAN SHALL NOT entice patients from his colleagues.

A PHYSICIAN SHALL observe the principles of the "Declaration of Geneva" approved by the World Medical Association.

DECLARATION OF GENEVA

AT THE TIME OF BEING ADMITTED AS A MEMBER OF THE MEDICAL PROFESSION:

I SOLEMNLY PLEDGE myself to consecrate my life to the service of humanity;

I WILL GIVE to my teachers the respect and gratitude which is their due;

I WILL PRACTICE my profession with conscience and dignity;

THE HEALTH OF MY PATIENT will be my first consideration;

I WILL RESPECT the secrets which are confided in me, even after the patient has died;

I WILL MAINTAIN by all the means in my power, the honor and the noble traditions of the medical profession;

MY COLLEAGUES will be my brothers;

I WILL NOT PERMIT considerations of religion, nationality, race, party politics or social standing to intervene between my duty and my patient;

I WILL MAINTAIN the utmost respect for human life from its beginning even under threat and I will not use my medical knowledge contrary to the laws of humanity.

I MAKE THESE PROMISES solemnly and freely, and upon my honor.

Source: World Medical Association, Inc. *International Code of Medical Ethics*, 1994.

The traditional physician-patient relationship began to take on new dimensions as more and different kinds of care became possible. The American Hospital Association, recognizing the hospital's responsibility to provide patients with a clear understanding of their rights when receiving care in that setting, created and affirmed A Patient's Bill of Rights. *This landmark document, which was written in 1972 and adopted by the American Hospital Association (AHA) in 1973, has no legal authority. However, when it was adopted as a guideline for members, more than 90 percent of all U.S. hospitals were members of the AHA. Some adopted it verbatim, while many others adapted it to fit their organizational culture. Some state legislatures also used the language of this document as the basis for laws. The AHA Patient Bill of Rights was updated and expanded in 1992.*

A Patient's Bill of Rights
American Hospital Association, 1973

The American Hospital Association presents a Patient's Bill of Rights with the expectation that observance of these rights will contribute to more effective patient care and greater satisfaction for the patient, his physician and the hospital organization. Further, the Association presents these rights in the expectation that they will be supported by the hospital on behalf of its patients, as an integral part of the healing process. It is recognized that a personal relationship between the physician and the patient is essential for the provision of proper medical care. The traditional physician-patient relationship takes on a new dimension when care is rendered within an organizational structure. Legal precedent has established that the institution itself also has a responsibility to the patient. It is in recognition of these factors that these rights are affirmed.

1. The patient has the right to considerate and respectful care.
2. The patient has the right to obtain from his physician complete current information concerning his diagnosis, treatment, and prognosis in terms the patient can be reasonably expected to understand. When it is not medically advisable to give such information to the patient, the information should be made available to an appropriate person in his behalf. He has the right to know, by name, the physician responsible for coordinating his care.
3. The patient has the right to receive from his physician information necessary to give informed consent prior to the start of any procedure and/or treatment. Except in emergencies, such information for informed consent should include but not necessarily be limited to the specific procedure and/or treatment, the medically significant risks involved, and the probable duration of incapacitation. Where medically significant alternatives for care or treatment exist, or when the patient requests information concerning medical alternatives, the patient has the right to such information. The patient also has the right to know the name of the person responsible for the procedures and/or treatment.
4. The patient has the right to refuse treatment to the extent permitted by law, and to be informed of the medical consequences of his action.
5. The patient has the right to every consideration of his privacy concerning his own medical care program. Care discussion, consultation, examination and treatment are confidential and should be conducted discreetly. Those not directly involved in his care must have the permission of the patient to be present.
6. The patient has the right to expect that all communications and records pertaining to his care should be treated as confidential.
7. The patient has the right to expect that within its capacity a hospital must make reasonable response to the request of a patient for services. The hospital must provide evaluation, service, and/or referral as indicated by the urgency of the case. When medically permissible a patient may be transferred to another facility only after he has received complete

information and explanation concerning the needs for and alternatives to such a transfer. The institution to which the patient is to be transferred must first have accepted the patient for transfer.

8. The patient has the right to obtain information as to any relationship of his hospital to other health care and educational institutions insofar as his care is concerned. The patient has the right to obtain information as to the existence of any professional relationships among individuals, by name, who are treating him.

9. The patient has the right to be advised if the hospital proposes to engage in or perform human experimentation affecting his care or treatment. The patient has the right to refuse to participate in such research projects.

10. The patient has the right to expect reasonable continuity of care. He has the right to know in advance what appointment times and physicians are available and where. The patient has the right to expect that the hospital will provide a mechanism whereby he is informed by the physician or a delegate of the physician of the patient's continuing health care requirements following discharge.

11. The patient has the right to examine and receive an explanation of his bill regardless of source of payment.

12. The patient has the right to know what hospital rules and regulations apply to his conduct as a patient.

Source: American Hospital Association, Chicago, IL, 1973.

The following principles were adopted by the American Medical Association in 1980 and then revised again in 1983 and 1990. These are not laws, but standards of conduct that seek to define the essentials of honorable behavior for physicians.

Principles of Medical Ethics, American Medical Association

I.   A physician shall be dedicated to providing competent medical service with compassion and respect for human dignity.

II. A physician shall deal honestly with patients and colleagues, and strive to expose those physicians deficient in character or competence, or who engage in fraud or deception.

III. A physician shall respect the law and also recognize a responsibility to seek changes in those requirements which are contrary to the best interests of the patient.

IV. A physician shall respect the rights of patients, of colleagues, and of other health professionals, and shall safeguard patient confidences within the constraints of the law.

V. A physician shall continue to study, apply and advance scientific knowledge, make relevant information available to patients, colleagues, and the public, obtain consultation, and use the talents of other health professionals when indicated.

VI. A physician shall, in the provision of appropriate patient care, except in emergencies, be free to choose whom to serve, with whom to associate, and the environment in which to provide medical services.

VII. A physician shall recognize a responsibility to participate in activities contributing to an improved community.

Source: American Medical Association. "Council Report—Guidelines," *Journal of the American Medical Association*, 273, no. 4 (25 January 1995): 334–335.

The guidelines provided for doctors have always left much room for interpretation and have relied on the honor of individuals to maintain high standards of integrity. This tradition of self-policing is being sorely tested by managed care, a bottom-line approach to the provision of health care services developed during the late 1980s in response to skyrocketing health care costs. Many people believe the implications of this approach for terminally ill patients are frightening, particularly if it becomes legal to assist patients to die before safeguards are in place to protect them from abuses. As resources become more and more limited, managed care could help widen the circle of those considered eligible for euthanasia to include the disabled and the elderly, bringing into play all of the slippery-slope concerns generated by practices in Nazi Germany. The American Medical Association's Council on Ethical and Judicial Affairs issued the following guidelines in 1994 in response to these and other concerns.

Guidelines: Council on Ethical and Judicial Affairs
American Medical Association

1. The duty and advocacy of the patient is a fundamental element of the physician-patient relationship that should not be altered by the system of health care delivery in which physicians practice. Physicians must continue to place the interests of their patients first.

2. When managed care plans place restrictions on the care that physicians in the plan may provide to their patients, the following principles should be followed:

   (a) Any broad allocation guidelines that restrict care and choices—which go beyond the cost-benefit judgments made by physicians as a part of their normal professional responsibilities—should be established at a policy-making level so that individual physicians are not asked to engage in ad hoc rationing.

(b) Regardless of any allocation guidelines or gatekeeper directives, physicians must advocate for any care that they believe will materially benefit their patients.

(c) Physicians should be given an active role in contributing their expertise to any allocation process and should advocate for guidelines that are sensitive to differences among patients. Managed care plans should create structures similar to hospital medical staffs that allow physicians to have meaningful input into the plan's development of allocation guidelines. Guidelines for allocating health care should be reviewed on a regular basis and updated to reflect advances in medical knowledge and changes in relative costs.

(d) Adequate appellate mechanisms for both patients and physicians should be in place to address disputes regarding medically necessary care. In some circumstances, physicians have an obligation to initiate appeals on behalf of their patients. Cases may arise in which a health plan has an allocation guideline that is generally fair but in particular circumstances results in unfair denials of care, i.e., denial of care that, in the physician's judgment, would materially benefit the patient. In such cases, the physician's duty as patient advocate requires that the physician challenge the denial and argue for the provision of treatment in the specific case. Cases may also arise in which a health plan has an allocation guideline that is generally unfair in its operation. In such cases, the physician's duty as patient advocate requires not only a challenge to any denials of treatment from the guideline but also advocacy at the health plan's policy-making level to seek an elimination or modification of the guideline. Physicians should assist patients who wish to seek additional appropriate care outside the plan when the physician believes that the care is in the patient's best interests.

(e) Managed care plans must adhere to the requirement of informed consent that patients be given full disclosure of material information. Full disclosure requires that managed care plans inform potential subscribers of limitations or restrictions on the benefits package when they are considering entering the plan.

(f) Physicians also should continue to promote full disclosure to patients enrolled in managed care organizations. The physician's obligation to disclose treatment alternatives to patients is not altered by limitations in the coverage provided by the patient's managed care plan. Full disclosure includes informing patients of all their treatment options, even those that may not be covered under the terms of the managed care plan. Patients may then determine whether an appeal is appropriate or whether they wish to seek care outside the plan for treatment alternatives that are not covered.

(g) Physicians should not participate in any plan that encourages or requires care at or below minimum professional standards.

3. When physicians are employed or reimbursed by managed care plans that offer financial incentives to limit care, serious potential conflicts are created between the physician's personal financial interests and the needs of their patients. Efforts to contain health care costs should not place patient welfare at risk. Thus, financial incentives are permissible only if they promote the cost-effective delivery of health care and not the withholding of medically necessary care.

(a) Any incentives to limit care must be disclosed fully to patients by plan administrators on enrollment and at least annually thereafter.

(b) Limits should be placed on the magnitude of fee withholds, bonuses, and other financial incentives to limit care. Calculating incentive payments according to the performance of a sizable group of physicians rather than on an individual basis should be encouraged.

(c) Health plans or other groups should develop financial incentives based on quality of care. Such incentives should complement financial incentives based on the quantity of services used.

4. Patients have an individual responsibility to be aware of the benefits and limitations of their health care coverage. Patients should exercise their autonomy by public participation in the formulation of benefits packages and by prudent selection of health care coverage that best suits their needs.

Source: Council on Ethical and Judicial Affairs, American Medical Association, *Journal of the American Medical Association* 273, no. 4 (25 January 1995): 334–335.

Spiritual-Social-Cultural
Religious Viewpoints

The following is an overview of the issues raised and defined by several religious groups.

To Affirm the Sacredness of Human Life
A resolution of the Missouri Synod of the Lutheran Church adopted in 1977.

WHEREAS, life is a gift from God and comes into being by an act that shares in the creative powers of God himself; and

WHEREAS, Scripture teaches that suffering has a purposes [sic] of God; and

WHEREAS, Life and death belong in the realm of God's providence; and

WHEREAS, Scripture teaches that suffering has a positive purpose and value in God's economy and is not to be avoided at all costs (2 Cor. 1:5-7; 2 Cor. 4:7-11; Heb. 12:5-11; Rom. 8:16-18,28, 35-39; Phil 3:10; Col. 1:24); and

WHEREAS, we sing of the positive purpose of suffering in our worship (TLH, 523, 528, 533, et al.); and

WHEREAS, The Commission on Theology and Church Relations (CTCR) and its Social Concerns Committee (SCC) currently have a study in progress regarding the question of euthanasia; and

WHEREAS, The willful taking of the life of one human being by another is contrary to the Word and the will of God (Ex. 20:13); therefore be it

RESOLVED, That the Synod affirm that human life is sacred and finds meaning and purpose in seeking and following God's will, not in self-centered pleasure, a concern for convenience, or a desire for comfort; and be it further

RESOLVED, That the Synod affirm the positive benefits of suffering, so that God's children may be comforted in Christ Jesus and have their sights focused more firmly on eternal values; and be it further

RESOLVED, That the Synod unequivocally declare that the practice known as euthanasia, namely, inducing death, is contrary to God's will and cannot be condoned or justified; and be it finally

RESOLVED, The CTCR and the SCC be urged to complete their study as soon as possible.

(The report affirmed this stance in October 1979)

Source: Resolution 3-30, "To Affirm the Sacredness of Human Life," The Lutheran Church—Missouri Synod, 1977 Convention Proceedings, 138.

Papal pronouncements condemning euthanasia have been issued periodically for several decades. The following is an excerpt from the landmark 1980 Declaration on Euthanasia as prepared by the Sacred Congregation for the Doctrine of the Faith, 5 May 1980.

Declaration on Euthanasia
Introduction
The rights and values pertaining to the human person occupy an important place among the questions discussed today. In this regard, the Second Vatican Ecumenical Council solemnly reaffirmed the lofty dignity of the human person, and in a special way his or her right to life. The Council therefore condemned crimes against life "such as any

type of murder, genocide, abortion, euthanasia, or willful suicide"
(Pastoral Constitution GAUDIUM ET SPES, no. 27).

More recently, the Sacred Congregation for the Doctrine of the
Faith has reminded all the faithful of Catholic teaching on procured
abortion. The Congregation now considers it opportune to set forth the
Church's teaching on euthanasia.

It is indeed true that, in this sphere of teaching, the recent Popes
have explained the principles, and these retain their full force; but the
progress of medical science in recent years has brought to the fore new
aspects of the question of euthanasia, and these aspects call for further
elucidation on the ethical level.

In modern society, in which even the fundamental values of
human life are often called into question, cultural change exercises an
influence upon the way of looking at suffering and death; moreover,
medicine has increased its capacity to cure and to prolong life in particular circumstances, which sometime give rise to moral problems. Thus
people living in this situation experience no little anxiety about the
meaning of advanced old age and death. They also begin to wonder
whether they have the right to obtain for themselves or their fellow
men an "easy death," which would shorten suffering and which seems
to them more in harmony with human dignity.

* * *

I. The Value of Human Life

Human life is the basis of all goods, and is the necessary source
and condition of every human activity and of all society. Most people
regard life as something sacred and hold that no one may dispose of
it at will, but believers see in life something greater, namely, a gift
of God's love, which they are called upon to preserve and make fruit-
ful. And it is this latter consideration that gives rise to the following
consequences:

1. No one can make an attempt on the life of an innocent person
   without opposing God's love for that person, without violating
   a fundamental right, and therefore without committing a crime
   of the utmost gravity.
2. Everyone has the duty to lead his or her life in accordance with
   God's plan. That life is entrusted to the individual as a good that
   must bear fruit already here on earth, but that finds its full per-
   fection only in eternal life.
3. Intentionally causing one's own death, or suicide, is therefore
   equally as wrong as murder; such an action on the part of a person is to be considered as a rejection of God's sovereignty and
   loving plan. Furthermore, suicide is also often a refusal of love
   for self, the denial of a natural instinct to live, a flight from the
   duties of justice and charity owed to one's neighbor, to various

communities or to the whole of society—although, as is generally recognized, at times there are psychological factors present that can diminish responsibility or even completely remove it.

However, one must clearly distinguish suicide from that sacrifice of one's life whereby for a higher cause, such as God's glory, the salvation of souls or the service of one's brethren, a person offers his or her own life or puts it in danger (cf. Jn. 15:14).

✓ II. Euthanasia

In order that the question of euthanasia can be properly dealt with, it is first necessary to define the words used.

Etymologically speaking, in ancient times EUTHANASIA meant an EASY DEATH without severe suffering. Today one no longer thinks of this original meaning of the word, but rather of some intervention of medicine whereby the suffering of sickness or of the final agony are reduced, sometimes also with the danger of suppressing life prematurely. Ultimately, the word EUTHANASIA is used in a more particular sense to mean "mercy killing," for the purpose of putting an end to extreme suffering, or saving abnormal babies, the mentally ill or the incurably sick from the prolongation, perhaps for many years, of a miserable life, which could impose too heavy a burden on their families or on society.

It is, therefore, necessary to state clearly in what sense the word is used in the present document.

By euthanasia is understood an action or an omission which of itself or by intention causes death, in order that all suffering may in this way be eliminated. Euthanasia's terms of reference, therefore, are to be found in the intention of the will and in the methods used.

It is necessary to state firmly once more that nothing and no one can in any way permit the killing of an innocent human being, whether a fetus or an embryo, an infant or an adult, an old person or one suffering from an incurable disease, or a person who is dying. Furthermore, no one is permitted to ask for this act of killing, either for himself or herself or for another person entrusted to his or her care, nor can he or she consent to it, either explicitly or implicitly, nor can any authority legitimately recommend or permit such an action. For it is a question of the violation of the divine law, an offense against the dignity of the human person, a crime against life, and an attack on humanity.

It may happen that, by reason of prolonged and barely tolerable pain, for deeply personal or other reasons, people may be led to believe that they can legitimately ask for death or obtain it for others. Although in these cases the guilt of the individual may be reduced or completely absent, nevertheless the error of judgment into which the conscience falls, perhaps in good faith, does not change the nature of this act of killing, which will always be in itself something to be rejected. The pleas of gravely ill people who sometimes ask for death are not to be understood as implying a true desire for euthanasia; in fact, it is almost always a case of an anguished plea for help and love. What a sick person needs, besides medical care, is love, the human and supernatural warmth with which the sick person can and ought to be surrounded by all those close to him or her, parents and children, doctors and nurses.

III. The Meaning of Suffering for Christians and the Use of Painkillers

Death does not always come in dramatic circumstances after barely tolerable sufferings. Nor do we have to think only of extreme cases. Numerous testimonies which confirm one another lead one to the conclusion that nature itself has made provision to render more bearable at the moment of death separations that would be terribly painful to a person in full health. Hence it is that a prolonged illness, advanced old age, or a state of loneliness or neglect can bring about psychological conditions that facilitate the acceptance of death.

Nevertheless the fact remains that death, often preceded or accompanied by severe and prolonged suffering, is something which naturally causes people anguish.

Physical suffering is certainly an unavoidable element of the human condition; on the biological level, it constitutes a warning of which no one denies the usefulness; but, since it affects the human psychological makeup, it often exceeds its own biological usefulness and so can become so severe as to cause the desire to remove it at any cost.

According to Christian teaching, however, suffering, especially suffering during the last moments of life, has a special place in God's saving plan; it is in fact a sharing in Christ's passion and a union with the redeeming sacrifice which He offered in obedience to the Father's will. Therefore, one must not be surprised if some Christians prefer to moderate their use of painkillers, in order to accept voluntarily at least a part of their sufferings and thus associate themselves in a conscious way with the sufferings of Christ crucified (cf. Mt. 27:34). Nevertheless it would be imprudent to impose a heroic way of acting as a general rule. On the contrary, human and Christian prudence suggest for the majority of sick people the use of medicines capable of alleviating or suppressing pain, even though these may cause as a secondary effect semiconsciousness and reduced lucidity. As for those who are not in a state to express themselves, one can reasonably presume that they wish to take these painkillers, and have them administered according to the doctor's advice.

But the intensive use of painkillers is not without difficulties, because the phenomenon of habituation generally makes it necessary to increase their dosage in order to maintain their efficacy. At this point it is fitting to recall a declaration by Pius XII, which retains its full force; in answer to a group of doctors who had put the question: "Is the suppression of pain and consciousness by the use of narcotics . . . permitted by religion and morality to the doctor and the patient (even at the approach of death and if one foresees that the use of narcotics will shorten life)?" the Pope said: "If no other means exist, and if, in the given circumstances, this does not prevent the carrying out of other religious and moral duties: Yes." In this case, of course, death is in no way intended or sought, even if the risk of it is reasonably taken; the intention is simply to relieve pain effectively, using for this purpose painkillers available to medicine.

However, painkillers that cause unconsciousness need special consideration. For a person not only has to be able to satisfy his or her moral duties and family obligations; he or she also has to prepare himself or herself with full consciousness for meeting Christ. Thus Pius XII warns: "It is not right to deprive the dying person of consciousness without a serious reason."

IV. Due Proportion in the Use of Remedies

Today it is very important to protect, at the moment of death, both the dignity of the human person and the Christian concept of life, against a technological attitude that threatens to become an abuse. Thus some people speak of a "right to die," which is an expression that does not mean the right to procure death either by one's own hand or by means of someone else, as one pleases, but rather the right to die peacefully with human and Christian dignity. From this point of view, the use of therapeutic means can sometimes pose problems.

In numerous cases, the complexity of the situation can be such as to cause doubts about the way ethical principles should be applied. In the final analysis, it pertains to the conscience either of the sick person, or of those qualified to speak in the sick person's name, or of the doctors, to decide, in the light of moral obligations and of the various aspects of the case.

Everyone has the duty to care for his or her own health or to seek such care from others. Those whose task it is to care for the sick must do so conscientiously and administer the remedies that seem necessary or useful.

However, is it necessary in all circumstances to have recourse to all possible remedies?

In the past, moralists replied that one is never obliged to use "extraordinary" means. This reply, which as a principle still holds good, is perhaps less clear today, by reason of the imprecision of the term and the rapid progress made in the treatment of sickness. Thus some people prefer to speak of "proportionate" and "disproportionate" means. In any case, it will be possible to make a correct judgment as to the means by studying the type of treatment to be used, its degree of complexity or risk, its cost and the possibilities of using it, and comparing these elements with the result that can be expected, taking into account the state of the sick person and his or her physical and moral resources.

In order to facilitate the application of these general principles, the following clarifications can be added:

- If there are no other sufficient remedies, it is permitted, with the patient's consent, to have recourse to the means provided by the most advanced medical techniques, even if these means are still at the experimental stage and are not without a certain risk. By accepting them, the patient can even show generosity in the service of humanity.
- It is also permitted, with the patient's consent, to interrupt these means, where the results fall short of expectations. But for such a decision to be made, account will have to be taken of the reasonable wishes of the patient and the patient's family, as also of the advice of the doctors who are specially competent in the matter. The latter may in particular judge that the investment in instruments and personnel is disproportionate to the results foreseen; they may also judge that the techniques applied impose on the patient strain or suffering out of proportion with the benefits which he or she may gain from such techniques.
- It is also permissible to make do with the normal means that medicine can offer. Therefore one cannot impose on anyone the obligation to have recourse to a technique which is already in use but which carries a risk or is burdensome. Such a refusal is not the equivalent of suicide; on the contrary, it should be considered as an acceptance of the human condition, or a wish to avoid the application of a medical procedure disproportionate to the results that can be expected, or a desire not to impose excessive expense on the family or the community.
- When inevitable death is imminent in spite of the means used, it is permitted in conscience to take the decision to refuse forms of treatment that would only secure a precarious and burdensome prolongation of life, so long as the normal care due to the sick person in similar cases is not interrupted. In such circumstances the doctor has no reason to reproach himself with failing to help the person in danger.

Conclusion

The norms contained in the present Declaration are inspired by a profound desire to service people in accordance with the plan of the Creator. Life is a gift of God, and on the other hand death is unavoidable; it is necessary, therefore, that we, without in any way hastening the hour of death, should be able to accept it with full responsibility and dignity. It is true that death marks the end of our earthly existence, but at the same time it opens the door to immortal life. Therefore, all must prepare themselves for this event in the light of human values, and Christians even more so in the light of faith.

As for those who work in the medical profession, they ought to neglect no means of making all their skill available to the sick and dying; but they should also remember how much more necessary it is to provide them with the comfort of boundless kindness and heartfelt charity. Such service to people is also service to Christ the Lord, who said: "As you did it to one of the least of these my brethren, you did it to me" (Mt. 25:40).

Source: The Vatican's Declaration on Euthanasia. Rome: Vatican, 1980.

The Right To Die with Dignity
Unitarian Universalist General Assembly, 1988

Guided by our belief as Unitarian Universalists that human life has inherent dignity, which may be compromised when life is extended beyond the will or ability of a person to sustain that dignity; and believing that it is every person's inviolable right to determine in advance the course of action to be taken in the event that there is no reasonable expectation of recovery from extreme physical or mental disability; and ...

WHEREAS, prolongation may cause unnecessary suffering and/or loss of dignity while providing little or nothing of benefit to the individual; and ...

WHEREAS, differences exist among people over religious, moral and legal implications of administering aid-in-dying when an individual of sound mind has voluntarily asked for such aid; and,

WHEREAS, obstacles exist within our society against providing support for an individual's declared wish to die; and

WHEREAS, many counselors, clergy and health-care personnel value prolongation of life regardless of the quality of life or will to live;

THEREFORE BE IT RESOLVED: That the Unitarian Universalist Association calls upon its congregations and individual Unitarian Universalists to examine attitudes and practices in our society relative to the ending of life, as well as those in other countries and cultures; and

BE IT FURTHER RESOLVED: That Unitarian Universalists reaffirm their support for the Living Will, as declared in a 1978 resolution of the General Assembly, declare support for the Durable Power of Attorney for Health Care, and seek assurance that both instruments will be honored.

BE IT FURTHER RESOLVED: That Unitarian Universalists advocate the right to self-determination in dying, and the release from civil or criminal penalties of those who, under proper safeguards, act to honor the right of terminally ill patients to select the time of their own deaths; and

BE IT FURTHER RESOLVED: That Unitarian Universalists advocate safeguards against abuses by those who would hasten death contrary to an individual's desires; and

BE IT FINALLY RESOLVED: That Unitarian Universalists, acting through their congregations, memorial societies, and appropriate organizations, inform and petition legislators to support legislation that will create legal protection for the right to die with dignity, in accordance with one's own choice.

Source: General Assembly of Unitarian Universalists, *1988 Proceedings*, 74.

The Rights and Responsibilities of Christians Regarding Human Death
A Resolution of the Rocky Mountain Conference United Church of Christ, 1990

WHEREAS: We live in an era of complex biomedical technologies, with various means to maintain or prolong physical life and postpone inevitable death; and

WHEREAS: There are ever-increasing anxieties about a prolonged dying process with hopeless deterioration, and its potentially devastating effects on the dignity of the dying person, the emotional and physical well-being of families as well as the responsible Christian Stewardship of resources; and

WHEREAS: Technology advances more quickly than public policy and public opinion is often ahead of legislative enactment; and

WHEREAS: Individuals have increasing responsibilities in these life and death decisions but often lack adequate information as to available options; and

WHEREAS: Life is sourced in God, and recognizes that our faith calls for commitment and work for the quality of human life, with mercy, justice and truth; and

WHEREAS: Affirming that the gift of abundant life is more than avoidance of death and that over-regard for the body, without proper concern for the needs of the person or the human spirit, can become a kind of biological idolatry. We are convinced that what is required is a balanced appreciation of the whole person; and

WHEREAS: General Synod 12 of the United Church of Christ has supported the legal recognition of living wills and the General Synod 9 addressed the rights and responsibilities of Christians regarding human death; and

WHEREAS: We support the right and responsibility of individuals to choose their own destiny, and recognizing the need for safeguards to protect persons who cannot make life and death choices for themselves.

BE IT THEREFORE RESOLVED: that the Church support the rights of individuals and families to make decisions regarding human death and dying;

Be it also resolved the the Churches within the Rocky Mountain Conference affirm the right of persons under hopeless and irreversible conditions to terminate their lives and emphasize that Christian understanding and compassion are appropriate with regard to suicide and euthanasia;

BE IT ALSO RESOLVED: that we call upon the Church to study and discuss these issues with resources provided by the Ministry Committee recognizing and respecting the rights of those who disagree;

BE IT ALSO RESOLVED: that we encourage legislation to safeguard all of these rights, including the rights of those who are unable to make decisions for themselves;...

Source: A Resolution of the Rocky Mountain Conference, United Church of Christ, 1990.

Personal and Cultural Insights

Arthur and Cynthia Koestler died on 1 March 1983 of an overdose of barbiturates and alcohol. He was 77 years old and she was 55 years old. Arthur Koestler was perhaps best known for his novel Darkness At Noon, *and other books, but he also was the president of the Voluntary Euthanasia Society (London). When he wrote the following note ten months before committing suicide, Arthur clearly assumed Cynthia would survive him. Before she took her life, Cynthia added her note to the end of her husband's.*

A Suicide Note
by Arthur Koestler, June 1982

To Whom It May Concern.

The purpose of this note is to make it unmistakably clear that I intend to commit suicide by taking an overdose of drugs without the knowledge or aid of any other person. The drugs have been legally obtained and hoarded over a considerable period. Trying to commit suicide is a gamble, the outcome of which will be known to the gambler only if the attempt fails, but not if it succeeds. Should this attempt fail and I survive it in a physically or mentally impaired state, in which I can no longer control what is done to me, or communicate my wishes, I hereby request that I be allowed to die in my own home and not be resuscitated or be kept alive by artificial means. I further request that my wife, or physician, or any friend present, should invoke habeus corpus against any attempt to remove me forcibly from my house to hospital.

My reasons for deciding to put an end to my life are simple and compelling. Parkinson's Disease and the slow-killing variety of leukemia (CCL). I kept the latter a secret even from intimate friends to save them distress. After a more or less steady physical decline over the last years, the process has now reached an acute state with added complications which make it advisable to seek self-deliverance now, before I become incapable of making the necessary arrangements.

I wish my friends to know that I am leaving their company in a peaceful state of mind, with some timid hopes for a de-personalized after-life beyond due confines of space, time and matter and beyond the limits of our comprehension. This "oceanic feeling" has often sustained me at difficult moments, and does so now, while I am writing this. What makes it nevertheless hard to take this final step is the reflection of the pain it is bound to inflict on my few surviving friends, above all my wife Cynthia. It is to her that I owe the relative peace and happiness that I enjoyed in the last period of my life—and never before.

Source: Mikes, George. *Arthur Koestler: The Story of a Friendship*. (London: André Deutsch, 1983), 78–79.

Footnote (by Cynthia Koestler):
I should have liked to finish my account of working for Arthur—a story which began when our paths happened to cross in 1949. However, I cannot live without Arthur, despite certain inner resources.

Source: Harris, Harold. *Stranger on the Square*, by Arthur and Cynthia Koestler. (New York: Random House, 1984), preface.

A Values Profile

I. Introduction

The following questionnaire is designed to guide your medical treatment after you have become incompetent (that is, you are unable to understand the nature and consequences of important medical decisions). The object is to instruct about what level of deterioration would warrant cessation of life-sustaining medical intervention on your behalf. Unless you indicate otherwise, you can assume that comfort care (care intended to keep you clean and comfortable) will always be provided.

Listed below are factors which some people consider important in shaping post-competence medical care. You are asked to give your own reactions to the various factors.

Some people's main concern is that their existence not be prolonged during the last stages of an unavoidable dying process (i.e., when they have been stricken with an incurable fatal condition). If that is your main concern, Section II below gives you a chance to indicate the time span which you consider the "last stage" of an unavoidable dying process.

Some people are more concerned about medical prolongation of their lives—whatever the possible survival period—after they have permanently deteriorated to a condition which they consider personally undignified and intolerable. If that is your main concern, Sections III through VIII below give you a chance to define the conditions which, for you, would be intolerable.

II.   A Terminal Condition

In my post-competence state, if I face an incurable condition which, according to medical judgment, will cause my death with or without medical intervention, I want life-sustaining care to cease, as follows:

_____ when I have less than a year to survive

_____ when I have less than six months to survive

_____ when I have less than a month to survive

_____ when I have less than a week to survive

_____ none of the above; I want all life sustaining care to be continued

_____ none of the above; I want my treatment to depend on my condition, not the remaining life span

III.   Pain and Suffering

In my post-competence state, I am concerned about extreme pain to the following extent: (check one)

_____ intolerable; I prefer death

_____ a very negative factor, to be weighed with other factors in determining my best interests

_____ unimportant

My attitude toward pain which can be controlled only by substances which leave me drowsy and confused most of the time:

_____ intolerable

_____ a very negative factor, to be weighed with other factors in determining my best interests

_____ unimportant

IV.   Mental Incapacity

In my post-competence state, I am concerned about the level of my mental deterioration to the following extent: (check one)

_____ a very critical factor

_____ important yet not determinative by itself, a factor to be weighed with other factors in determining my best interests

_____ unimportant

My attitude toward a permanently unconscious state, confirmed by up-to-date medical tests, showing no hope of ever regaining consciousness:

_____ intolerable; I prefer death

_____ tolerable, so long as insurance or other non-family sources are paying the bills

My reaction to profound dementia to the point where I can no longer recognize and interact with my loved ones:

_____ intolerable; I prefer death

_____ a very negative factor to be weighed with other factors in determining my best interests

_____ tolerable

My reaction to dementia to the point where I can no longer read and understand written material:

_____ intolerable, I prefer death

_____ a very negative factor, to be weighed with other factors in determining my best interests

_____ tolerable

V.   Physical Immobility

In my post-competence state, I am concerned about physical immobility to the following extent:

_____ important

_____ unimportant

My reaction to being permanently bedridden:

_____ intolerable; I prefer death

_____ a very negative factor, to be weighed with other factors in determining my best interests

_____ tolerable

My reaction to being non-ambulatory, meaning I can leave my bed but can only move around in a wheelchair:

_____ intolerable; I prefer death

_____ a very negative factor, to be weighed with other factors in determining my best interests

_____ tolerable

VI.   Physical Helplessness

In my post-competence state, I am concerned about my independence and my ability to tend to my own physical needs to the following extent:

_____ a very critical factor

_____ important yet not determinative by itself, a factor to be weighed in determining my best interests

_____ unimportant

My reaction to being incapable of feeding myself:

_____ intolerable; I prefer death

_____ a very negative factor, to be weighed with other factors in determining my best interests

_____ a somewhat negative factor

_____ unimportant

My reaction to being incapable of dressing myself:

_____ intolerable; I prefer death

_____ a very negative factor, to be weighed with other factors in determining my best interests

_____ a somewhat negative factor

_____ unimportant

My reaction to being incontinent:
_____ intolerable; I prefer death
_____ a very negative factor, to be weighed with other factors in determin-
ing my best interests
_____ a somewhat negative factor
_____ unimportant

VII.　Interests of Loved Ones

In my post-competence state, the emotional and financial burdens imposed on my loved ones are of concern to the following extent:
_____ a critical factor
_____ an important factor, depending on degree of burden
_____ unimportant

My reaction to emotional strain posed for my spouse or other loved ones surrounding me during my incompetency:
_____ an important factor
_____ a somewhat important factor
_____ irrelevant; they owe it to me

My reaction to a financial burden being imposed on my spouse or other loved ones:
_____ an important factor
_____ a somewhat important factor
_____ irrelevant; they can afford it
_____ irrelevant; my life is the critical factor

My reaction to my assets being depleted by heavy medical expenses being used for my care:
_____ an important factor
_____ somewhat important
_____ irrelevant; I earned it

VIII.　Living Arrangements

I would find any of the following living arrangements intolerable so that, if there were no alternative, I would prefer cessation or withdrawal of life sustaining medical care:
_____ living at home, but with need for full-time help
_____ living permanently in the home of one of my children or other relative
_____ living permanently in a nursing home or other long-term care facility
_____ being confined to a hospital with little or no hope of ever leaving

Source: Cantor, Norman L. *Advance Directives and the Pursuit of Death with Dignity* (Indiana University Press, 1993), 166–171.

Impact of Illness on Patients' Families

Family Impact Questions/Family Impact Survey Items Used in the Analysis

  1. Since (you/the patient) left the hospital on (date of discharge), how much help has been needed from someone in the family? A great deal, a moderate amount, or none at all?

2. Since (you/the patient) left the hospital on (date of discharge), has anyone in the family had to quit work or make any other major changes to provide personal care for the patient? (answered yes/no)
3. Please tell me about these changes. (recorded verbatim)
4. Has anyone else in the family become ill or unable to function normally in part because of the stress and strain of (your/the patient's) illness? (answered yes/no)
5. Has (your/the patient's) illness meant having to use all or most of the family's savings? (answered yes/no)
6. Has (your/the patient's) illness meant the loss of the major source of income for the family? (answered yes/no)
7. Have the costs of care for (your/the patient's) illness required the family to move to a less expensive place to live? (answered yes/no)
8. Have the costs of care for (your/the patient's) illness required putting off important medical care for anyone in the family? (answered yes/no)
9. Have the costs of care for (your/the patient's) illness required putting off plans for education or otherwise greatly changing the plans for anyone in the family? (answered yes/no)
10. Please tell me about these changes. (recorded verbatim)

Source: Covinsky, Kenneth E., M.D., M.P.H., et al. "Impact of Illness on Patients' Families," *Journal of the American Medical Association* 272 no. 23 (21 December 1994): 1840.

Legal-Political

A Legislative Overview

Many hope that the U.S. Constitution will ultimately determine whether or not individuals in the United States have a right to die. Constitutional rights provide greater legal protection than do rights based in case law, so those in favor of euthanasia work toward this protection and those in opposition struggle to ensure that euthanasia does not become a constitutional choice. The following excerpts from the Constitution are provided to help clarify the legal arguments made in right-to-die cases.

The Constitution of the United States
Preamble

We the people of the United States, in order to form a more perfect Union, establish Justice, insure domestic Tranquillity, provide for the common defense, promote the general Welfare, and secure the Blessings of Liberty to ourselves and our Posterity, do ordain and establish this CONSTITUTION for the United States of America.

A Bill of Rights of the United States of America Effective December 15, 1791

Article IV
Security from Unwarranted Search and Seizure

The right of the people to be secure in their persons, houses, papers, and effects, against unreasonable searches and seizures, shall not be violated, and no Warrants shall issue, but upon probable cause, supported by Oath or affirmation, and particularly describing the place to be searched, and the persons or things to be seized.

Article V
Life, Liberty and Property

No person shall be held to answer for a capital, or otherwise infamous crime, unless on a presentment or indictment of a Grand Jury, except in cases arising in the land or naval forces, or in the Militia, when in actual service in time of War or public danger; nor shall any person be subject for the same offense to be twice put in jeopardy of life or limb; nor shall be compelled in any criminal case to be a witness against himself, nor be deprived of life, liberty, or property, without due process of law; nor shall private property be taken for public use, without just compensation.

Article XIV
Citizenship, Congressional Apportionment, Insurrection, Public Debt

Section 1. All persons born or naturalized in the United States, and subject to the jurisdiction thereof, are citizens of the United States and of the State wherein they reside. No state shall make or enforce any law which shall abridge the privileges or immunities of citizens of the United States; nor shall any State deprive any person of life, liberty or property, without due process of law; nor deny any person within its jurisdiction the equal protection of the laws.

Source: *United States Constitution*, 1791.

The Kansas state legislature was the first to legally define brain death by passing House Bill 1961 on 17 March 1970. The work of both the Ad Hoc Committee to Examine the Definition of Brain Death formed by Harvard scholars in 1968 and the World Medical Assembly, which took place that same year in Sydney, Australia, formed the foundation of this landmark legislation.

Kansas House Bill No. 1961 (1970)

AN ACT relating to and defining death.

Be it enacted by the Legislature of the State of Kansas:
Section 1. *Definition of death.* A person will be considered medically and legally dead if, in the opinion of a physician, based on ordinary

standards of medical practice, there is the absence of spontaneous respiratory and cardiac function and, because of the disease or condition which caused, directly or indirectly, these functions to cease, or because of the passage of time since these functions ceased, attempts at resuscitation are considered hopeless; and, in this event, death will have occurred at the time these functions ceased; or

A person will be considered medically and legally dead if, in the opinion of a physician, based on ordinary standards of medical practice, there is the absence of spontaneous brain function; and if based on ordinary standards of medical practice, during reasonable attempts to either maintain or restore spontaneous circulatory or respiratory in the absence of the aforesaid brain function, it appears further attempts at resuscitation or supportive maintenance will not succeed, death will have occurred at the time when these conditions first coincide. Death is to be pronounced before artificial means of supporting respiratory and circulatory function are terminated and before any vital organ is removed for purposes of transplantation.

These alternative definitions of death are to be utilized for all purposes in this state, including the trials of civil and criminal cases, any laws to the contrary notwithstanding.

Section 2. This act shall take effect and be in force from and after its publication in the statute book.

Approved March 17, 1970.

Source: 1970 KAN.SESS.LAWS 378; KAN.STAT.ANN. SS 77-202 (1971).

The first living will was developed in 1967 by Luis Kutner, a Chicago attorney, along with the Euthanasia Society. The first attempt to pass living-will legislation occurred in 1968 in Florida, when Dr. Walter Sackett introduced a bill. Fifteen other states introduced bills before the Natural Death Act was passed in California in September 1976. This statute made living wills binding for the first time and specifically allowed patients to refuse treatment. The culmination of nearly 20 years of work by lawmakers around the country, it was only applicable in California. Seven more states (Arkansas, Idaho, Nevada, New Mexico, North Carolina, Oregon, and Texas) passed laws similar to the California Natural Death Act the following year. The full text of this landmark legislation follows.

Natural Death Act, 1976
Guidelines for Signers:

The DIRECTIVE allows you to instruct your doctor not to use artificial methods to extend the natural process of dying.

Before signing the DIRECTIVE, you may ask advice from anyone you wish, but you do not have to see a lawyer or have the DIRECTIVE signed by a notary public.

If you sign the DIRECTIVE, talk it over with your doctor and ask that it be made a part of your medical record.

The DIRECTIVE must be WITNESSED by two adults who 1) are not related to you by blood or marriage, 2) are not mentioned in your will, and 3) would have no claim on your estate.

The DIRECTIVE may NOT be witnessed by your doctor or anyone working for your doctor. If you are in a HOSPITAL at the time you sign the DIRECTIVE, none of its employees may be a witness. If you are in a SKILLED NURSING FACILITY, one of your two witnesses MUST be a "patient advocate" or "ombudsman" designated by the State Department of Aging.

You may sign a DIRECTIVE TO PHYSICIANS if you are at least 18 years old and of sound mind, acting of your own free will in the presence of two qualified witnesses.

No one may force you to sign the DIRECTIVE. No one may deny you insurance or health care services because you have chosen *not* to sign it. If you *do* sign the DIRECTIVE, it will not affect your insurance or any other rights you may have to accept or reject medical treatment.

Your doctor is bound by the DIRECTIVE only 1) if he/she is satisfied that your DIRECTIVE is valid, 2) if another doctor has certified your condition as terminal, and 3) at least 14 days have gone by since you were informed of your condition. (California only.)

If you sign a DIRECTIVE while in good health, your doctor may respect your wishes but is not bound by the DIRECTIVE.

The DIRECTIVE is valid for a period of five years, at which time you may sign a new one.

The DIRECTIVE is not valid during pregnancy.

Revocation

You may revoke the DIRECTIVE *at any time*, even in the final stages of a terminal illness, by 1) destroying it, 2) signing and dating a written statement, or 3) by informing your doctor. No matter how you revoke the DIRECTIVE, be sure your doctor is told of your decision.

Source: CA. Stats. 1976, c. 1439.ss.1

The Patient Self-Determination Act (PSDA), introduced by Sen. John Danforth (R-Missouri), was a critical first step toward clarifying the responsibilities of the physician, the patient/family, and health care facilities. At the time the law was passed, only Nebraska and Pennsylvania lacked living-will legislation. The passage of the PSDA made this a moot point, as it superseded all state-level legislation of this nature. The PSDA went into effect on 1 December 1991, creating the first advance directives. Only the salient portions of this lengthy document are included; asterisks (* * *) indicate locations where text has been omitted.

United States Congress
Patient Self-Determination Act Title IV in the Omnibus Budget Reconciliation Act of 1990
Signed by President George Bush, November 5, 1990

SEC. 420c. MEDICARE PROVIDER AGREEMENTS ASSURING THE IMPLEMENTATION OF A PATIENT'S RIGHT TO PARTICIPATE IN AND DIRECT HEALTH CARE DECISIONS AFFECTING THE PATIENT.

* * *

(Q) in the case of hospitals, skilled nursing facilities, home health agencies, and hospice programs, to comply with the requirement of subsection (f) (relating to maintaining written policies and procedures respecting advance directives); and

(2)   by inserting after subsection (e) the following new subsection:
"(f)(1) For purposes of subsection (a)(1)(Q) and sections 1819(c)(2)(E), 1833(r), 1876(c)(8), and 1891 (a)(6), the requirement of this subsection is that a provider of services or prepaid or eligible organization (as the case may be) maintain written policies and procedures with respect to all adult individuals receiving medical care by or through the provider or organization—

"(A)   to provide written information to each individual concerning

"(i)   an individual's rights under State law (whether statutory or as recognized by the courts of the State) to make decisions concerning such medical care, including the right to accept or refuse medical or surgical treatment and the right to formulate advance directives (as defined in paragraph (3)), and

"(ii)   the written policies of the provider or organization respecting the implementation of such rights;

"(B)   to document in the individual's medical record whether or not the individual has executed an advance directive;

"(C)   not to condition the provision of care or otherwise discriminate against an individual based on whether or not the individual has executed an advance directive;

"(D)   to ensure compliance with requirements of State law (whether statutory or as recognized by the courts of the State) respecting advance directives at facilities of the provider or organization; and

"(E) to provide (individually or with others) for education for staff and the community on issues concerning advance directives.

Subparagraph (C) shall not be construed as requiring the provision of care which conflicts with an advance directive.

"(2) The written information described in paragraph (1)(A) shall be provided to an adult individual—

"(A) in the case of a hospital, at the time of the individual's admission as an inpatient,

"(B) in the case of a skilled nursing facility, at the time of the individual's admission as a resident,

"(C) in the case of a home health agency, in advance of the individual coming under the care of the agency,

"(D) in the case of a hospice program, at the time of initial receipt of hospice care by the individual from the program, and

"(E) in the case of an eligible organization (as defined in section 1876(b)) or an organization provided payments under section 1833(a)(1)(A), at the time of enrollment of the individual with the organization.

"(3) In this subsection, the term 'advance directive' means a written instruction, such as a living will or durable power of attorney for health care, recognized under State law (whether statutory or as recognized by the courts of the State) and relating to the provision of such care when the individual is incapacitated."

* * *

(c) EFFECT ON STATE LAW.—Nothing in subsections (a) and (b) shall be construed to prohibit the application of a State law which allows for an objection on the basis of conscience for any health care provider or any agent of such provider which, as a matter of conscience, cannot implement an advance directive.

* * *

"(57) provide that each hospital, nursing facility, provider of home health care or personal care services, hospice program, or health maintenance organization (as defined in section 1903(m)(1)(A)) receiving funds under the plan shall comply with the requirements of subsection (w);

* * *

(2) by adding at the end the following new subsection:

"(u)(1) For purposes of subsection (a)(57) and sections 1903(m)(1)(A) and 1919(c)(2)(E), the requirement of this subsection is that a provider or organization (as the case may be) maintain written policies and procedures with respect to all adult individuals receiving medical care or through the provider organization—

"(A) to provide written information to each such individual concerning—

"(i) an individual's rights under State law (whether statutory or as recognized by the courts of the State) to make decisions concerning such medical care, including the right to accept or refuse medical or surgical treatment and the right to formulate advance directives (as defined in paragraph (3)), and

"(ii) the provider's or organization's written policies respecting the implementation of such rights;

"(B) to document in the individual's medical record whether or not the individual has executed an advance directive;

"(C) not to condition the provision of care or otherwise discriminate against an individual based on whether or not the individual has executed an advance directive;

"(D) to ensure compliance with requirements of State law (whether statutory or as recognized by the courts of the State) respecting advance directives; and

"(E) to provide (individually or with others) for education for staff and the community on issues concerning advance directives.

Subparagraph (C) shall not be construed as requiring the provision of care which conflicts with an advance directive.

"(2) The written information described in paragraph (1)(A) shall be provided to an adult individual—

"(A) in the case of a hospital, at the time of the individual's admission as an inpatient,

"(B) in the case of a nursing facility, at the time of the individual's admission as a resident,

"(C) in the case of a provider of home health care or personal care services, in advance of the individual coming under the care of the provider,

"(D) in the case of a hospice program, at the time of initial receipt of hospice care by the individual from the program, and

"(E) in the case of a health maintenance organization, at the time of enrollment of the individual with the organization.

"(3) Nothing in this section shall be construed to prohibit the application of a State law which allows for an objection on the basis of conscience for any health care provider or any agent of such provider which as a matter of conscience cannot implement an advance directive.

"(4) In this subsection, the term 'advance directive' means a written instruction, such as a living will or durable power of attorney for health care, recognized under State law (whether statutory or as recognized by the courts of the State) and relating to the provision of such care when the individual is incapacitated."

* * *

(d) PUBLIC EDUCATION CAMPAIGN.—

(1) IN GENERAL.—The Secretary, no later than 6 months after the date of enactment of this section, shall develop and implement a national campaign to inform the public of the option to execute advance directives and of a patient's right to participate and direct health care decisions.

(2) DEVELOPMENT AND DISTRIBUTION OF INFORMATION.—The Secretary shall develop or approve nationwide informational materials that would be distributed by providers under the requirements of this section, to inform the public and the medical and legal profession of each person's right to make decisions concerning medical care, including the right to accept or refuse medical or surgical treatment, and the existence of advance directives.

(3) PROVIDING ASSISTANCE TO STATES.—The Secretary shall assist appropriate State agencies, associations, or other private entities in developing the State-specific documents that would be distributed by providers under the requirements of this section. The Secretary shall further assist appropriate State agencies, associations, or other probate entities in ensuring that providers are provided a copy of the documents that are to be distributed under the requirements of the section.

(4) DUTIES OF SECRETARY.—The Secretary shall mail information to Social Security recipients, add a page to the Medicare handbook with respect to the provisions of this section.

Source: 104 STAT. 1388-15, 42 USC.

Living Wills and Powers of Attorney

The following advance directives were promulgated by the Patient Self-Determination Act. Living wills allow individuals to express their end-of-life wishes while competent, and durable powers of attorney for health care are the vehicle by which individuals can assign these decisions to a specific person in the event of a tragedy or incompetency. Each state has versions that reflect its specific provisions. The directives used in the state of Colorado follow. State-specific documents may be obtained through Choice in Dying, 200 Varick Street, New York, NY 10014-4810, (800) 989-WILL.

Sample Living Will

I, _____, being of sound mind and at least eighteen years of age, direct that my life shall not be artificially prolonged under the circumstances set forth below and hereby declare that:

1. If at any time my attending physician and one other physician certify in writing that:
   a. I have an injury, disease, or illness which was not curable or reversible and which, in their judgment, is a terminal condition, and
   b. For a period of seven (7) days (or the amount of time specified by me), I have been unconscious, comatose, or otherwise incompetent so as to be unable to make or communicate responsible decisions concerning my person, then

I direct that, IN ACCORDANCE WITH COLORADO LAW, life-sustaining procedures shall be withdrawn and witheld PURSUANT TO THE TERMS OF THIS DECLARATION, it being understood that life-sustaining procedures shall not include any medical procedure or intervention for nourishment considered necessary by the attending physician to provide comfort or alleviate pain. However, I may specifically direct, in accordance with Colorado law, that artificial nourishment be withdrawn or withheld pursuant to the terms of the Declaration.

2. IN THE EVENT THAT THE ONLY PROCEDURE I AM BEING PROVIDED IS ARTIFICIAL NOURISHMENT, I DIRECT THAT ONE OF THE FOLLOWING ACTIONS BE TAKEN:
   ___ a. ARTIFICIAL NOURISHMENT SHALL NOT BE CONTINUED WHEN IT IS THE ONLY PROCEDURE BEING PROVIDED; OR
   ___ b. ARTIFICIAL NOURISHMENT SHALL BE CONTINUED FOR __ DAYS WHEN IT IS THE ONLY PROCEDURE BEING PROVIDED; OR
   ___ c. ARTIFICIAL NOURISHMENT SHALL BE CONTINUED WHEN IT IS THE ONLY PROCEDURE BEING PROVIDED.

3. I EXECUTE THIS DECLARATION AS MY FREE AND VOLUNTARY ACT THIS _____ day of _____ 19____.

By_____
The foregoing instrument was signed and declared by _____ to be his/her declaration, in the presence of us, who, in his/her presence of each other, and at his/her request, have signed our names below as witnesses, and we declare that, at the time of execution of this instrument, the declarant, according to our best knowledge and belief, was of sound mind and under no constraint or undue influence.

Dated at _____, Colorado, this day of _____, 19____.

Name and Address   Name and Address

_____   _____

_____   _____

_____   _____

Sample Durable Power of Attorney for Health Care

THIS IS AN IMPORTANT LEGAL DOCUMENT, A POWER OF ATTORNEY FOR MEDICAL DECISIONS IN THE EVENT YOU BECOME LEGALLY INCAPACITATED. DO NOT SIGN THIS DOCUMENT UNLESS YOU UNDERSTAND IT COMPLETELY. IF THERE IS ANYTHING IN THIS DOCUMENT WHICH YOU DO NOT UNDERSTAND, YOU SHOULD ASK AN ATTORNEY OR OTHER QUALIFIED PERSON TO EXPLAIN IT TO YOU.

I, _____, who live at _____, now nominate, constitute and appoint _____, who lives at _____, as my true and lawful attorney-in-fact to act for me, in my name, in my place and as my substitute.

(*Optional:* If _____ is unable for any reason to act as my attorney-in-fact, I nominate

_____ who lives at

_____ to substitute as my attorney-in-fact and who will have all the same power and authority contained herein.)

1. Power Arises upon Incapacitation. This power of attorney will become effective only if I become impaired such that I do not have a sufficient understanding or capacity to make or communicate responsible medical decisions concerning myself, whether the impairment is due to mental illness, mental deficiency, physical illness, advanced age, chronic use of drugs, chronic intoxication or other cause.

2. Duration of Power. I understand that this power of attorney will exist indefinitely from the date I sign it unless I expressly revoke it or indicate below a specific day on which it ends. If I indicate a specific day on which this power of attorney ends and if I am incapacitated on that day, the authority I have granted to my attorney-in-fact will continue to exist until the time when I am no longer incapacitated.

This power of attorney shall:

A. _____ Continue indefinitely until I expressly revoke it, or

B. _____ End on the following date:
(Initial either A or B and, if B, write in the date.)

3. Cancellation of Power. This power of attorney may be cancelled by me, verbally or in writing, at any time, by notifying my attorney-in-fact, my physician or any hospital employee caring for me.

4. Cancellation of Prior Powers. By signing this document, I now expressly cancel any prior power of attorney for medical decisions which I may have signed. However, this document does not affect any other powers previously given by me through a general or limited power of attorney, and those powers are to continue in full force and effect until cancelled by me or terminated by their own terms.

5. *Powers.* In the event that I am incapacitated, I now give to my attorney-in-fact the full power and authority to make medical decisions for me, including consent, refusal of consent, or withdrawal of consent to any care, treatment, service or procedure to maintain, diagnose or treat a physical or mental condition.

I expressly confer upon my attorney-in-fact the power to make decisions and to consent on my behalf to the performance of major surgical procedures.

In the event that my medical condition becomes so irreversible and terminal that my death is imminent, I expressly confer upon my attorney-in-fact the power to make decisions and to consent on my behalf to the withholding, withdrawal or discontinuation of any life-sustaining procedures or any mechanically induced nourishment, but not medications to provide comfort or alleviate pain.

My attorney-in-fact shall have the right to exercise any of these specified powers without the necessity of seeking prior court approval or authorization.

6. *Other Provisions.*

_____

_____

_____

(Specify any other conditions or limitations which you want to place on the powers granted to your attorney-in-fact.)

7. *Specimen Signature.* The following is a sample of the signature of my attorney-in-fact for medical decisions:

_____   _____
(Signature of attorney-in-fact)   (Signature of substitute if chosen)

This document was signed by me on the _____ day of _____, 19____.

_____
(Signature of patient)

STATE OF COLORADO   ]
                           ] ss.
COUNTY OF   ]

This document was acknowledged before me this _____ day of _____, 19____. (SEAL)

_____

Notary Public

Address: _____

My commission expires: _____

The first serious attempt to enact legislation that would legalize physician aid-in-dying took place in Washington State in 1991, three years after a preliminary attempt in California proved that there was substantial interest in pursuing this type of legislation in the United States. Signatures were collected throughout 1990 and 1991 to place the initiative on the ballot, and almost twice as many signatures as needed were amassed. Developed by Rev. Ralph Mero, a Unitarian minister and director of the Northwest Region chapter of the Hemlock Society, Initiative #119 was the first to take end-of-life decision making beyond passive measures into the realm of physician aid-in-dying. It defined a persistent vegetative state as a terminal illness, and nutrition and hydration as artificial life supports. Although this initiative was defeated (811,104–701,818), the nine safeguards for terminally ill patients that were written into the initiative have formed the basis for other legislative efforts. These are listed below.

Washington State Initiative for Death with Dignity #119
Safeguards

1. The aid-in-dying provisions of #119 are totally voluntary for patients, physicians, and hospitals.
2. Only conscious, mentally competent, terminally ill patients with less than six months to live may voluntarily request aid-in-dying.
3. No one can request aid-in-dying for anyone else.
4. Two impartial people must witness the written request of the terminal patient for aid-in-dying. They cannot be family members, heirs, or employees of the physician or health care facility.
5. A terminally ill patient may revoke his or her request at any time.
6. Two doctors must indicate in writing that the terminally ill patient has less than six months to live. One of the physicians must be the patient's primary doctor.
7. Physicians may require a psychological evaluation to ensure that the patient is mentally competent, not depressed, and that the request is voluntary.
8. Aid-in-dying may only be requested at the time it is to be provided, not in advance.
9. Terminally ill patients and their physicians may seek advice from any family members or clergy they choose.

Source: Cox, Donald. *Hemlock's Cup* (Buffalo, NY: Prometheus Books, 1993), 151.

When living-will bills were first proposed in the 1970s and 1980s, it was standard procedure to keep a patient alive for as long as possible.

This often involved CPR, artificial hydration and nutrition, and artificial ventilation. The concept of overtreatment was not argued at the bedside. Since that time, the courts have rendered many of these life-saving procedures optional. By the 1990s this shift had prompted a response from the pro-life community. The following document represents an effort by the National Right to Life Committee (NRLC) to prevent what they see as a slide down the "slippery slope" toward involuntary euthanasia, and to protect life at all cost. Like the living wills available through Choice in Dying, state-specific wills to live have been prepared by the NRLC for every state in the union. The Washington State version that follows is representative.

Washington State Durable Power of Attorney—Will To Live Form

I, (your name), domiciled and living in the state of Washington, hereby designate (name of attorney-in-fact) living at (address and telephone number) as my attorney-in-fact. If the attorney-in-fact appointed above is unable to serve, then I appoint (successor attorney-in-fact) living at (address and telephone number) to serve as successor attorney-in-fact in place of the person who is unable to serve. If neither is able to serve, then I appoint (successor attorney-in-fact) living at (address and telephone number) to serve as successor attorney-in-fact in place of the persons who are unable to serve.

In the event I become disabled or incompetent, my attorney-in-fact shall have all powers as are necessary to provide for my health and to consent to health care as provided in the Revised Code of Washington Annotated section 7.70.065(b) in accordance with the following instructions.

General Presumption for Life

I direct my health care provider(s) and attorney-in-fact to make health care decisions consistent with my general desire for the use of medical treatment that would preserve my life, as well as for the use of medical treatment that can cure, improve, or reduce, or prevent deterioration in, any physical or mental condition.

Food and water are not medical treatment, but basic necessities. I direct my health care provider(s) and attorney-in-fact to provide me with food and fluids orally, intravenously, by tube, or by other means to the full extent necessary both to preserve my life and to assure me the optimal health possible.

I direct that medication to alleviate my pain be provided, as long as the medication is not used in order to cause my death.

I direct that the following be provided:

- the administration of medication;
- cardiopulmonary resuscitation (CPR); and

- the performance of all other medical procedures, techniques, and technologies, including surgery, all to the full extent necessary to correct, reverse, or alleviate life-threatening or health-impairing conditions, or complications arising from those conditions.

I also direct that I be provided basic nursing care and procedures to provide comfort care.

I reject, however, any treatments that use an unborn or newborn child, or any tissue or organ of an unborn or newborn child, who has been subject to an induced abortion. This rejection does not apply to the use of tissues or organs obtained in the course of the removal of an ectopic pregnancy.

I also reject any treatments that use an organ or tissue of another person obtained in a manner that causes, contributes to, or hastens that person's death.

The instructions in this document are intended to be followed even if suicide is alleged to be attempted at some point after it is signed.

I request and direct that medical treatment and care be provided to me to preserve my life without discrimination based on my age or physical or mental disability or the "quality" of my life. I reject any action or omission that is intended to cause or hasten my death.

I direct my health care provider(s) and attorney-in-fact to follow the above policy, even if I am judged to be incompetent.

During the time I am incompetent, my attorney-in-fact, as named above, is authorized to make medical decisions on my behalf, consistent with the above policy, after consultation with my health care provider(s), utilizing the most current diagnoses and/or prognosis of my medical condition, in the following situations with the written special conditions.

When My Death Is Imminent

A. **If I have an incurable terminal illness or injury**, and I will die imminently—meaning that a reasonably prudent physician, knowledgeable about the case and the treatment possibilities with respect to the medical conditions involved, would judge that I will live only a week or less even if lifesaving treatment or care is provided to me—the following may be withheld or withdrawn:

(Be as specific as possible: See Suggestions.):

(Cross off any remaining blank lines.)

When I Am Terminally Ill

B. **Final Stage of Terminal Condition.** If I have an incurable terminal illness or injury and even though death is not imminent I am in the final stage of that terminal condition—meaning that a reasonably prudent physician, knowledgeable about the case and the treatment possibilities with respect to the medical conditions involved, would judge that I will live only three months or less, even if lifesaving treatment or care is provided to me—the following may be withheld or withdrawn:

(Be as specific as possible: See Suggestions.):

(Cross off any remaining blank lines.)

C. **Other Special Conditions:** (Be as specific as possible: See Suggestions.):

(Cross off any remaining blank lines.)

If I Am Pregnant

D. **Special Instructions for Pregnancy.** If I am pregnant, I direct my health care provider(s) and attorney(s)-in-fact to use all lifesaving procedures for myself with none of the above special conditions applying if there is a chance that prolonging my life might allow my child to be born alive. I also direct that lifesaving procedures be used even if I am legally determined to be brain dead if there is a chance that doing so might allow my child to be born alive. Except as I specify by writing my signature in the box below, no one is authorized to consent to any procedure for me that would result in the death of my unborn child.

If I am pregnant, and I am not in the final stage of a terminal condition as defined above, medical procedures required to prevent my death are authorized even if they may result in the death of my unborn child provided every possible effort is made to preserve both my life and the life of my unborn child.

_____

(Signature of Principal)

This power of attorney shall become effective in the event I become disabled or incompetent. This power of attorney may be revoked in writing by my giving written notice to the attorney-in-fact, or if applicable, to the successor attorney-in-fact.

DATED , 19____

_____

(your signature)

STATE OF WASHINGTON

COUNTY OF

I certify that I know or have satisfactory evidence that (name) signed this instrument and acknowledged it to be his or her free and voluntary act for the use and purposes mentioned in the instrument.

Dated: _____ (Notary Public)

My Appointment Expires: _____

How To Use the Washington form—
Suggestions and Requirements:

1. This document allows you to name an attorney-in-fact for health care who will make health care decisions for you whenever you are unable to make them for yourself. It also allows you to give instructions concerning medical treatment decisions that the attorney-in-fact must follow. You must sign and date this document before a Notary Public.
2. None of the following persons may act as your attorney-in-fact: any of your doctors, your doctors' employees, or the owners, administrators, or employees of the health care facility in which you reside or receive care. However, you may name as your attorney-in-fact any person listed above if that person is your spouse, or your adult child, or your brother or sister.
3. It is helpful to appoint a successor(s) attorney-in-fact, in the event that your first attorney-in-fact is unable to serve. There is a space on the form for you to name two successors to the attorney-in-fact.
4. You should tell your doctor about this document and ask him or her to keep a copy of it in your medical file.
5. Your attorney-in-fact's authority takes effect only when you no longer have the capacity to make health care decisions.
6. This type of document has been authorized by Washington State law.
7. No fee may be charged for the preparation of this document.
8. If you have questions about this document, or want assistance in filling it out, please consult an attorney.

Suggestions for Preparing Will To Live/Durable
Power of Attorney

(Please read the document itself before reading this. It will help you better understand the suggestions.)

You are not required to fill out any part of this "Will To Live" or any other document such as a Living Will or durable power of attorney for health care. No one may force you to sign this document or any other of its kind.

The Will To Live form starts from the principle that the presumption should be for life. If you sign it without writing any "SPECIAL CONDITIONS," you are giving directions to your health care provider(s) and attorney-in-fact to do their best to preserve your life.

Some people may wish to continue certain types of medical treatment when they are terminally ill and in the final stages of life. Others may not.

If you wish to refuse some specific medical treatment, the Will To Live form provides space to do so ("SPECIAL CONDITIONS"). You may make special conditions for your treatment when your death is imminent, meaning you will live no more than a week even if given all available medical treatment; or when you are incurably terminally ill, meaning you will live no more than three months even if given all available medical treatment. There is also space for you to write down special conditions for circumstances you describe yourself.

The important thing for you to remember if you choose to fill out any part of the "SPECIAL CONDITIONS" sections of the Will To Live is that you must be very specific in listing what treatments you do not want. Some examples of how to be specific will be given shortly, or you may ask your physician what types of treatment might be expected in your specific case.

Why is it important to be specific? Because, given the pro-euthanasia views widespread in society and particularly among many (not all) health care providers, there is great danger that a vague description of what you do not want will be misunderstood or distorted so as to deny you treatment that you do want.

Many in the medical profession as well as in the courts are now so committed to the quality of life ethic that they take as a given that patients with severe disabilities are better off dead and would prefer not to receive either life-saving measures or nutrition and hydration. So pervasive is this "consensus" that it is accurate to say that in practice it is no longer true that the "presumption is for life" but rather for death. In other words, instead of assuming that a now incompetent patient would want to receive treatment and care in the absence of clear evidence to the contrary, the assumption has virtually become that since any "reasonable" person would want to exercise a "right to die," treatment and care should be withheld or withdrawn unless there is evidence to the contrary. The Will To Live is intended to maximize the chance of providing that evidence.

It is important to remember that you are writing a legal document, not holding a conversation, and not writing a moral textbook. The language you or a religious or moral leader might use in discussing what is and is not moral to refuse is, from a legal standpoint, often much too vague. Therefore, it is subject to misunderstanding or deliberate abuse.

The person you appoint as your attorney-in-fact may understand general terms in the same way you do. But remember that the person you appoint may die, or become incapacitated, or simply be unavailable when decisions must be made about your health care. If any of these happens, a court might appoint someone else you don't know in that person's place. Also remember that since the attorney-in-fact has to follow the instructions you write in this form, a health care provider could try to persuade a court that the attorney-in-fact isn't really following your wishes. A court could overrule your attorney-in-fact's insistence on treatment in cases in which the court interprets any vague language you put in your "Will To Live" less protectively than you meant it.

So, for example, do not simply say you don't want "extraordinary treatment." Whatever the value of that language in moral discussions, there is so much debate over what it means legally that it could be interpreted very broadly by a doctor or a court. For instance, it might be interpreted to require starving you to death when you have a disability, even if you are in no danger of death if you are fed.

For the same reason, do not use language rejecting treatment which has a phrase like "excessive pain, expense or other excessive burden." Doctors and courts may have a very different definition of what is "excessive" or a "burden" than you do. Do not use language that rejects treatment that "does not offer a reasonable hope of benefit." "Benefit" is a legally vague term. If you had a significant disability, a health care provider or court might think you would want no medical treatment at all, since many doctors and judges unfortunately believe there is no "benefit" to life with a severe disability.

What sort of language is specific enough if you wish to write exclusions? Here are some examples of things you might—or might not—want to list under one or more of the "Special Conditions" described on the form. Remember that any of these will prevent treatment ONLY under the circumstances—such as when death is imminent—described in the "Special Condition" you list it under. (The examples are not meant to be all inclusive—just samples of the type of thing you might want to write.)

"Cardiopulmonary resuscitation (CPR)." (If you would like CPR in some but not all circumstances when you are terminally ill, you should try to be still more specific: for example, you might write "CPR if cardiopulmonary arrest has been caused by my terminal illness or a complication of it." This would mean that you would still get CPR if, for example, you were the victim of smoke inhalation in a fire.) "Organ transplants." (Again, you could be still more specific, rejecting, for example, just a "heart transplant.")

"Surgery that would not cure me, would not improve either my mental or my physical condition, would not make me more comfortable, and would not help me to have less pain, but would only keep me alive longer."

"A treatment that will itself cause me severe, intractable, and long-lasting pain but will not cure me."

Pain Relief. Under the "General Presumption for Life" of your Will To Live, you will be given medication necessary to control any pain you may have "as long as the medication is not used in order to cause my death." This means that you may be given pain medication that has the secondary, but unintended, effect of shortening your life. If this is not your wish, you may want to write something like one of the following under the third set of "Special Conditions" (the section for conditions you describe yourself):

"I would like medication to relieve my pain but only to the extent the medication would not seriously threaten to shorten my life."

OR

"I would like medication to relieve my pain but only to the extent
it is known, to a reasonable medical certainty, that it will not shorten
my life."

**Think carefully about any special conditions you decide to write
in your "Will To Live."** You may want to show them to your intended
attorney-in-fact and a couple of other people to see if they find them
clear and if they mean the same thing to them as they mean to you.
**Remember that how carefully you write may literally be a matter of
life or death—your own.**

AFTER WRITING DOWN YOUR SPECIAL CONDITIONS, IF
ANY, YOU SHOULD MARK OUT THE REST OF THE BLANK LINES
left on the form for them (just as you do after writing out the amount
on a check) to prevent any danger that somebody other than you could
write in something else.

It is wise to review your Will To Live periodically to ensure that it
still gives the directions you want followed.

Source: National Right to Life Committee, "Will To Live," Washington,
D. C. April, 1992. To request a state-specific "Will To Live," see p. 265.

*The movement toward legally sanctioned physician-assisted sui-
cide has continued to gain strength in the United States. Every year,
several states attempt to write legislation. As a result of all this activity, the New York-based organization Choice in Dying released a position statement on physician-assisted suicide in 1994.*

Choice in Dying's Position Statement on Physician-Assisted Suicide

Recognizing the need of those desperately ill individuals who
suffer intractable pain and anguish and seek the right to have the aid of
their physicians in dying, Choice in Dying is committed to stimulating
informed public discussion of physician-assisted suicide.

Choice in Dying recognizes that the request for physician-assisted
suicide is a complex and grave issue for society and that the debate
about physician-assisted suicide is in a formative phase. Choice in
Dying therefore supports programs to increase public understanding of
physician-assisted suicide and to develop compassionate public policy
in this area.

Choice in Dying devotes itself to ensuring that dying persons are
treated with dignity and respect, advocating for individuals' rights to
participate fully in decisions about their medical treatment at the end of
life, and securing dying persons' rights to receive adequate pain medication and other appropriate palliative treatment.

Source: *Choices* 4, no. 2 (Summer 1995): 5.

In November 1994 the landmark Oregon Death with Dignity Act was passed by voters 52 to 48 percent. It is the world's first assisted-suicide law. This important document is reproduced in its entirety below.

The Oregon Death with Dignity Act

Section I
General Provisions
1.01 Definitions

The following words and phrases, whenever used in this Act, shall have the following meanings:

(1) "Adult" means an individual who is 18 years of age or older.

(2) "Attending physician" means the physician who has primary responsibility for the care of the patient and treatment of the patient's disease.

(3) "Consulting physician" means the physician who is qualified by specialty or experience to make a professional diagnosis and prognosis regarding the patient's disease.

(4) "Counseling" means a consultation between a state licensed psychiatrist or psychologist and a patient for the purpose of determining whether the patient is suffering from a psychiatric or psychological disorder, or depression causing impaired judgment.

(5) "Health care provider" means a person licensed, certified, or otherwise authorized or permitted by the law of this State to administer health care in the ordinary course of business or practice of a profession, and includes a health care facility.

(6) "Incapable" means that in the opinion of a court or in the opinion of the patient's attending physician or consulting physician, a patient lacks the ability to make and communicate health care decisions to health care providers, including communication through persons familiar with the patient's manner of communicating if those persons are available. "Capable" means not incapable.

(7) "Informed decision" means a decision by a qualified patient, to request and obtain a prescription to end his or her life in a humane and dignified manner, that is based on an appreciation of the relevant facts and after being fully informed by the attending physician of:

(a) his or her medical diagnosis;

(b) his or her prognosis;

(c) the potential risks associated with taking the medication to be prescribed;

(d) the probable result of taking the medication to be prescribed;

(e) the feasible alternatives, including, but not limited to, comfort care, hospice care and pain control.

(8) "Medically confirmed" means the medical opinion of the attending physician has been confirmed by a consulting physician who has examined the patient and the patient's relevant medical records.

(9) "Patient" means a person who is under the care of a physician.

(10) "Physician" means a doctor of medicine or osteopathy licensed to practice medicine by the Board of Medical Examiners for the State of Oregon.

(11) "Qualified patient" means a capable adult who is a resident of Oregon and has satisfied the requirements of this Act in order to obtain a prescription for medication to end his or her life in a humane and dignified manner.

(12) "Terminal disease" means an incurable and irreversible disease that has been medically confirmed and will, within reasonable medical judgment, produce death within six (6) months.

Section 2
Written Request for Medication to End One's Life in a Humane and Dignified Manner

2.01 Who may initiate a written request for medication

An adult who is capable, is a resident of Oregon, and has been determined by the attending physician and consulting physician to be suffering from a terminal disease, and who has voluntarily expressed his or her wish to die, may make a written request for medication for the purpose of ending his or her life in a humane and dignified manner in accordance with this Act.

2.02 Form of the written request

(1) A valid request for medication under this Act shall be in substantially the form described in Section 6 of this Act, signed and dated by the patient and witnessed by at least two individuals who, in the presence of the patient, attest that to the best of their knowledge and belief the patient is capable, acting voluntarily, and is not being coerced to sign the request. (2) One of the witnesses shall be a person who is not: (a) A relative of the patient by blood, marriage or adoption; (b) A person who at the time the request is signed would be entitled to any portion of the estate of the qualified patient upon death under any will or by operation of law; or (c) An owner, operator or employee of a health care facility where the qualified patient is receiving medical treatment or is a resident. (3) The patient's attending physician at the time the request is signed shall not be a witness. (4) If the patient is a patient in a long term care facility at the time the written request is made, one of the witnesses shall be an individual designated by the facility and having the qualifications specified by the Department of Human Resources by rule.

Section 3
Safeguards

3.01 Attending physician responsibilities

The attending physician shall: (1) Make the initial determination of whether a patient has a terminal disease, is capable, and has made the request voluntarily; (2) Inform the patient of; (a) his or her medical diagnosis; (b) his or her prognosis; (c) the potential risks associated with taking the medication to be prescribed; (d) the probable result of taking the medication to be prescribed; (e) the feasible alternatives, including, but not limited to, comfort care, hospice care and pain control. (3) Refer the patient to a consulting physician for medical confirmation of the diagnosis, and for determination that the patient is capable and acting voluntarily; (4) Refer the patient for counseling if appropriate pursuant to Section 3.03; (5) Request that the patient notify next of kin; (6) Inform the patient that he or she has an opportunity to rescind the request at any time and in any manner, and offer the patient an opportunity to rescind at the end of the 15 day waiting period pursuant to Section 3.06; (7) Verify, immediately prior to writing the prescription for medication under this Act, that the patient is making an informed decision; (8) Fulfill the medical record documentation requirements of Section 3.09; (9) Ensure that all appropriate steps are carried out in accordance with this Act prior to writing a prescription for medication to enable a qualified patient to end his or her life in a humane and dignified manner.

3.02 Consulting physician confirmation

Before a patient is qualified under this Act, a consulting physician shall examine the patient and his or her relevant medical records and confirm, in writing, the attending physician's diagnosis that the patient is suffering from a terminal disease, and verify that the patient is capable, is acting voluntarily and has made an informed decision.

3.03 Counseling referral

If in the opinion of the attending physician or the consulting physician a patient may be suffering from a psychiatric or psychological disorder, or depression causing impaired judgment, either physician shall refer the patient for counseling. No medication to end a patient's life in a humane and dignified manner shall be prescribed until the person performing the counseling determines that the person is not suffering from a psychiatric or psychological disorder, or depression causing impaired judgment.

3.04 Informed decision

No person shall receive a prescription for medication to end his or her life in a humane and dignified manner unless he or she has made an informed decision as defined in Section 1.01(7). Immediately prior to writing a prescription for medication under this Act, the attending physician shall verify that the patient is making an informed decision.

3.05 Family notification

The attending physician shall ask the patient to notify next of kin of his or her request for medication pursuant to this Act. A patient who declines or is unable to notify next of kin shall not have his or her request denied for that reason.

3.06 Written and oral requests

In order to receive a prescription for medication to end his or her life in a humane and dignified manner, a qualified patient shall have made an oral request and a written request, and reiterate the oral request to his or her attending physician no less than fifteen (15) days after making the initial oral request. At the time the qualified patient makes his or her second oral request, the attending physician shall offer the patient an opportunity to rescind the request.

3.07 Right to rescind request

A patient may rescind his or her request at any time and in any manner without regard to his or her mental state. No prescription for medication under this Act may be written without the attending physician offering the qualified patient an opportunity to rescind the request.

3.08 Waiting periods

No less than fifteen (15) days shall elapse between the patient's initial and oral request and the writing of a prescription under this Act. No less than 48 hours shall elapse between the patient's written request and the writing of a prescription under this Act.

3.09 Medical record documentation requirements

The following shall be documented or filed in the patient's medical record: (1) All oral requests by a patient for medication to end his or her life in a humane and dignified manner; (2) All written requests by a patient for medication to end his or her life in a humane and dignified manner; (3) The attending physician's diagnosis and prognosis, determination that the patient is capable, acting voluntarily and has made an informed decision; (4) The consulting physician's diagnosis and prognosis, and verification that the patient is capable, acting voluntarily and has made an informed decision; (5) A report of the outcome and determinations made during counseling; (6) The attending physician's offer to the patient to rescind his or her request at the time of the patient's second oral request pursuant to Section 3.06; and (7) A note by the attending physician indicating that all requirements under this Act have been met and indicating the steps taken to carry out the request, including a notation of the medication prescribed.

3.10 Residency requirements

Only requests made by Oregon residents, under this Act, shall be granted.

3.11 Reporting requirements

(1) The Health Division shall annually review a sample of records maintained pursuant to this Act. (2) The Health Division shall make rules to facilitate the collection of information regarding compliance with this Act. The information collected shall not be a public record and may not be made available for inspection by the public. (3) The Health Division shall generate and make available to the public an annual statistical report of information collected under Section 3.11(2) of this Act.

3.12 Effect on construction of wills, contracts and statutes

(1) No provision in a contract, will or other agreement, whether written or oral, to the extent the provision would affect whether a person may make or rescind a request for medication to end his or her life in a humane and dignified manner, shall be valid. (2) No obligation owing under any currently existing contract shall be conditioned or affected by the making or rescinding of a request, by a person, for medication to end his or her life in a humane and dignified manner.

3.13 Insurance or annuity policies

The sale, procurement, or issuance of any life, health, or accident insurance or annuity policy or the rate charged for any policy shall not be conditioned upon or affected by the making or rescinding of a request, by a person, for medication to end his or her life in a humane and dignified manner. Neither shall a qualified patient's act of ingesting medication to end his or her life in a humane and dignified manner have an effect upon a life, health, or accident insurance or annuity policy.

3.14 Construction of Act

Nothing in this Act shall be construed to authorize a physician or any other person to end a patient's life by lethal injection, mercy killing or active euthanasia. Actions taken in accordance with this Act shall not, for any purpose, constitute suicide, assisted suicide, mercy killing or homicide, under the law.

Section 4
Immunities and Liabilities

4.01 Immunities

Except as provided in Section 4.02:

(1) No person shall be subject to civil or criminal liability or professional disciplinary action for participating in good faith compliance with this Act. This includes being present when a qualified patient takes the prescribed medication to end his or her life in a humane and dignified manner.

(2) No professional organization or association, or health care provider, may subject a person to censure, discipline, suspension, loss of license, loss of privileges, loss of membership or other penalty for participating or refusing to participate in good faith compliance with this Act.

(3) No request by a patient for or provision by an attending physician of medication in good faith compliance with the provisions of this Act shall constitute neglect for any purpose of law or provide the sole basis for the appointment of a guardian or conservator.

(4) No health care provider shall be under any duty, whether by contract, by statute or by any other legal requirement to participate in the provision to a qualified patient of medication to end his or her life in a humane and dignified manner. If a health care provider is unable or unwilling to carry out a patient's wishes, that health care provider shall transfer, upon request, a copy of the patient's relevant medical records to the new health care provider.

4.02 Liabilities

(1) A person who without authorization of the patient willfully alters or forges a request for medication or conceals or destroys a rescission of that request with the intent or effect of causing the patient's death shall be guilty of a Class A felony.

(2) A person who coerces or exerts undue influence on a patient to request medication for the purpose of ending the patient's life, or to destroy a rescission of such a request, shall be guilty of a Class A felony.

(3) Nothing in this Act limits further liability for civil damages resulting from other negligent conduct or intentional misconduct by any persons.

(4) The penalties in this Act do not preclude criminal penalties applicable under other law for conduct which is inconsistent with the provisions of this Act.

Section 5
Severability

5.01 Severability

Any section of this Act being held invalid as to any person or circumstance shall not affect the application of any other section of this Act which can be given full effect without the invalid section or application.

Section 6
Form of the Request

6.01 Form of the request

A request for a medication as authorized by this Act shall be in substantially the following form:

REQUEST FOR MEDICATION TO END MY LIFE IN A HUMANE AND DIGNIFIED MANNER

I, (name), am an adult of sound mind.

I am suffering from (illness), which my attending physician has determined is a terminal disease and which has been medically formed by a consulting physician.

I have been fully informed of my diagnosis, prognosis, the nature of medication to be prescribed and potential associated risks, the expected result, and the feasible alternatives, including comfort care, hospice care and pain control.

I request that my attending physician prescribe medication that will end my life in a humane and dignified manner.

INITIAL ONE:

_____ I have informed my family of my decision and taken their opinions into consideration.

_____ I have decided not to inform my family of my decision.

_____ I have no family to inform of my decision.

_____ I understand that I have the right to rescind this request at any time.

_____ I understand the full import of this request and I expect to die when I take the medication to be prescribed.

_____ I make this request voluntarily and without reservation and I accept full moral responsibility for my actions.

DECLARATION OF WITNESSES

We declare that the person signing this request: (a) Is personally known to us or has provided proof of identity; (b) Signed this request in our presence; (c) Appears to be of sound mind and not under duress, fraud or undue influence; (d) Is not a patient for whom either of us is attending physician.

Witness 1/_____

Date_____

Witness 2/_____

Date_____

Note: One witness shall not be a relative (by blood, marriage or adoption) of the person signing this request, shall not be entitled to any portion of the person's estate upon death and shall not own, operate or be employed at a health care facility where the person is a patient or resident. If the patient is an inpatient at a health care facility, one of the witnesses shall be an individual designated by the facility.

Source: http://www.right~.org/-Deathnet/ergo_orlaw.html.

The outline of the Northern Territory Rights of the Terminally Ill Act is reproduced along with pertinent excerpts showing the aspects of this landmark act that differ from provisions included in Oregon's Measure 16.

The Northern Territory Rights of the Terminally Ill Act
Passed May 25, 1995

Table of Provisions

An Act to confirm the right of a terminally ill person to request assistance from a medically qualified person to voluntarily terminate his or her life in a humane manner; to allow for such assistance to be given in certain circumstances without legal impediment to the person rendering the assistance; to provide procedural protection against the possibility of abuse of the rights recognized by this Act; and for related purposes.

Section

Part 1—Preliminary

1. Short Title
2. Commencement
3. Interpretation

. . . "assist," in relation to the death or proposed death of a patient, includes the prescribing of a substance, the preparation of a substance and the giving of a substance to the patient for self administration, and the administration of a substance to the patient; . .

"terminal illness," in relation to a patient, means an illness which, in reasonable medical judgment will, in the normal course, without the application of extraordinary measures or of treatment unacceptable to the patient, result in the death of the patient.

. . .

Part 2 —Request for and Giving Assistance

4. Request for assistance to voluntarily terminate life.

A patient who, in the course of a terminal illness, is experiencing pain, suffering and/or distress to an extent unacceptable to the patient, may request the patient's medical practitioner to assist the patient to terminate the patient's life.

5. Response of medical practitioner.

A medical practitioner who receives a request referred to in section 4, if satisfied that the conditions of section 7 have been met, but subject to section 8, may assist the patient to terminate the patient's life in accordance with this Act or, for any reason and at any time, refuse to give that assistance.

6. Response of medical practitioner, &c., not to be influenced by extraneous considerations.

7. Conditions under which a medical practitioner may assist
    (1) A medical practitioner may assist a patient to end his or
         her life only if all of the following conditions are met:
         (a) the patient has attained the age of 18 years;
         (b) the medical practitioner is satisfied, on reasonable
              grounds, that—
              (i) the patient is suffering from an illness that will,
                   in the normal course and without the applica-
                   tion of extraordinary measures, result in the
                   death of the patient;
              (ii) in reasonable medical judgment, there is no
                   medical measure acceptable to the patient that
                   can reasonably be undertaken in the hope of
                   effecting a cure; and
              (iii) any medical treatment reasonably available to
                    the patient is confined to the relief of pain, suf-
                    fering and / or distress with the object of allow-
                    ing the patient to die a comfortable death; . . .

8. Palliative care
9. Patient who is unable to sign certificate of request
10. Right to rescind request
11. Improper conduct

Part 3 —Records and Reporting of Death
12. Medical records to be kept
13. Certification as to death
14. Medical records to be sent to coroner
15. Coroner may report on operation of act

Part 4 —Miscellaneous
16. Construction of act
17. Certificate of request is evidence
18. Effect on construction of wills, contracts and statutes
19. Insurance or annuity policies
20. Immunities
21. Regulations

Source: The Northern Territory Rights of the Terminally Ill Act (Act
No. 12 of 1995).

Legal Cases at the Forefront of the Contemporary Debate

*The victory enjoyed by the proponents of death with dignity was short-
lived. A declaratory injunction was handed down by Judge Michael
Hogan on 7 December 1994 that prevented the Oregon Death with
Dignity Act from going into effect the following day. The following
injunction is important because it is based on allegations that the act*

violates the Fourteenth Amendment of the Constitution. This challenge may force the issue to be heard by the Supreme Court.

IN THE UNITED STATES DISTRICT COURT FOR THE DISTRICT OF OREGON GARY LEE, et al., Plaintiffs, STATE OF OREGON, et al., Defendants. Civil No. 94-6467-HO

DECLARATORY JUDGMENT AND PERMANENT INJUNCTION

The court, having considered the parties' dispositive motions, having granted plaintiffs' motion for summary judgment as to the Equal Protection Clause claim, and having granted certain of defendants' motions for summary judgment as to standing, intervention and immunity, grants plaintiffs Dutson, Elsner, Willows Residential Care Facility, and Maryville Nursing Home a declaratory judgment and permanent injunction against the remaining defendants.

IT IS HEREBY ORDERED, ADJUDGED, AND DECREED that:

(1) Oregon's Death with Dignity Act ("Measure 16") violates the Equal Protection Clause of the Fourteenth Amendment (page one) of the Constitution of the United States;

(2) Defendants are permanently enjoined from recognizing the constitutionality of Measure 16;

(3) Defendant District Attorney Harcleroad is permanently enjoined from recognizing any exceptions from criminal law created by Oregon Ballot Measure 16 in the exercise of his criminal enforcement duties;

(4) Defendant members of the State Board of Medical Examiners are permanently enjoined from recognizing any exceptions from law or regulation governing physicians' conduct created by Oregon Ballot Measure 16 in the exercise of their duties involving licensure, quality control, continuing education, and discipline of physicians.

Nominal security is set in this matter in the amount of $1.00, to be posted in the form of cash or bond with the clerk of this court.

This injunction is binding upon the defendants, their agents, servants, employees, and attorneys, and upon those persons in active concert or participation with them who receive actual notice of this order by personal service or otherwise.

IT IS SO ORDERED.

DATED this 3rd day of August, 1995.

Michael Hogan
United States District Judge

Source: Declaratory Judgment—http://www.right~.org/-deathnet/ergo Hogan4.html

Compassion in Dying v. State of Washington *is the first right-to-die case that any U.S. federal court of appeals has decided. The plaintiffs are four physicians who treat terminally ill patients, three terminally ill patients, and Choice in Dying, a Washington-based nonprofit organization. This case forced the court to weigh the state's interest in preserving human life against the desire of individuals to die peacefully and with dignity. Should the decision made by the Ninth Circuit Court in early 1996 be upheld, competent adults who wish to hasten their own deaths may legally be assisted by a physician in doing so, providing they reside in the western states that fall under the jurisdiction of the Ninth Circuit Court. The excerpt included herein eloquently summarizes the sentiment of the court.*

Compassion in Dying v. State of Washington
No. 94-35534, United States Court of Appeals for the Ninth Circuit
March 6, 1996
REINHARDT, Circuit Judge:
I.

This case raises an extraordinarily important and difficult issue. It compels us to address questions to which there are no easy or simple answers, at law or otherwise. It requires us to confront the most basic of human concerns—the mortality of self and loved ones—and to balance the interest in preserving human life against the desire to die peacefully and with dignity. People of good will can and do passionately disagree about the proper result, perhaps even more intensely than they part ways over the constitutionality of restricting a woman's right to have an abortion. Heated though the debate may be, we must determine whether and how the United States Constitution applies to the controversy before us, a controversy that may touch more people more profoundly than any other issue the courts will face in the foreseeable future.

Today we are required to decide whether a person who is terminally ill has a constitutionally protected liberty interest in hastening what might otherwise be a protracted, undignified, and extremely painful death. If such an interest exists, we must decide whether or not the state of Washington may constitutionally restrict its exercise by banning a form of medical assistance that is frequently requested by terminally ill people who wish to die. We first conclude that there is a constitutionally protected liberty interest in determining the time and manner of one's own death, an interest that must be weighed against the state's legitimate and countervailing interests, especially those that relate to the preservation of human life. After balancing the competing interests, we conclude by answering the narrow question before us: We hold that insofar as the Washington statute prohibits physicians from prescribing life-ending medication for use by terminally ill, competent adults who wish to hasten their own deaths, it violates the Due Process Clause of the Fourteenth Amendment.

* * *

VII. Conclusion

We hold that a liberty interest exists in the choice of how and when one dies, and that the provision of the Washington Statute banning assisted suicide, as applied to competent, terminally ill adults who wish to hasten their deaths by obtaining medication prescribed by their doctors, violates the Due Process Clause [FOOTNOTE 140]. We would add that those whose services are essential to help the terminally ill patient obtain and take that medication and who act under the supervision or direction of a physician are necessarily covered by our ruling. That includes the pharmacist who fills the prescription; the health care worker who facilitates the process; the family member or loved one who opens the bottle, places the pills in the patient's hand, advises him how many pills to take, and provides the tea, water or other liquids; or the persons who help the patient to his death bed and provide the love and comfort so essential to a peaceful death. We recognize that this decision is a most difficult and controversial one, and that it leaves unresolved a large number of equally troublesome issues that will require resolution in the years ahead. We also recognize that other able and dedicated jurists, construing the Constitution as they believe it must be construed, may disagree not only with the result we reach but with our method of constitutional analysis. Given the nature of the judicial process and the complexity of the task of determining the rights and interests comprehended by the Constitution, good faith disagreements within the judiciary should not disturb or surprise anyone who follows the development of the law. For these reasons, we express our hope that whatever debate may accompany the future exploration of the issues we have touched on today will be conducted in an objective, rational, and constructive manner that will increase, not diminish, respect for the Constitution.

There is one final point we must emphasize. Some argue strongly that decisions regarding matters affecting life or death should not be made by the courts. Essentially, we agree with that proposition. In this case, by permitting the individual to exercise the right to choose we are following the constitutional mandate to take such decisions out of the hands of the government, both state and federal, and to put them where they rightly belong, in the hands of the people. We are allowing individuals to make the decisions that so profoundly affect their very existence—and precluding them from intruding excessively into that critical realm. The Constitution and the courts stand as a bulwark between individual freedom and arbitrary and intrusive governmental power. Under our constitutional system, neither the state nor the majority of the people in a state can impose its will upon the individual in a matter so highly "central to personal dignity and autonomy," Casey, 112 S.Ct. at 2807. Those who believe strongly that death must come without physician assistance are free to follow that creed, be they doctors or patients. They are not free, however, to force their views, their religious convictions, or their philosophies on all the other members of a democratic society, and to compel those whose values differ with theirs to die painful, protracted, and agonizing deaths.

AFFIRMED

Source: Internet: http://www.islandnet.com/~deathnet/us9.html.

The second constitutional challenge of assisted-suicide law was decided by the Second Circuit Court of Appeals in the state of New York on 2 April 1996. It was brought by Drs. Timothy Quill, Samuel Klagsburn, and Howard Grossman, as well as a cancer patient and two AIDS patients. The lawsuit was sponsored by Seattle-based Compassion in Dying. The following three excerpts explain why the New York State assisted-suicide law was deemed to violate the Equal Protection Clause of the United States Constitution.

Quill v. Vacco
U.S. Court of Appeals Second Circuit, 2 April 1996

"... it seems clear that New York does not treat similarly circumstanced persons alike: those in the final stages of terminal illness who are on life-support systems are allowed to hasten their deaths by directing the removal of such system; but those who are similarly situated, except for the previous attachment of life-sustaining equipment are not allowed to hasten death by self-administering prescribed drugs...

... Moreover, the writing of a prescription to hasten death, after consultation with a patient, involves a far less active role for the physician than is required in bringing about death through asphyxiation, starvation and/or dehydration...

... The New York Statutes criminalizing assisted suicide violate the Equal Protection Clause because to the extent that they prohibit a physician from prescribing medications to be self-administered by a mentally competent, terminally-ill person in the final stages of his terminal illness, they are not rationally related to any legitimate state interest."

Source: U.S. Second Circuit Court of Appeals, *Quill v. Vacco*, decided 2 April 1996.

Quotations

This section contains words that have been written or spoken by key individuals illuminating important facets of the debate currently raging over end-of-life issues. Opinions that favor the right to die are followed by those in opposition to euthanasia and physician aid-in-dying. Each of these sections is divided into Medical-Bioethical, Spiritual-Social-Cultural, and Legal-Political subsections.

Opinions in Favor of Euthanasia or Physician-Assisted Suicide

Medical-Bioethical

The euthanasia debate has intensified in recent years. One of the catalysts for this has been the concept of patient autonomy, only recently addressed by law (Patient Self-Determination Act, 1991). Patient-oriented decision making has driven many questions about health care into a highly public forum. Author David Rothman reflects on the way things were just a few decades ago.

> Issues of life and death remained relatively obscure in the 1960s, largely because doctors, inside the closed world of the intensive care units, turned off the machines when they believed the patient's death was imminent and irreversible.... The intensive care units were a private domain, whatever the formal definition of death, and doctors exercised their discretion.
> — David J. Rothman, *Strangers at the Bedside*
>   (New York: Basic Books, 1991), 160.

Nancy Dickey, a former chairwoman of the Council on Ethical and Judicial Affairs of the American Medical Association, addresses the highly individual nature of end-of-life decisions.

> We would all draw a different line at which we wouldn't want to live any longer. We have a strong recognition in this country that you are the master of your body. If we begin to deny the freedom of an individual to participate or not in medical care, we could become a medical police state.
> — As quoted in Donald Cox, *Hemlock's Cup*
>   (Buffalo, NY: Prometheus Books, 1993), 79.

The problems that have attended the development of life-saving medical interventions have their roots in the noble desire of the physician to save lives. In this quest, however, it is possible for even the best-intentioned health care provider to lose sight of the patient and to strive to conquer death at all costs. This heroic attitude on the part of the physician can come at the expense of those they are charged with helping. Anna Quindlen wrote a piece in the *New York Times* that addressed this issue, suggesting it may be a reason for the huge popularity of Derek Humphrey's book, *Final Exit*.

> Perhaps they are also people [those buying the book] who have gone to doctors and who know that when you become a patient, often you cease to be an actor and become acted upon. They are people who know from experience that certain illnesses leave the sick stripped of everything they think makes life worth living, prisoners of pain and indignity.
> — Anna Quindlen, "Death: The Best Seller,"
> *New York Times* (14 August 1991): A19.

Sherwin Nuland, M.D., questions the values of a medical paradigm that requires patients to undergo painful, dehumanizing treatments virtually alone. He poignantly describes a patient in the final stages of septic shock.

> ...the anguished patient...has begun to wonder whether enough can be done *for* him to justify what is being done *to* him. Although he cannot know it, his doctors are beginning to wonder the same thing. And yet everyone continues on, because the battle is not yet lost. But all this time, something unnoticed has been happening—despite the best of intentions, the staff members have begun to separate themselves from the man whose life they are fighting to save. A process of depersonalization has set in. The patient is every day less a human being and more a complicated challenge in intensive care.
> — Sherwin Nuland, *How We Die: Reflections on Life's Final Chapter* (New York: Alfred A. Knopf, 1993), 148–149.

Medical professionals may find they are forced to ask themselves if their actions are helping or hurting their patients. Dr. Timothy Quill describes an instance in which he performed CPR on a critically ill 80-year-old male patient. The patient subsequently died.

> The bones in his chest were so frail that they fractured easily. His heart compressions were accompanied by a sickening crunch of broken ribs...I left the room profoundly disturbed. I felt that not only had we violated this dying man, but I too had been violated by being forced to act in a way I found both personally and professionally intolerable. How could we repeatedly brutalize this poor man in the name of extending life? Could this possibly be what the Hippocratic Oath intended?
> — Dr. Timothy Quill, *Death and Dignity: Making Choices and Taking Charge* (New York: W. W. Norton, 1993), 35–36.

Addressing issues raised in the case of Elizabeth Bouvia, a handicapped woman who wished to die but was force-fed against her will by the medical establishment and the legal system, Boston lawyer and ethicist George J. Annas wrote:

> Where are nursing and medical students schooled in the martial art of restraint, forced treatment, intimidation, and violence?...Medical care must be consensual or it loses its legitimacy.
> — George J. Annas, "When Suicide Prevention Becomes Brutality: The Case of Elizabeth Bouvia," *Hastings Center Report* (April 1984): 46.

Elisabeth Kübler-Ross, noted researcher and author, addresses the dual issues of quality of life and the futility of some medical procedures:

> It says nowhere in the Hippocratic Oath that you have to prolong suffering.... That subtle line between prolonging life and dying is part of the art of medicine. Unfortunately, that chapter isn't in medical school text books.
> — As quoted in Derek Humphrey and Ann Wickett, *The Right To Die* (Eugene, OR: The Hemlock Society, 1990), 96.

As a physician who has lived and worked through the period of the most rapid medical advances in history, world-renowned heart surgeon Dr. Christiaan Barnard considers the care of the dying patient an important facet of a physician's responsibility.

My career has spanned an era of great strides in medical knowledge, from the days when we felt we had done our utmost in merely diagnosing a heart condition to the point that we can now do something constructive about most, if not all, heart problems. Yet I do not subscribe to the view that the aim of every doctor is to conquer death. What is more relevant is to look at the problem in a slightly different way and recognize that from the instant of conception in the womb we are all dying.... I have learned from my life in medicine that death is not always an enemy. Often it is good medical treatment. Often it achieves what medicine cannot achieve—it stops suffering.

— Dr. Christiaan Barnard, *Good Life, Good Death:*
A Doctor's Case for Euthanasia and Suicide
(Englewood Cliffs, NJ: Prentice Hall, 1980), vii, 15.

The physicians who provided Barney Clark with the first artificial heart on 2 December 1982 also provided Mr. Clark with a key that allowed him to turn off the machine that enabled him to live. Dr. Willem Kolff, founder of the artificial heart program, reveals his team's awareness that there can be a downside to high-tech medical interventions and that patients should not be left unwillingly in its grip against their will.

If the man suffers and feels it isn't worth it any more, he has a key that he can apply.... I think it is entirely legitimate that this man whose life has been extended should have the right to cut it off if he doesn't want it, if life ceases to be enjoyable.... The operation won't be a success unless he is happy. This has always been our criteria—to restore happiness.

— *Commercial Appeal* (Memphis, TN),
5 December 1982, C2, as cited in James Rachels,
The End of Life (Oxford, England: Oxford University
Press, 1986), 79.

But modern medicine has removed many physicians from prolonged periods at the bedside where empathy for the patient and family is nurtured. Nurses now provide much of the comfort and care ordered by the doctor. When the doctor, who makes treatment decisions, no longer participates in the aftermath of those decisions, ethical questions and conflicts can arise with those who are actively engaged in carrying out those orders. The following quote was taken from a study of critical care nurses who were asked to examine their attitudes toward euthanasia and assisted suicide.

> I have experienced tremendous frustration and anger with physicians who either stress the possibility of a good prognosis, giving false hope—or place their belief system above that of their patients. The physician spends 5 to 10 minutes each day with the patient and then leaves me to carry out his orders and deal with the patient and his/her family for 8 to 12 hours. I'm left with the dilemma of carrying out orders that I believe—and sometimes know—are not in the patient's best interest or what the patient or family has expressed as their desires.
> — David A. Asch, M.D. "The Role of Critical Care Nurses in Euthanasia and Assisted Suicide," *New England Journal of Medicine* 334, no. 21 (23 May 1996): 1374.

Paul Ramsey, a prominent theological ethicist, suggests a scenario illustrating how hard it is to reach a uniform definition of extraordinary versus ordinary medical treatment. By using an example of an "ordinary" treatment that can have "extraordinary" life-saving results, he reveals the dilemmas encountered when these difficult distinctions must be made and how challenging it is to codify or decide these issues for anyone other than ourselves.

> Suppose that a diabetic long accustomed to self-administration of insulin falls victim to terminal cancer, or suppose a terminal cancer patient suddenly develops diabetes. Is he in the first case obliged to continue, and in the second case obliged to begin, insulin treatment and die painfully of cancer, or in either or both cases may the patient choose rather to pass into diabetic coma and an earlier death?
> — Paul Ramsey, *The Patient as Person*
> (New Haven, CT: Yale University Press, 1970), 115–116.

Many have come to view artificial nutrition and hydration as among the many medical interventions that are inappropriate for some patients. In the case of Clarence Herbert, a man who died after physicians Neil Barber and Robert Nedjdl removed his feeding tube, the judge stated that:

> Medical procedures to provide nutrition and hydration are more similar to other medical procedures than to

typical human ways of providing nutrition and hydration. Their benefits and burdens ought to be evaluated in the same manner as any other medical procedure.
— *Barber v. Superior Ct.,*
147 App. 3d 1006, 195 Cal. Rptr. 484 (1983).

Medical technology is not of neutral value. It can have unforeseen and often painful consequences. The need for guidelines to help administer these new treatments becomes greater with every new development. Arthur Caplan, director of biomedical ethics at the University of Minnesota, suggests that it is our own lack of foresight regarding the outcome of these new treatments that has forced the right-to-die debate into high gear.

They're developing an artificial liver machine...there's a sophisticated new respirator for infants in the pipeline. The possibilities are endless. But no one is writing the rules.
— Arthur Caplan, Director of Biomedical Ethics,
University of Minnesota as quoted in Donald Cox,
Hemlock's Cup (Buffalo, NY: Prometheus Books, 1993).

There is an increasing awareness of the dark side of new technology and society's responsibility to address it. Sen. Albert Gore addressed such matters in a session of the 101st Congress during a discussion of genetic-engineering.

The Human Genome initiative is, in my view, a good example of the contrast between how well we are able to recognize the scientific exploration of questions of science and how difficult we find it to delve into ethical and societal concerns that are also raised. Here, as is so often the case, our cleverness has outpaced our wisdom.
— U.S. Congress. Senator Albert Gore, Chairman of the
Subcommittee on Science, Technology, and Space of the
Committee on Commerce, Science and Transportation.
Human Genome Initiative and the Future of Biotechnology.
101st Congress, 9 November 1989, 3.

The Dutch have developed a legal construct that provides room for the practice of physician-assisted suicide. Dr. Herbert Cohen, a Dutch family physician, explains why a euthanasia law was passed in that country in 1993. Similar reasoning is behind current legal efforts in other parts of the world, including the United States.

We need a counterweight for the enormous technology
of present medicine. We are talking mostly about older
people, who in other times, would have died from their
condition. If we can keep people alive but give them a
life that is no life, we must be consistent and give them
the choice to end it.
— As quoted in Marlise Simons, "Dutch Move To Enact
  Law Making Euthanasia Easier," *New York Times*
  (9 February 1993): 1, 9.

There are those who are physically unable to take their own
lives without assistance. The question of whether these people,
and others, should be able to obtain assistance in dying from
their physicians represents the cutting edge of the contemporary
debate. Rev. Ralph Mero, president of Compassion in Dying,
shared the story of a friend whose planned death he attended.
The friend had prepared two glasses, which, when consumed
together, would administer a lethal mixture of medication. After
drinking the first, he requested a spoonful of pudding because
the mixture had an unpleasant taste. While Rev. Mero went to
get the pudding, his friend passed out from the effects of the
first glass and was unable to take the second dose. He remained
in a coma for seven days before he died. Rev. Mero realized that
it is important for someone with experience and knowledge to
be present to assist a person in dying.

> This was the most difficult day of my life. If someone
> could have been there to help him—I didn't know what
> to do—someone better informed, then he would not
> have suffered for seven days before he died.
> — The Reverend Ralph Mero, speaking at the monthly
>   meeting of Hemlock Colorado on 20 May 1995 in
>   Denver, Colorado.

Ronald Dworkin looks at the added complications of self-
determination as experienced by those who are unable to act on
their own behalf and how this results in choices that are often
exceedingly painful and brutal.

> ...Many very sick or handicapped people, though fully
> conscious, are unable to commit suicide unaided.... But
> the laws of all western countries (except, in practice, The
> Netherlands) still prohibit doctors or others from
> directly killing people at their own request.... So the

law produces the apparently irrational result that people can choose to die lingering deaths by refusing to eat, by refusing treatment that keeps them alive, or by being disconnected from respirators and suffocating, but they cannot choose a quick, painless death that their doctors could easily provide.
— Ronald Dworkin, *Life's Dominion: An Argument about Abortion, Euthanasia and Individual Freedom* (New York: Alfred A. Knopf, 1993), 183–184.

Dr. Anthony Shaw, a writer on the subject of physician-assisted death, describes what happens when a decision is made to let a baby with Down's syndrome die, rather than allow a physician to administer a lethal injection.

When surgery is denied [the doctor] must try to keep the infant from suffering while natural forces sap the baby's life away. As a surgeon whose natural inclination is to use the scalpel to fight off death, standing by and watching a salvageable baby die is the most emotionally exhausting experience I know. It is easy at a conference, in a theoretical discussion, to decide that such infants should be allowed to die. It is altogether different to stand by in the nursery and watch as dehydration and infection wither a tiny being over hours and days. This is a terrible ordeal for me and the hospital staff—much more so than for the parents who never set foot in the nursery.
— Anthony Shaw, M.D., "Doctor, Do We Have a Choice?," *New York Times Magazine* (30 January 1972): 44–54.

For many physicians, the end of life and the elimination of suffering occupy two sides of a very fine line. In prescribing powerful pain medications for patients, doctors are also often shortening their lives—a double effect. In the landmark report by the President's Commission titled *Supportive Care for the Dying Patient*, this method of foreshortening life is sanctioned.

No death is more agonizing for the aware patient... than one from respiratory insufficiency. Untreated, the patient will struggle for air until exhausted.... With the consent of the family morphine may be given.... If the patient is already quite exhausted, the slowed respirations will induce hypercapnia [substantial amounts of

carbon dioxide in the blood], which will perpetuate the sedation and the patient will die in the ensuing sleep.
— President's Commission for the Study of Ethical Problems in Medicine and Biomedical and Behavioral Research, *Decisions To Forego Life-Sustaining Treatment* (Washington, DC: U.S. Government Printing Office, 1983), 294–295.

Spiritual-Social-Cultural

Fear of death and denial of its inevitability often prevents a rational approach to end-of-life decisions. This fear has its basis in our cultural and spiritual understanding of life and death. Many consider the spirit, or the essence of the person, and his or her ability to contribute to society to be that which makes life worth living—not the wasted shell alone in a room with no other sound but the mechanical hiss of a ventilator. Dr. Elisabeth Kübler-Ross reflects on how this dichotomy affects end-of-life decisions.

Once more people become aware that our physical form is not the person, but the cocoon, we may have fewer problems in letting go and less guilt that we did not prolong a life at all costs.
— Elisabeth Kübler-Ross, *On Children and Death* (New York: Macmillan, 1983), 59.

Norman Cousins, writing as editor of the *Saturday Review* in June 1975, expresses a view of life and death that succinctly addresses the quality-of-life issue:

Death is not the greatest loss in life. The greatest loss is what dies inside us while we live. The unbearable tragedy is to live without dignity or sensitivity.
— As quoted in Derek Humphrey and Ann Wickett, *The Right To Die* (Eugene, OR: The Hemlock Society, 1990), 106.

Knowing what loved ones want is usually easiest for those who have loved and lived with them. Christy Cruzan White and her family felt they knew Nancy Cruzan well enough to decide what Nancy would have wanted, given her prognosis of a life-long persistent vegetative state.

How do you make the best decision? The answer was, we didn't make the decision—our loved one made the decision.... Chances are—if you haven't already—you will probably make some sort of treatment decision for yourself or a loved one someday.
— Christy Cruzan White in "Taking the 'Right To Die' Issue to the Supreme Court," a presentation to the Hospice of Boulder (CO) County, 10 March 1996.

George Annas, professor of health and law at Boston University, suggests that the outcome of Nancy Cruzan's case demonstrated that there had been an unacceptable degree of state control over the individual in the United States.

Our challenge is to resist the State's inherent normalization program by striving to give meaningful content to our stated goals for forming our country: "Life, liberty and the pursuit of happiness." We cannot, of course, have liberty or pursue happiness without life. But life without liberty or happiness, in the sense of self-realization and benevolence, translates into mindless vitalism: life reduced to the biology of cell division.
— George J. Annas, *Standard of Care: The Law of American Bioethics* (Oxford, England: Oxford University Press, 1993), 97.

Euthanasia brings up deep, spiritual questions regarding death that many believe can only be answered on an individual basis. In a chapter titled "Understanding Fears of Death," authors Janet Maurer and Patricia Strasberg suggest that this existential internal debate on these issues may sometimes prevent us from respecting the needs of the dying.

To deal with his own fears of death, a child or other surviving person may put great effort into vain attempts at saving the dying person's life. It is much more difficult to respect the dying person's decision and mourn with them.
— Janet Maurer, M.D., and Patricia Strasberg, Ed.D., *Building a New Dream: A Family Guide to Coping with Chronic Illness and Disability* (Reading, MA: Addison-Wesley, 1989), 202.

In a view that is nearly the mirror image of the right-to-life stance on abortion and euthanasia, the late Lesley Weatherhead, a British Methodist clergyman, acknowledges:

We do not leave birth to God.... We space births. We prevent births. We arrange births. Many should learn to become the lord of death as well as the master of birth.
— Lesley Weatherhead as quoted in Nancy Gibbs, "Love and Let Die," *Time* (18 March 1990): 68.

How are patients who have no reasonable hope of recovery treated? They are, after all, kept alive by machines, considered by some a feeble excuse for long-term care. Studies have shown that these patients are often ignored by their physicians.

... [dying patients] will not feed a doctor's narcissism by responding and getting well. Their care is demanding, frustrating, and far from helpful to the medical magician's self-esteem.
— C. G. Schoenfeld, "Mercy Killing and the Law: A Psychoanalytically Oriented Analysis," *Journal of Psychiatry and Law* 6, no. 2 (1978): 53.

How we die in this world of medical miracles depends to a great degree on our physician's education and attitude toward death.

Our modern doctor is the sworn enemy of death, a specialist waging a battle in the medical arena. To lose a patient is to fail. All effort is organized and centered around the science of saving lives. In this all-out war, the human needs of the individual patient or family may often be forgotten or ignored.
— Judith Ahronheim, M.D., and Doron Weber, *Final Passages: Positive Choices for the Dying and Their Loved Ones* (New York: Simon & Schuster, 1992), 18.

In every decision made in a hospital pertaining to life and death, there are at least two elements to be considered: the culture of the individual patient and that of the doctor.

Every step of the medical decision-making process is affected by both the patient's and the physician's cultural background. In the emotionality of life-and-death decisions, cultural beliefs are likely to be perceived as absolute beliefs about what is right and wrong...
— Lillian Burke, M.D., Researcher, National Institute of Diabetes, Digestive and Kidney Diseases, National Institutes of Health, Bethesda, MD, as quoted in Donald

Irish et al., eds., *Ethnic Variations in Dying, Death and Grief* (Washington, DC: Taylor and Francis 1993), 170.

Tibetan meditation master Sogyal Rinpoche addresses the difficulty of dying a meaningful death in a highly technological care setting:

> ...Being in an intensive care unit will make a peaceful death very difficult, and hardly allows for spiritual practice at the moment of death. As the person is dying, there is no privacy: They are hooked up to monitors, and attempts to resuscitate them will be made when they stop breathing or their heart fails...our state of mind at death is all-important. If we die in a positive frame of mind, we can improve our next birth.... And if we are upset and distressed, it may have a detrimental effect, even though we may have used our lives well.... To use life-support mechanisms when a person has no chance of recovery is pointless. It is far better to let them die naturally in a peaceful atmosphere and perform positive actions on their behalf. When the life-support machinery is in place, but there is no hope, it is not a crime to stop it, since there is no way in which the person can survive, and you are only holding on to their life artificially.
> — Sogyal Rinpoche, *The Tibetan Book of Living and Dying* (San Francisco: Harper, 1992), 185, 224, 372.

In contemporary medical settings, machines often replace a patient's most important sources of strength during the final moments when comfort is most needed. Catholic psychiatrist Frank J. Ayd speaks to the painful separation of family members during the last moments of life.

> Why, when they face the greatest of all crises together, must they be shoved out of the room, displaced by gadgets and personnel striving to delay the inevitable?
> — Frank J. Ayd, "The Hopeless Case: Medical and Moral Considerations," *Journal of the American Medical Association* 181, no. 13 (29 September 1962): 1100.

The Cruzan family felt alienated from decisions about Nancy's life, not only by the intrusion of the courts into a very personal matter, but also by the lack of clear communication with health care professionals:

[The hospital was like a] foreign land where we often
did not speak the language.
— Christy Cruzan White in "Taking the 'Right To Die' Issue
to the Supreme Court," a presentation at the Hospice of
Boulder (CO) County, 10 March 1996.

Daniel Callahan, director of the Hastings Center and a highly
respected figure in the field of medical ethics, discusses the
impact of pain on the process of aging and death:

[Death should] not be marked by unbearable and de-
grading pain.... Pain, whether physical or psychological, can destroy the personality, the sense of self, and the
ability to relate to others. It separates a person, not only
from himself, but from others as well.
— Daniel Callahan, *Setting Limits: Medical Goals in an Aging
Society* (New York: Simon & Schuster, 1987), 72.

What is suffering? Can sufficient pain medication and high-
quality palliative care relieve it? These questions are central to
the hospice movement and to much of the end-of-life debate.

Although modern techniques of pain management can
substantially alleviate physical pain for many, not all
forms of pain and distress can be controlled; sedation to
the point of unconsciousness *will* block pain, of course,
but only by creating a deathlike state in which the person
has no conscious experience, no significant communication with others, no joy, no movement toward personal
goals—in short, no life. More crucial to death control
decisions is the fact that pain relief is not equivalent to the
relief of *suffering*. The latter encompasses psychological
phenomena such as the frustration of not being able to do
the things one enjoys, hopelessness about the possibility
of returning to an acceptable quality of life, and the sense
of being a burden to others. Pain medication cannot erad-
icate these nonphysical forms of suffering.
— Barbara J. Logue, *Last Rights: Death Control and
the Elderly in America* (New York: Lexington Books,
1993), 126–127.

The spiritual value of suffering, an argument against euthanasia often raised by Christians, is addressed by Dr. Christiaan
Barnard following his years of experience with critically ill
patients:

Long acquaintance with human fallibility, most of it my
own, has taught me never to be adamant on any subject.
But if ever I were tempted to stick my neck out, it would
be on this topic—and my first categorical statement
would be that there is no nobility in pain, bravely borne
or otherwise.
— Christiaan Barnard, *Good Life, Good Death: A Doctor's Case
for Euthanasia and Suicide* (Englewood Cliffs, NJ: Prentice
Hall, 1980), 115.

Dr. Timothy Quill discusses pain in the context of the many
types of death he has witnessed as a physician and a former hospice medical director. His words might be particularly frightening to the roughly 400,000 people who have been diagnosed
with AIDS since 1982.

For a few patients, even those in hospice programs, the
end can be agonizing and completely out of control.…
Some patients infected with human immunodeficiency
virus (HIV) experience such ends.
 Those who have witnessed difficult deaths of patients in hospice programs are not reassured by the glib
assertion that we always know how to make death tolerable, and they fear that physicians will abandon them
if their course becomes difficult or overwhelming in the
face of comfort care. In fact, there is no empirical evidence that all physical suffering associated with incurable illness can be effectively relieved.
— Dr. Timothy Quill, *Death and Dignity: Making Choices
and Taking Charge* (New York: W. W. Norton, 1993), 106,
166.

Larry Beresford addresses the changes in community structure in the United States and its impact on hospice care. If hospice care can only be accessed by those who have a caregiver in
their home, doesn't this make hospice care a luxury for many?

If an aging and mobile society helped to shape the demand for hospice care in the 1970s and 1980s, an increasingly aged and mobile society in the 1990s will demand
some modifications to the basic hospice approach. It is
becoming harder for hospices to expect all or even most
of their patients to have a willing, available, and reliable
family caregiver in the home.…

— Larry Beresford, *The Hospice Handbook*
(Boston: Little, Brown, 1993), 131.

Many Christians argue that only God can decide when a person will die. In 1784 philosopher David Hume made a point that, to this day, has not been given adequate attention by those who would maintain life at any cost.

Were the disposal of human life so much reserved as the peculiar providence of the Almighty that it were an encroachment on his right for men to dispose of their own lives, it would be equally criminal to act for the preservation of life as for its destruction. If I turn aside a stone which is falling upon my head, I disturb this course of nature, and I invade the peculiar providence of the Almighty by lengthening out my life beyond the period which by the general laws of matter and motion he had assigned it.

— As quoted in James Rachels, *The End of Life:
Euthanasia and Morality* (Oxford, England: Oxford
University Press, 1986), 163.

The issue of suffering, and release from it through suicide, has been discussed throughout recorded history and has often played a role in fiction. Sir Thomas More, a Catholic and a statesman in the court of Henry VIII, published *Utopia* in 1516, in which he expressed his vision of a utopian death-by-choice:

If, besides being incurable, the disease also causes constant excruciating pain, some priests and government officials visit the person concerned and say.... Since your life's a misery to you, why hesitate to die? You're imprisoned in a torture chamber—why don't you break out and escape to a better world.... If the patient finds these arguments convincing, he either starves himself to death, or is given a soporific and put painlessly out of his misery. But this is strictly voluntary.

— Sir Thomas More (Paul Turner, trans.), *Utopia*
(New York: Penguin Books, 1981), 102.

The Renaissance was similar to modern times in that there was an enormous increase in scientific knowledge, including the discovery of many new medical technologies. This increase was attended by a heightened sense of individualism and an awareness that technology is not always benign.

When the disease would not reduce us, [God] sent a second and worse affliction, ignorant and torturing physicians. I must say the same of this case, that in punishment of Adam's sins God cast upon us an infectious death with so much horror and fright that it can hardly be made wholesome and agreeable to us.
— John Donne (William A Clebesch, ed.), *Suicide* (Chico, CA: Scholars Press, 1983), 96.

Author Gavin Fairbairn, who has written extensively about the ethics of the caring professions, makes a distinction between euthanasia and suicide.

In an act of euthanasia, steps are taken to allow a person who is dying to die a death that he wishes to die, in preference to a death he wishes to avoid.

In an act of suicide a person arranges his death to avoid a life that he does not wish to live, or in order to die a death that he wishes to die.
— Gavin J. Fairbairn, *Contemplating Suicide* (London, New York: Routledge, 1995), 123.

Legal-Political

The individual's right to choose is the foundation of one of the most significant legal arguments for the right to die. Kansas Supreme Court Justice Alfred Schroeder clarified the basis for informed consent in 1960:

Anglo-American law starts with the premise of thoroughgoing self-determination. It follows that each man is considered to be master of his own body, and he may, if he be of sound mind, expressly prohibit the performance of life-saving surgery, or other medical treatment.
— *Natanson v. Kline*, 186 Kan. 393, 350 P.2d 1093 (1960).

There are those who maintain that the rights of the individual supersede the best interests of society and that personal autonomy should be the guiding force in determining quality of life and the time of death. This right, although well accepted by many contemporary individuals, is not always respected by the medical community. When patients and hospitals face off, the courts and politicians are sure to follow.

...respect for a competent patient's control over medical intervention has now become the legal and medical norm. This development reflects a widespread sentiment that individual self-determination is an integral element of human dignity and humane medical treatment.

Yet there are still uncertainties about the source and bounds of a patient's prerogative to reject life-preserving medical intervention. The roots of patient autonomy are found in common-law sources.... It is important to decide the precise degree of constitutional protection accorded to patient autonomy. For if a patient's right to reject life-preserving medical intervention is indeed anchored in a constitutional source, both state legislatures and state judiciaries must respect the constitutional constraint.

— Norman L. Cantor, *Advance Directives and the Pursuit of Death with Dignity* (Bloomington: Indiana University Press, 1993), 2.

On 3 May 1994 Judge Barbara Rothstein ruled that Washington State's law RCW 9A.36.060, known as "Promoting a Suicide Attempt," was unconstitutional. The law had been called into question by the group Compassion in Dying in the case *Compassion in Dying et al. v. Washington State.*

The liberty interest protected by the Fourteenth Amendment is the freedom to make choices according to one's individual conscience about those matters which are essential to personal autonomy and basic human dignity. There is no more profoundly personal decision, nor one which is closer to the heart of personal liberty, than the choice which a terminally ill person makes to end his or her suffering and hasten an inevitable death. From a constitutional perspective, the court does not believe that a distinction can be drawn between refusing life-sustaining medical treatment and physician-assisted suicide by an uncoerced, mentally competent, terminally ill adult.

— Chief District Judge Barbara Rothstein,
Compassion in Dying et al. v. Washington State
(850 F. Supp. 3 May 1994).

In his speech on 22 February 1995 to the Northern Australian Legislative Assembly, Marshall Perron introduced the "Rights of the Terminally Ill" bill, addressing the difficult question: Who decides?

This is not a political issue; it is a human rights issue.... Through the laws in place today, society has made an assessment for all of us that our quality of life, no matter how wretched, miserable or painful, is never so bad that any of us will be allowed to put an end to it. I am not prepared to allow society to make that decision for me or for those I love.... If we as legislators wring our hands and turn our backs, we are compelling suffering citizens to beg their loved ones to take the law into their own hands by whatever means they have available because current laws forbid the medical profession to do what is humane.
— Marshall Perron, excerpted from the First Reading
   Speech presented at the 22 February 1995 meeting of the
   Northern Territory Legislative Assembly. Available on
   the World Wide Web at:
   http://www.nla.gov.au/nt/rotti/speech.html.

Philosopher Marvin Kohl feels that comparisons are inaccurately drawn between the acts called euthanasia that were committed in Nazi Germany and the needs of individuals dying in our highly technological medical milieu.

The motivation behind and the nature and consequences of acts of beneficent euthanasia are radically different. In the Nazi example, the motivation, aside perhaps from sadism, was solely that of maximizing "benefit" for the state. In cases of beneficent euthanasia, the motivation is essentially and predominantly that of maximizing benefit for the recipient, of helping most where and when the individual needs it most. The Nazi form was involuntary; the form advocated here is voluntary.
— Marvin Kohl, ed., *Beneficent Euthanasia*
   (Buffalo, NY: Prometheus Books, 1975), 137.

Several quotes from the opinions of the three affirming members of the Supreme Court in the Cruzan decision follow:

The 14th Amendment provides that no state shall "deprive any person of life, liberty, or property, without due process of law."...But determining that a person has a liberty interest under the Due Process Clause does not end the inquiry; whether respondent's constitutional rights have been violated must be determined by balancing his liberty interests against the relevant state interests.

— Justice William Rehnquist, excerpted from U.S. Supreme Court Majority Opinions on *Cruzan v. Director, Missouri Department of Health* (25 June 1990).

As the court notes, the liberty interest in refusing medical treatment flows from decisions involving the state's invasions into the body. Because our notions of liberty are inextricably entwined with our idea of physical freedom and self-determination, the Court has often deemed state incursions into the body repugnant to the interests protected by the Due Process Clause [of the Fifth Amendment].

— Justice Sandra Day O'Connor, ibid.

The various opinions in this case portray quite clearly the difficult, indeed agonizing, questions that are presented by the constantly increasing power of science to keep the human body alive for longer than any reasonable person would want to inhabit it.

— Justice Antonin Scalia, ibid.

Justice Brennan's decision was essentially a pro decision, but Brennan dissented because of the procedural obstacles mentioned above. Justices Thurgood Marshall and Harry Blackmun essentially agreed with this view.

Because I believe that Nancy Cruzan has a fundamental right to be free of unwanted artificial nutrition and hydration, which right is not outweighed by any interests of the state, and because I find that the improperly biased procedural obstacles imposed by the Missouri Supreme Court impermissibly burden that right, I respectfully dissent. Nancy Cruzan is entitled to choose to die with dignity.

— Justice William Brennan Jr., excerpted from U.S. Supreme Court Majority Opinions on *Cruzan v. Director, Missouri Department of Health* (25 June 1990).

The language of the courts, although not concrete, is beginning to shift toward an acceptance of physician-assisted death to relieve suffering.

The majority's approach to subjects such as [terminally ill] patients to unwanted and needless suffering... The right to die with dignity falls squarely within the privacy right recognized by the Supreme Court. The right to die with dignity accords with the American values of self-determination and privacy regarding personal decisions.
— Hon. Eugene A. Wright, appeals court judge,
dissenting in *Compassion in Dying et al. v. State of Washington*, 49 F. 3d 586 (Ninth Circuit, 1995).

On 6 March 1996 the Ninth U.S. Circuit Court of Appeals ruled that Washington State's ban on physician-assisted suicide should be struck down. Judge Stephen Reinhardt wrote in the 8–3 decision:

A competent, terminally ill adult, having lived nearly the full measure of his life, has a strong liberty interest in choosing a dignified and humane death, rather than being reduced at the end of his existence to a childlike state of helplessness, diapered, sedated, incompetent.
— *Compassion in Dying et al. v. State of Washington*,
62 F. 3d 299 (Ninth Circuit, 1995).

Opinions against Euthanasia or Physician-Assisted Death

There are those who believe that sanctioning any form of voluntary choice in dying will push our society down the slippery slope toward involuntary mercy killing and perhaps even genocide. Some believe that this process has already begun. The acceptance of passive euthanasia by withholding or withdrawing medical care is offered as evidence of this trend. The following quotes illustrate various aspects of the position held by those who believe that euthanasia is, at best, a questionable practice and, at worst, legalized murder. Others feel that all life is sacred and that all questions of life and death should be left to a higher power.

Medical-Bioethical

Medical ethics for the past 20 years has focused on patient autonomy. But is it possible for patients to fully understand the language used by highly trained professionals? Is it a doctor's job to educate patients or to heal them? David Karnofsky, a cancer specialist, felt in the 1960s that the patient's wishes should not be the guiding force behind a physician's actions.

The physician who treasures his patient's life, without trying to judge its value to the patient, his family, or to his community, in the end will make fewer mistakes, will learn more about the disease he is treating, and will have the satisfaction of giving his best efforts against difficult odds.
— Derek Humphrey and Ann Wickett, *The Right To Die* (Eugene, OR: The Hemlock Society, 1990), 76.

We are living in a time when the decision to terminate a life can be based on more comprehensive medical criteria than has ever before been available. But there are those who feel that we do not do justice to the fighting spirit of the individual by offering an early death. Do we focus too much on the percentages and not enough on the potential of the human spirit?

At best, confidence in predicting death is possible only in the last few hours. Patients with the same stage of disease but with different family settings, personalities, and "things to live for" actually do live for strikingly varied periods of time.
— President's Commission for the Study of Ethical Problems in Medicine and Biomedical and Behavioral Research, *Deciding To Forego Life-Sustaining Treatment: A Report on the Ethical, Medical and Legal Issues in Treatment Decisions* (Washington, DC: U.S. Government Printing Office, 1983), 25–26.

Is it possible to determine an ethical stance on life-and-death issues that can be applied by all doctors to real-life situations? The late Franz Ingelfinger, a renowned editor of the *New England Journal of Medicine*, addresses this question:

This is the heyday of the ethicist in medicine. He delineated the rights of patients, of experimental subjects, of fetuses, of mothers, of animals, and even of doctors.... With impeccable logic—once certain basic assumptions are granted—and with graceful prose, the ethicist develops his arguments.... Yet his precepts are essentially the products of armchair exercise and remain abstract and idealistic until they have been tested in the laboratory of experience.
— Franz J. Ingelfinger, "Bedside Ethics for the Hopeless Case," *New England Journal of Medicine* 289 (1973), 914.

Terminology plays an enormous role in discussions of life and death and who will exercise power or make decisions in this critical arena. Quality-of-life discussions imply that some life is not worthy of our resources, which then leaves open the possibility that personal biases could determine how resources are allocated.

> In many cases, disagreements over [medical] futility are actually debates over the prudent allocation of limited health care resources. Terming an intervention "futile" may allow people to deny that value judgments and trade-offs are being made or that the cost of trying to save some lives is too high.
> — Ann Alpers, J. D., and Bernard Lo, M.D.,
>   "When Is CPR Futile?," *Journal of the American Medical Association* 273, no. 2 (1995), 158.

Considering the causes of the German Euthanasia Programme, Dr. Leo Alexander, an investigator for the War Crimes Tribunal, attributed much of the moral decline of that society as a whole to the attitudes of its physicians.

> The beginnings at first were merely a subtle shifting in emphasis in the basic attitudes of the physicians. It started with the acceptance of the attitude, basic in the euthanasia movement, that there is such a thing as a life not worthy to be lived. This attitude in its early stages concerned itself merely with the severely and chronically sick. Gradually the sphere of those to be included in this category was enlarged to encompass the socially unproductive, the ideologically unwanted and finally all non-Germans. But it is important to realize that the infinitely small wedged-in lever from which this entire trend of mind received its impetus was the attitude toward the nonrehabilitable sick.
> — Dr. Leo Alexander, "Medical Science under
>   Dictatorship," *New England Journal of Medicine* 241 (14 July 1949), 39–47.

Karl Brandt, a physician who was tried at Nuremburg for his role as a key player in the Euthanasia Programme, expresses physician policy toward congenitally compromised children during the Weimar Republic.

> In the case of children, the purpose was to prevent their development at an early age, if only for reasons of family

difficulties, etc. The goal was to make it possible to locate and kill these cases of congenital malformation as soon as possible after birth.
— Alexander Mitserlich, *Doctors of Infamy*
(New York: Henry Schuman, 1949), 105–106.

After an anonymous account that chronicled a gynecologist-in-training's decision to end a patient's life ("It's Over, Debbie") appeared in the *Journal of the American Medical Association* in January 1988, four prominent physicians shared their concerns about the effect they felt the legalization of physician-assisted suicide would have on the medical profession.

The very soul of medicine is on trial. For this is not one of those peripheral issues about which pluralism and relativism can be tolerated.... This issue touches medicine at its very moral center; if this moral center collapses, if physicians become killers or are even merely licensed to kill, the profession—and, therewith, each physician—will never again be worthy of trust and respect as healer and comforter of life in all its frailty.
— Willard Gaylin, M.D., Leon Kass, M.D.,
Edmund Pellegrino, M.D., and Mark Siegler, M.D.,
"Doctors Must Not Kill," *Journal of the American Medical Association* 259, no. 14 (8 April 1988), 2139–2140.

A physician's power over a patient does not need to be exercised overtly to be coercive. A U.S. government commission cautions us to be wary of the powerful sway a physician holds over a vulnerable patient.

How information is communicated and continuing care is provided can forcefully induce a patient to make certain choices. In many medical care situations, patients are dependent and professionals are relatively powerful.
— President's Commission, *Deciding To Forego Life-Sustaining Treatment* (Washington, DC: U.S. Government Printing Office, 1983), 44–45.

Perhaps the legalization of physician-assisted death raises the greatest concern for those populations most vulnerable to abuse. If we are not able to meet the needs of these populations in areas such as adequate nutrition and equal employment while they are still healthy, how can we possibly expose the disabled, poor, homeless, mentally impaired, elderly, female, ethnic and homosexual to the potentially fatal bigotry of physician-assisted death? Barbara Logue speaks to the issues faced today by women and the poor. Women make up approximately three-fourths of nursing home residents over the age of 65. In addition, Logue points out, many women have been raised to be submissive, which sets the stage for coercion in health care decision making.

> In the American health care system, reports of disrespect for women are frequent because health workers often reflect the disregard for women so prevalent in the larger culture.... There are also differences in the way men and women are diagnosed and treated. For instance, women suffering from end-stage renal disease are less likely to receive dialysis than men with the same condition.... Higher income elders, and their advisors and care givers, are more sophisticated at manipulating the system to obtain good care. They can better afford deductibles, co-payments and medigap policies and thus are more attractive clients to doctors, hospitals and nursing homes.
> — Barbara J. Logue, *Last Rights: Death Control and the Elderly in America* (New York: Macmillan, 1993), 261–278.

In 1991 Dr. C. Everett Koop (U.S. surgeon general 1981–1989) expressed his concerns about the increasing interest in physician-assisted suicide:

> We are pulling the plug on a great medical history. If you ask your doctor to be both the killer and the healer, then when you get sick you won't know which doctor is approaching your bed.
> — Donald Cox, *Hemlock's Cup* (Buffalo, NY: Prometheus Books, 1993), 209.

In addition to the philosophical implications of legalizing physician-assisted death, possibly fatal loopholes are being created by changes in the U.S. health care delivery system. How is it possible to trust a physician whom you barely know and who barely knows you? Author David Rothman, professor of social medicine and history, notes the huge shifts that have taken place in the doctor-patient relationship over the past 50 years. He feels these shifts make giving physicians additional life-and-death power a dangerous gamble.

Practically every development in medicine in the post–World War II period distanced the physician and the hospital from the patient and community, disrupting personal connections and severing bonds of trust. Whatever the index—whether ties of friendship, religion, ethnicity, or intellectual activity—the results highlight a sharp division between the lay world and the medical world. By the 1960s the two had moved so far apart that one could have asked a lay audience about the last time they spoke to a physician and had their clothes on, and they would have been unable to remember an occasion.
— David J. Rothman, *Strangers at the Bedside*
(New York: Basic Books, 1991), 127.

If physicians can no longer focus on the needs of patients, but must instead think about cost control, many think that patient abuse is almost inevitable.

By forcing primary care doctors out of private practice through impossibly low fixed-payment rates, the insurance companies have cleared the way to hire new doctors to come in and work for them.

Now … not only do the insurance companies control the patients; they employ the doctors who care for these people.
— Vince Passaro, "On the Examining Table: A Patient's Wary Encounter with Managed Health Care,"
Harper's (May 1994): 70.

Many are unwilling to legalize euthanasia because they do not believe we are doing everything possible to address the needs of the dying. Dr. Richard Lamberton, a British hospice director, reminds us of this.

If anyone really wants euthanasia, he must have pretty poor doctors and nurses. It is not that the question of euthanasia is right or wrong, desirable or repugnant, practical or unworkable. It is just that it is irrelevant. We as doctors have a duty to so care for our patients that they never ask to be killed off.
— Dr. Richard Lamberton as quoted by Sandol Stoddard in
The Hospice Movement: A Better Way To Care for the Dying
(New York: Vintage Books, 1978).

It is often the nurse who follows the doctor's orders to administer increased medication that will result in death (known as the double effect).

> ...It's my patient who stopped breathing, it doesn't feel like a side effect. It feels like I killed him.
> — *Chicago Tribune,* 7 May 1979.

Nurses are put in a double bind when their obligation to the patient conflicts with the doctor's orders. If physician-assisted suicide is legalized, how will subtle coercion of medical personnel be addressed? Will nurses and others be fired if they fail to perform certain tasks associated with assisted death?

> In general, nurses are expected to obey a written "No Code" order which follows hospital policy. However, neither the physician's orders nor the agency's policies protect the nurse from legal and ethical accountability for her actions....Often the nurse's implementation of professional legal and ethical duties may be hampered by the legal privilege and conventional ethical rights of the physician who is considered to have ultimate accountability for patient care or by institutional limits on the nurse's authority to act.
> — "Nurses Speak Out: Does a Terminal Patient Have the Right To Die?" *Good Housekeeping* (May 1984).

Many point to the Netherlands as an example of a progressive country in matters of death with dignity. In his study of the decision-making process between a physician and the parents of a Dutch newborn with Down's Syndrome, Carlos Gomez notes serious communication errors. For some medical conditions, these errors are minor and can easily be rectified. In this case, the baby was euthanized by the doctor's lethal injection.

> The power of consent here devolves to the parents, who refuse further treatments for the child. I note, moreover, that it is unclear whether parents actively consent to euthanasia in this case or whether the request for euthanasia is inferred from the mother's plea that the child not suffer any further. The ethicist relating the case takes the mother's statement as a tacit plea for euthanasia.
> — Carlos F. Gomez, M.D., *Regulating Death: Euthanasia and the Case of the Netherlands* (New York: The Free Press, 1991), 107.

Spiritual-Social-Cultural

Authors James Hoefler and Brian Kamoie suggest that in the United States, the focus on individualism has created a society in which the burden of caring for the young, the old, or the otherwise vulnerable is no longer shared. They imply that the traditional value of community has been lost.

> Ultimately, in a culture that emphasizes the value of power and control of one's own destiny, death, by definition, represents the lack of both power and control, and for that reason must be avoided at all costs. Moreover, when it is not avoided, Americans tend to see the death as an individual loss that really has very little to do with the community at large.
> — James M. Hoefler with Brian E. Kamoie, *Deathright: Culture, Medicine, Politics and the Right To Die* (Boulder, CO: Westview Press, 1994), 28.

Given what many consider the current deplorable state of care for the elderly in this country, would legalizing the right to die lead to abuses?

> Elder abuse...is dependent upon the vulnerability of the victim. Frail, lonely, and trusting elders become high-risk victims, pawns in the hands of unscrupulous care givers and others who would prey upon them. This troubling national problem...is expected to worsen as the population of elders in our society increases ... Present studies suggest that some four percent of elders, about one million per year, are abused, but it is estimated that only one out of six cases is reported...as many elders have no way to assert their rights and some lack the physical and mental capability to present their cases.... many professionals and paraprofessionals who would ordinarily record abuses have not been adequately trained in recognizing the signs of elder abuse.
> — S. J. Quinn and S. K. Tomita, *Elder Abuse and Neglect* (New York: Springer Publishing, 1986), 2.

Our increasingly callous attitudes toward the elderly and their care underline author Robert Kastenbaum's fear that history could repeat itself.

> Is it absurd to suppose that one of these days panic-level concern about overpopulation and its impact, a back-

ground of extreme social tension, fear and disorganiza-
tion, *and* our mental preparation to accept the death of
old people as "natural" (and by implication, desirable)
may bring about a new kind of "final solution"?
— Robert Kastenbaum et al., eds., *Psychosocial Aspects of
Terminal Care* (New York: Columbia University Press,
1972), 119.

When euthanasia or physician-assisted death is viewed in
light of the current economic situation, it must be remembered
that scarce resources helped the Nazi regime convince the
German people that euthanizing "life not worthy of life" was
the best way to a better society. This quote marks the shift in
German attitudes toward an almost society-wide neglect of the
ill and indigent:

It could almost seem as if we have witnessed a change in
the concept of humanity. I simply mean that we were
forced by the terrible exigencies of war to ascribe a different value to the life of the individual than was the
case before, and that in the years of starvation during the
war, we had to get used to watching our patients die of
malnutrition in vast numbers, almost approving of this,
in the knowledge that perhaps the healthy could be kept
alive through these sacrifices. But in emphasizing the
right of the healthy to stay alive, which is an inevitable
result of periods of necessity, there is also a danger of
going too far: a danger that the self-sacrificing subordi-
nation of the strong to the needs of the helpless and ill,
which lies at the heart of any true concern for the sick,
will give ground to the demand of the healthy to live.
— Karl Bonhoeffer, in his May 1920 address to the
German Psychiatric Association, of which he was
chairman, as quoted in Michael Burleigh, *Death and
Deliverance — "Euthanasia" in Germany c. 1900–1945*
(Cambridge, England: Cambridge Univ. Press, 1994), 12.

The question of whether or not an assisted suicide law
would open the door to abuse by family members gains legiti-
macy and immediacy in the words of George Delury, who
helped his wife take her own life on 4 July 1995. He currently
awaits trial for second-degree manslaughter in New York.
During his wife's final months with multiple sclerosis, he kept a
journal, which is being used as evidence in his trial. The journal

indicates that he may well have coerced his wife into taking her life. On 28 March, roughly four months before his wife's death, he wrote of his frustration:

> I have fallen prey to the tyranny of a victim. You [his wife] are sucking my life out of me like a vampire.
> — George Delury as quoted in Thomas Fields-Meyer and Lorna Grisby, "A Death Foretold: Does George Delury's Diary Reveal a Loving Husband—or a Man Who Encouraged His Wife's Suicide?" *People* (26 February 1996): 89–92.

Our rights as individuals, even on a spiritual level, are still subject to the rules of moral behavior that hold us together as a society. Former Surgeon General C. Everett Koop asserts that plenty of case law indicates that there is no constitutional right to die.

> Members of the Jehovah's Witnesses sect have been legally shown not to have the right to refuse a blood transfusion on religious grounds nor to withhold such from a minor who has not reached the age of consent.
> — C. Everett Koop, *The Right To Live, The Right To Die* (Wheaton, IL: Tyndale House, 1976), 102–111.

Jesuit scholar Gerald Kelly argues that, although it is acceptable to kill those who are aggressors, a line must be drawn at taking the lives of the innocent. This view represents the most commonly held interpretation of the Bible's sixth commandment, "Thou shalt not kill."

> ...Innocent human life is absolutely inviolable. By reason of this principle, we exclude all direct killing of the innocent, e.g. by ... "mercy killing."...
> — Gerald Kelly, S. J., "The Duty of Using Artificial Means of Preserving Life," *Theological Studies II*, 1950, as cited in James Rachels, *The End of Life: Euthanasia and Morality* (Oxford, England: Oxford University Press, 1986), 69.

Some people will not engage in any discussion of euthanasia because it conflicts with their religious or philosophical beliefs. This attitude is quite succinctly stated by Monsignor Robert E. McCormick in his response to Dr. Charles Potter (president of the Euthanasia Society during the 1940s) when asked to participate in a debate about euthanasia:

There is only one law and I have stated it: the law of
God. This is not a debatable issue.
— *New York Times* (9 December 1946): 28.

Catholic Bishop Joseph Sullivan believed, like many, that
once a "wedge" is allowed to open the closed door to killing one
another, there will be no way to draw the line and stop the
killing from spreading through society at large.

To permit in a single instance the direct killing of an
innocent person would be to admit a most dangerous
wedge that might eventually put all life in a precarious
condition. Once a man is permitted on his own authority
to kill an innocent person directly, there is no way of
stopping the advancement of that wedge. There exists no
longer any rational grounds for saying that the wedge
can advance so far and no further. Once the exception
has been made it is too late; hence the grave reason why
no exception may be allowed. That is why euthanasia
under any circumstances must be condemned.
— Marvin Kohl, ed., *Beneficent Euthanasia*
(Buffalo, NY: Prometheus Books, 1975), 14.

Many believe that there is courage in relieving suffering by
prematurely ending one's own life. But is there not equal or
greater courage shown by those who choose to continue to fight
on? Do not those who surround the bedside of the dying find
courage and meaning there? These questions are poignantly
addressed by Elisabeth Kübler-Ross.

Those who have the strength and love to sit with a
dying patient in the silence that goes beyond words will
know that this moment is neither frightening nor
painful, but a peaceful cessation of the functioning of
the body.... To be a therapist to a dying patient makes
us aware of the uniqueness of each individual in this vast
sea of humanity. It makes us aware of our finiteness, our
limited lifespan.
— Elisabeth Kübler-Ross, *On Death and Dying*
(New York: Simon & Schuster, 1993), 272.

When is it morally acceptable to give up on a life? Despite our
technical expertise, there is no way to know for sure when, for
instance, someone in a coma might emerge. Although his prognosis was grim, policeman Gary Dockery emerged from a vegetative

state after seven and a half years. The very day before, his family
had argued at his bedside about whether they should allow doctors to perform a surgical operation to prolong his life. His former
partner, who administered CPR and revived Dockery after he suffered a gunshot wound to the head, was quoted as saying:

"I felt guilty about bringing him back, because I
knew he wouldn't want to live like this."

But after Dockery emerged from his coma and was able to
speak, Cox said:

"I had done the right thing after all."
— Gail Wescott, "I Love You, Dad: A Father Awakens; His
Faithful Family Rejoices," *People* (4 March 1996): 66.

Scholars of suicide have provided ample reason to question
whether a rational decision-making process can lead to suicide.
Can a decision made by a depressed person ever be entirely
rational? Isn't society responsible for keeping hope alive for
those who have lost their will to live in a moment of extreme
anguish? English poet A. Alvarez wrote of the "closed world of
suicide," in which the depressed person ceases to be influenced
by rational thinking once a fatal decision has been made.

Once a man decides to take his own life he enters a shut-
off, impregnable but wholly convincing world...where
every detail fits and every incident reinforces his decision....Each of these deaths has its own inner logic and
unrepeatable despair.... [Suicide is] a terrible but utterly
natural reaction to the strained, narrow, unnatural
necessities we sometimes create for ourselves.
— A. Alvarez, *The Savage God: A Study of Suicide* (New York:
Random House, 1972) as quoted in Edwin Shneidman,
Voices of Death (New York: Harper
& Row, 1980), 57.

Even those who support the right to die take issue with the
wholesale acceptance of suicide that is implied when dosages
and methods are made available to the general public. Donald
McKinney, president of the pro–assisted-suicide group *Concern
for Dying*, condemned Derek Humphrey's book *Let Me Die before
I Wake*, which was published in 1981.

We oppose the publication of material offering advice or
counseling on specific aspects of suicide because we
believe that such material is likely to be misused and

that it is not possible to give effective standardized advice about drug dosage for the purpose of suicide.
— As quoted in Derek Humphrey and Ann Wickett,
    The Right To Die (Eugene, OR: The Hemlock Society,
    1990), 117.

The concern surrounding a societal acceptance of intentional death has been backed up by a report issued in 1989 by the Centers for Disease Control's National Center for Injury Prevention discussing the risks of what it terms "suicide contagion," a process by which exposure to the suicide or suicidal behavior of one or more persons influences others to commit or attempt suicide. The report recommends that:

All parties [health officials and the media] should understand that a scientific basis exists for concern that news coverage of suicide may contribute to the causation of suicide.... Describing technical details about the method of suicide is undesirable...providing details of the mechanism and procedures used to complete the suicide may facilitate imitation...by other at risk persons.
— Centers for Disease Control and Prevention,
    "Suicide Contagion and the Reporting of Suicide:
    Recommendation from a National Workshop,"
    MMWR 43, no. RR-6 (1994), 13–17.

Depression must be treated before patients become so despondent that they want to take their own lives. This problem is especially prevalent among the elderly.

...A very large proportion of the elderly men and women who kill themselves do it because they suffer from quite remediable depression.... I have more than once seen a suicidal old person emerge from depression.... When such men or women return to a less despondent vision of reality, their loneliness seems...less stark and their pain more bearable because life has become interesting again and they realize that there are people who need them.
— Sherwin Nuland, *How We Die: Reflections on Life's Final Chapter* (New York: Alfred A. Knopf, 1993), 152.

The late Senator Hubert Humphrey spoke to the U.S. Senate on 25 October 1977 after an 11-week leave of absence caused by cancer, which took his life three months later. In his speech, he addresses the importance of support and faith when battling a terminal illness with dignity.

> The greatest healing therapy is friendship and love, and over this land I have sensed it. Doctors, chemicals, radiation, pills, nurses, therapists are all very helpful. But without faith in yourself and your own ability to overcome your own difficulties, faith in divine Providence and without the friendship and kindness and generosity of friends, there is no healing.
> — *New York Times* (26 October 1977). Also quoted in Edwin Shneidman, *Voices of Death* (New York: Harper & Row, 1980), 137.

Author and thanatologist Edwin Shneidman elegantly reflects on the grace with which Humphrey fought his final battle.

> Humphrey salvaged some redeeming elements from his defeats by using his own special approach to the hollows in the waves of life. He saved for himself (and bequeathed to the rest of us) some worthwhile elements in his dying. There was a consistency in his living while he was well and his living when he was ill.... Humphrey did not lie to us about his cancer. He did not conceal from us its ravaging effects. We all knew that he wore a colostomy bag. But he did all this with a dignity and a good humor that undercut the baleful metaphors associated with that disease. In his openness and sharing, he helped change our notions of cancer itself. He is an important figure in the history of medicine.
> — Edwin Shneidman, *Voices of Death*
> (New York: Harper & Row, 1980), 139.

The most effective source of support to relieve the suffering of the terminally ill has been the hospice movement. The founder of the modern hospice, Dame Cicely Saunders, sums up the movement:

> You matter because of who you are. You matter to the last moment of your life, and we will do all we can not only to help you die peacefully, but also to live until you die.
> — Dame Cicely Saunders as quoted in Larry Beresford, *The Hospice Handbook* (Boston: Little, Brown, 1993), vi.

The hospice perspective challenges us to look at and enhance the way we care for the terminally ill, rather than attempting to take the easy way out by offering death.

> With adequate counseling and the emphasis on the enhancement of the spiritual quadrant, the patients grow in leaps and bounds, and many of my terminal patients have emphasized to me that the last six months of their life were the most valuable months of their entire existence.
> — Elisabeth Kübler-Ross as quoted in Larry Beresford, *The Hospice Handbook* (Boston: Little, Brown, 1993), xi-xii.

Pope John Paul II, in a Doctrine of the Faith given 5 May 1980 in Vatican City, Rome, made the Catholic position on suffering clear.

> According to Christian teaching...suffering, especially suffering during the last moments of life, has a special place in God's saving plan; it is in fact a sharing in Christ's passion and a union with the redeeming sacrifice which he offered in obedience to the Father's will.
> — Pope John Paul II, *Declaration on Euthanasia: Prepared by the Sacred Congregation for the Doctrine of the Faith,* 5 May 1980.

Rev. Napoleon Gilbert, speaking in opposition to the acquittal of Dr. Hermann Sanders, a physician charged with killing one of his patients to relieve her suffering, also views suffering as meaningful and important.

> Suffering is useful in the sight of God.
> — As quoted in Derek Humphrey and Ann Wickett, *The Right To Die* (Eugene, OR: The Hemlock Society, 1986), 44.

Jewish scholars, writing on medical ethics, assert:

> The Jewish attitude towards euthanasia as well as towards suicide, is based on the premise that "only He who gives life may take it away."...
> For Judaism, human life is, "created in the image of God." Although life is considered to be God's creation and good, human life is related to God in a special way: it is sacred. The sanctity of human life prescribes that, in

any situation short of self-defense or martyrdom, human life be treated as an end in itself. It may thus not be terminated or shortened because of considerations of the patient's convenience or usefulness, or even sympathy with the suffering of the patient. Thus euthanasia may not be performed either in the interest of the patient or of anyone else. Even individual autonomy is secondary to the sanctity of human life and, therefore, a patient is not permitted to end his or her life or be assisted in such a suicide by anyone else, be he or she a health care professional, family member, friend or bystander. In Judaism suicide and euthanasia are both forms of prohibited homicide. No human life is more or less sacred.
— Feldman, David M. and Fred Rosner, eds. *Compendium on Medical Ethics* 6th ed. (New York: Federation of Jewish Philanthropies of New York, 1984), 106.

Would physicians lose respect for life if they became accustomed to helping their patients die? Would medical training that included killing in the curriculum be reinforcing this loss of respect? Author and psychologist Dave Grossman believes that our constant exposure to killing and violence through video games, television news reports, and other media acts on the average person in the same way that desensitization training acts on soldiers to prepare them for combat. He attributes the breakdown of the taboo against killing in contemporary society to this subtle and inadvertent desensitization process.

We are reaching that stage of desensitization at which the inflicting of pain and suffering has become a source of entertainment: vicarious pleasure rather than revulsion. We are learning to kill, and we are learning to like it.
— Dave Grossman, *On Killing: The Psychological Cost of Learning To Kill in War and Society* (Boston: Little, Brown, 1995), 310–311.

Legal-Political

In 1939 Louis Repouille, a man on trial for taking the life of his 13-year-old disabled son, was convicted of manslaughter in the second degree. Repouille told the court that the actions of another man, Louis Greenfield, had influenced his decision to take his son's life. Mr. Greenfield had previously taken the life of his 17-year-old son and been acquitted. The Judge, after suspending Repouille's sentence, stated:

> This type of killing has become associated in the public mind with the thought that, on certain occasions, it is an act of mercy. The words mercy killing have no sanction in our law. The fact that you were the father of an imbecile did not give you the right to kill him. There is grave danger that the leniency extended to you may encourage others to do what you did.
>
> — *New York Times* (25 December 1941), as quoted in Derek Humphrey and Ann Wickett, *The Right To Die* (Eugene, OR: The Hemlock Society, 1990), 18.

Medical technology has added several degrees of complexity to the issue of suffering. The Rev. Billy Graham, speaking to an audience of 6,000 about the trial of Dr. Hermann Sanders, recommended he be prosecuted to set an example.

> Anyone who voluntarily, knowingly, or premeditatedly takes the life of another, even one minute prior to death, is a killer. I don't say Dr. Sander deserves death, but if we let this pass, who is to say who is to live and who is to die?
>
> — *New York Times* (9 January 1950), as quoted in Derek Humphrey and Ann Wickett, *The Right To Die* (Eugene, OR: The Hemlock Society, 1990), 44.

If killing is legalized, perhaps there is a risk of sliding so far down the slippery slope that a political leader, such as Adolf Hitler, can say:

> The law of existence prescribes uninterrupted killing, so that the better may live.
>
> — Adolf Hitler in 1941, as quoted in Gerald Fleming, *Hitler and the Final Solution* (Berkeley: University of California Press, 1982), 27.

In a 1995 editorial in the *Journal of the American Medical Association*, Dr. Edmund Pelligrino speaks of the devastating conditions in the Soviet health care system. His editorial points to a disturbing facet of the Russian health care system during Communist rule, which he calls "the subversion of medical ethics to the ideology of the Marxist-Stalinist state." He questions the creation of statutes and laws that open a Pandora's box that may be impossible to close.

First, corruption inevitably afflicts any health system not designed with care of the patient as its primary driving force. Second, medical ethics must maintain independence from political exigency.

...A morally responsive profession is an indispensable safeguard for the sick against the statistical morality of utilitarian politics, even in democracies.... Totalitarian regimes always recognize the power of medicine as an instrument for social control. Just as surely, traditional medical ethics stands in the way of such subversion.... For the Nazi physicians, killing was reinterpreted as "healing" if their "patients" were retarded, psychotic, or Jewish.

...The integrity of medical ethics is not immune to corrosion in democratic countries. In democracies, that corrosion will not be as stark and abrupt as it was in Soviet Russia. It is apt to be more subtle and grow through legislation of small increments of accommodation to expediency.

— Edmund Pelligrino, M.D., "Guarding the Integrity of Medical Ethics: Some Lessons from Soviet Russia," *Journal of the American Medical Association* 273, no. 20 (24/31 May 1995), 1622–1623.

In advancing the slippery-slope argument, many assert that the government has an overarching responsibility to avoid any course of action that could result in the destruction of lives, particularly those of our most vulnerable citizens. If the government becomes party to questionable practices, abuse on a large scale could occur. Henrich Himmler in 1940, writing to another Reich official, demonstrated the level of premeditated thought that went into the Nazi propaganda program to convince the public that euthanizing patients in their mental institutions was a good idea.

I hear there is a great unrest in the Württemberg mountains on account of the Grafneck institution. The people know the gray SS bus and think they know what happens in the crematory with its ever-smoking chimney. What does happen there is a secret, and yet it is a secret no longer. The public temper is ugly and in my opinion there is nothing to do but to stop using this particular institution. Possibly one might initiate a skillful and reasonable program of enlightenment by running films on

heredity and mental disease in this particular region.
May I ask you to let me know how this difficult problem
was solved.
— As quoted in Gerald Fleming, *Hitler and the Final Solution*
(Berkeley: University of California Press,
1982), 112.

A German man named Roland Gerkan who was dying of
lung disease, wrote a proposed draft of a euthanasia law in 1913
and submitted it to the German publication *Das monistische Jar-
hundert*. Although he died a week later, his letter caused considerable debate among members of the medical profession. One
doctor, M. Beer, who opposed the concept of state-sanctioned
euthanasia, stated:

> I also believe that this (euthanasia) would be the first
> step, but whether it would be the last appears to me to
> be very doubtful.... Once respect for the sanctity of hu-
> man life has been diminished by introducing voluntary
> mercy killing for the mentally-healthy incurably ill, and
> involuntary killing for the mentally ill, who is going to
> ensure that matters stop there?
> — M. Beer as quoted in Michael Burleigh, *Death and
> Deliverance—"Euthanasia" in Germany c. 1900–1945*
> (Cambridge, England: Cambridge Univ. Press, 1994), 15.

There are nuances to the meaning of euthanasia that only
become clear in retrospect—after the deed is done and there is
no turning back. It is this irrevocableness that for some makes
assisted suicide such a great hazard.

> Our slippery slope might yet be analogous to Nazi
> Germany's in a more abstract way. If we consider the
> rationale which gives social utility or economic returns
> precedence over individual freedom, then we might see
> how our society could approach the kind of thinking
> that underlay the Nazi experience. There, racism over-
> rode personal autonomy; here it might be an economic
> rationale—the attitude that we won't spend so much
> per year to keep somebody alive on the slim chance of
> recovery. The slippery slope then is not the precipitating
> act; it's the context in which that act takes place.
> — Laurence McCullough, a postdoctoral fellow, speaking
> at a Hastings Center conference on "Biomedical Ethics
> and the Shadow of Nazism," as quoted in Derek

Humphrey and Ann Wickett, *The Right To Die* (Eugene, OR: The Hemlock Society, 1990), 32.

Author Nancy Gibbs points out how radically our ideas and values changed after World War II:

> It took no more than three decades to transform a war crime into an act of compassion.
> — Nancy Gibbs, "To Love and Let Die," *Time* (19 March 1990): 62–71.

During his interviews with Dutch physicians, euthanasia researcher Dr. Carlos Gomez found that many Dutch physicians were not applying the guidelines required by law in the Netherlands when deciding whether or not to honor a patient's request for physician-assisted death. He explains his interview process:

> I called into question whether the requirement of "voluntariness" stipulated by the protocol had been followed. In some cases, the respondents would add details that they had left out of the earlier narrative. In others, the respondents would say that they did not remember. In still others, it became obvious that particular points had been either overlooked or not sufficiently considered.
> — Carlos F. Gomez, M.D., *Regulating Death: Euthanasia and the Case of the Netherlands* (New York: The Free Press, 1991), 64.

Dr. Gomez then points out institutional irregularities pertaining to the practice of euthanasia in the Netherlands. He asks, if the Dutch are so comfortable with this practice, why do they neglect to track it and assure the population that guidelines are being followed?

> ...The Dutch central and provincial governments gather and analyze extensive records pertaining to the health of their people. On the question of euthanasia, however, the government publishes no regular records.
> — Ibid., 50.

Dr. Gomez found that there is greater concern about the rights of the individual than about the public control of euthanasia needed to protect vulnerable citizens. He warns that governments that allow physician-assisted suicide but neglect to track the practice and provide for a public review of physician actions are asking for trouble.

> Those who would challenge my assessment here have to contend with several features highlighted in this study. The most obvious is that the formal, judicial level of this regulatory scheme is routinely bypassed. It is commonly agreed that public prosecutors do not review the vast majority of euthanasia cases in The Netherlands.... Yet tolerance of euthanasia in The Netherlands—at least officially—rests on the supposition that the practice has an institutional, extra-medical check to it, that is, that there is a *public* process regulating the practice.... However, the data I gather in this study, both the clinical narratives and data available from formal and informal sources, strongly suggest that this situation does not obtain. At least at this most formal level, then, the public policy of regulating euthanasia fails in meeting its stated objective.... it is not so benign—and certainly not so well regulated—as its defenders have suggested. I have pointed to deficiencies in the theory of regulation and have noted how these deficiencies play themselves out in practice. I have, moreover, suggested that if euthanasia is to be allowed, a stronger case needs to be made if what I have called the public institution of medicine not be corrupted for private purposes.
> — Ibid., 121, 136–137.

Some find the lack of public accountability in the Netherlands as described by Dr. Gomez to be disturbingly reminiscent of the cover-ups that surrounded the euthanasia program in Nazi Germany, described below.

> A nonexistent registry, documents with false reports and circumstances of death, the pretense of an epidemic hazard as justification for the cremation of corpses, cover names for physicians and officials, fabricated medical histories, gas chambers disguised as tiled shower facilities with dummy shower nozzles, hypocritical demonstration of sympathy and condolence, deceptive claims about the purpose of patient relocations and the registration forms: this is what actually constituted the euthanasia program, which was so readily termed a program of "mercy killing."

— Gerald Fleming, *Hitler and the Final Solution* (Berkeley: University of California Press, 1982), 27, as quoted in Derek Humphrey and Ann Wickett, *The Right To Die* (Eugene, OR: The Hemlock Society, 1990), 23.

After the courts allowed the hospital to remove the nutrition and hydration tubes from Nancy Cruzan, right-to-life groups stood vigil outside the hospital. They entered the building on 19 December 1990 in an attempt to reattach her feeding tube. They were arrested. Joseph Foreman, one of the founders of Operation Rescue (an antiabortion group), predicted:

> I think the next few years will see an entire industry spring up around putting people to death whom family and friends have deemed to be no longer of use to anybody. There will be wings in hospitals devoted to putting people to death like this.... I have no sympathy for a family who solves their problems by starving their daughter to death when there were hundreds of bonafide offers to care for her regardless of her condition. Even a dog in Missouri cannot be legally starved to death.
> — As quoted in Lisa Belkin, "As Family Protests, Hospital Seeks an End to Woman's Life Support," *New York Times* (10 January 1991): 1, 10.

How can patients be sure that their physician has their best interests in mind? While the country awaited the outcome of Washington's Initiative #119, James Vorenberg, a professor of criminal law, analyzed the legal aspects of physician-assisted suicide.

> In effect, existing law on assisted suicide places virtually unlimited discretionary power in the hands of doctors and prosecutors, and gives patients no assurances that they can decide when to end their lives if they are terminally ill.
> — James Vorenberg, "The Limits of Mercy," *New York Times*, op-ed (5 November 1991).

Judges are charged with the responsibility of upholding the highest moral values for society as a whole. They have the difficult task of determining the best course for a culturally, politically, spiritually, and economically diverse society.

The State's interest is not in quality of life... were quality of life at issue, all manner of handicaps might find the State to terminate their lives. Instead, the State's interest is in life; that interest is unqualified.
— *Cruzan v. Director, Missouri Department of Health*, 109 S. Ct. 3240 (1989).

A dissenting Supreme Court opinion in the Cruzan case considers the best interests of patients and the constitutional right to be free from unwanted medical treatment:

The portion of this Court's opinion that considers the merits of this case is similarly unsatisfactory. It, too, fails to respect the best interests of the patient. It, too, relies on what is tantamount to a waiver rationale: the dying patient's best interests are put to one side and the entire inquiry is focused on her prior expressions of intent.

An innocent person's constitutional right to be free from unwanted medical treatment is thereby categorically limited to those patients who had the foresight to make an unambiguous statement of their wishes while competent.
— Justice John Paul Stevens in U.S. Supreme Court Minority Opinions on *Cruzan v. Director, Missouri Department of Health* (25 June 1990).

In the case of infants or young children who are deemed by the courts to be incompetent by virtue of their youth or lack of maturity, the court has consistently upheld the highest standard of life, even in the face of parents who would see the child's life ended. In one well-publicized case, Robert and Pamela Mueller, parents of Siamese, or conjoined, twins, had made the decision to starve their children to death because there was no way the twins could be separated surgically. When an anonymous complaint was filed with the state of Illinois, the twins were taken into the custody of the state.

Perhaps the most important practical lesson of the Danville case is the reminder that non-treatment of handicapped infants is subject to criminal prosecution. Causing the death of an infant by intentional withholding of food or necessary medical treatments by a parent, or by a physician who has undertaken to treat the infant,

may constitute a series of crimes ranging from murder and manslaughter to conspiracy and child abuse.
— John A. Robertson, "Involuntary Euthanasia of Defective Newborns: A Legal Analysis," *Stanford Law Review* 27 (1975): 213.

Other countries are concerned about legally protecting society's most vulnerable citizens as well. After the Medical Treatment Bill of 1995 (a voluntary euthanasia bill introduced by Legislative Minister Michael Moore) was defeated in Australia, Margaret Tighe, chairperson of Right to Life Australia, stated:

Those who are most vulnerable and least able to speak up for themselves have been given a reprieve.
— *International Anti-Euthanasia Task Force Newsletter* 9 (November–December 1995): 12.

References

Allen, J. Linn. "The Case for Dying with Dignity Is Muddied by the Kevorkian Debate," *Chicago Tribune* (20 January 1995): 1.

Alzheimer's Disease and Related Disorders Association, Inc. *Alzheimer's Disease: Statistics* (December 1994).

American Cancer Society. *Cancer Facts & Figures 1996: Costs of Cancer*, 1996.

Anthony, Joseph. "Your Aging Parents: Document Their Wishes," in *American Health* 14, no. 4 (1995): 58, 61.

Arras, J. D., as quoted in Robert Kane and Rosalie A. Kane. "Long-Term Care," *Journal of the American Medical Association* 273, no. 21 (1995): 1690–1691.

Asche, David A. "The Role of Critical Care Nurses in Euthanasia and Assisted Suicide," *New England Journal of Medicine* 334 (23 May 1996): 1374–1379.

Bachman, Jerald G., et al. "Attitudes of Michigan Physicians and the Public toward Legalizing Physician-Assisted Suicide and Voluntary Euthanasia," *New England Journal of Medicine* 334, no. 5 (1 February 1996): 303-309.

Barnard, Christiaan. *Good Life, Good Death: A Doctor's Case for Euthanasia and Suicide*. Englewood Cliffs, NJ: Prentice Hall, 1980.

Beresford, Larry. *The Hospice Handbook*. Boston: Little, Brown, 1993.

Bristow, Lonnie R., M.D. "Euthanasia/Physician-Assisted Suicide: Lessons in the Dutch Experience—Report of the Board of Trustees,

American Medical Association," *Issues in Law and Medicine* 10 (Summer 1994): 81–90.

Canella, David. "Doctors Face the Dilemma of Assisted Suicide," *Arizona Republic* (14 May 1995): A9.

CBS. Population forecasts in 1993 as cited in Vanderberg Jeths, Anneke Thorslund, and M. Thorslund. "Will Resources for Elder Care Be Scarce?," *Hastings Center Report* 5 (September–October 1994): 7.

Choices 4, no. 2 (Summer 1995): 1, 7.

Committee to Study the Medical Practice concerning Euthanasia. *Medical Decisions about the End of Life.* 2 vols. The Hague, 19 September 1991.

Cox, Donald. *Hemlock's Cup.* Buffalo, NY: Prometheus Books, 1993.

Curtis, J. Randall, et al. "Use of the Medical Futility Rationale in Do-Not-Attempt-Resuscitation Orders," *Journal of the American Medical Association* 273, no. 2 (11 January 1995): 124.

Davol, Samuel, ed. "Legal Briefs," *Choices* 4, no. 2 (1995): 7.

"Death," *The New Grolier Encyclopedia* on CD-ROM. Grolier Publishing Company, 1993.

Dillman, Wal G. "Euthanasia in the Netherlands," *British Medical Journal* 308 (1994): 1346–1349.

Donovan, M., P. Dillon, and L. McGuire. "Incidence and Characteristics of Pain in a Sample of Medical/Surgical In-Patients," *Pain* 30 (1987): 69–87.

Famighetti, Robert, ed. *The World Almanac Book of Facts 1995.* Mahwah, NJ: Funk and Wagnalls, 1994.

Family Caregiver Alliance. *Selected Caregiver Statistics and Factsheet,* 1996.

Fenigsen, Richard. "The Report of the Dutch Governmental Committee on Euthanasia," *7 Issues in Law and Medicine* 339 (1991).

Goldfluss, Howard. *Living Wills and Wills.* New York: Wings Books, 1994.

Henry J. Kaiser Family Foundation and KAPMG Peat Marwick. Employer survey on health reform, *Med Benefits* 11 (1994): 9.

Henry J. Kaiser Family Foundation/Commonwealth Fund/Louis Harris and Associates poll. *Poll, August 6, 1993,* Storrs, CT: Roper Center for Public Opinion Research.

Hoefler, James M., with Brian E. Kamoie. *Deathright: Culture, Medicine, Politics, and the Right To Die.* Boulder, CO: Westview Press, 1994.

Humber, James M., Robert Almeder, and Gregg Kasting, eds. *Physician-Assisted Death*. Totowa, NJ: Humana Press, 1994.

Jones, Priscilla Samuel, ed. "Death Is Painless, Quiet for Most," *Aging Magazine*, no. 363–364 (1992): 5.

Kinella, David. "ALS Ruins Body as Mind Watches Helplessly: Cause, Cure Are Elusive. Drug Might Slow Disease," *Arizona Republic* (14 May 1995): A8.

Lane, Dee. "Americans' Interest in Suicide Heightens," *Oregonian* 1 (January 1995): B1.

Lear, Dick. "Physicians Face Wrenching Choices," *Boston Globe* (27 April 1993).

Lee, Melinda A., et al. "Legalized Assisted Suicide: Views of Physicians in Oregon," *New England Journal of Medicine* 344, no. 5 (1 February 1996): 310–315.

Marwick, Charles. "Longevity Requires Policy Revolution," *Journal of the American Medical Association* 273, no. 17 (3 May 1995).

Mehra, Leila. "Science Academies Call for Action on Population," *World Health* 7 (May–June 1994): 7.

Multi-Society Task Force on PVS. "Medical Aspects of the Persistent Vegetative State," *New England Journal of Medicine* 330, no. 22 (2 June 1994): 1572, 1576.

National Center for Health Statistics, *Health, United States, 1992*. Hyattsville, MD: Public Health Service, 1993.

"1991 Roper Poll of the West Coast," *Hemlock Quarterly* 44 (1991): 9–11.

Oye R. K., and P. E. Bellamy. "Patterns of Resource Consumption in Medical Intensive Care," *99 Chest* (March 1991): 685–689.

President's Commission for the Study of Ethical Problems in Medicine and Biomedical and Behavioral Research. *Deciding To Forego Life-Sustaining Treatment*. Washington, DC: U.S. Government Printing Office, 1983a.

———. *Making Health Care Decisions: The Ethical and Legal Implications of Informed Consent in the Patient-Practitioner Relationship* 2, App. B (Washington, DC: U.S. Government Printing Office, 1983b): 56.

Schmall, Vicki, and Ruth Stiehl. From an Oregon State University study quoted in the "News Notes Section" of *Aging Magazine* 365 (1993): 52.

Simons, Marlise. "Dutch Move To Enact Law Making Euthanasia Easier," *New York Times* (9 February 1993): 1–9.

———. "Dutch Doctors To Tighten Rules on Mercy Killings," *New York Times* (11 September 1995).

Solomon, Mildred Z., et al. "Decisions near the End of Life," *American Journal of Public Health* 83, no. 1 (January 1993): 16–17 (table).

Support Principal Investigators. "A Controlled Trial To Improve Care for Seriously Ill, Hospitalized Patients," *Journal of the American Medical Association* 274, no. 20 (22–29 November 1995): 1591–1598.

Susman, Carolyn. "Pharmacists Seek Guidance on Suicide-Assisting Drug," *Palm Beach Post* (13 May 1995): 1D.

Taffet, Teasdale, and Lucci Taffet. "In-Hospital Cardiopulmonary Resuscitation," *Journal of the American Medical Association* 260 (1988): 2069–2072.

Takken, Teresa. "Mercy-Killing in California and The Netherlands," *BioLaw* 4 (1987): 4.

U.S. Bureau of the Census *Bureau Income, Poverty and Valuation of Non-Cash Benefits: 1993.* Washington, DC: U.S. Bureau of the Census.

Van Der Maas, P., et al. "Euthanasia and Other Medical Decisions Concerning the End of Life," *Healthy Policy* 22 (Special Issue: Elsevier, Amsterdam, 1992).

Wachter, Robert M., et al. "Cost and Outcome of Intensive Care for Patients with AIDS, Pneumocystis Carinii Pneumonia, and Severe Respiratory Failure," *Journal of the American Medical Association* 273, no. 3 (18 January 1995): 230–235.

Warden, John. "Euthanasia around the World," *British Medical Journal* 304 (4 January 1992): 7.

Waxma, Sharon. "The Dutch Way of Death: Euthanasia Is Accepted but It's Not Easy," *Washington Post* (31 January 1995): B1.

Wegman, Myron E. "Annual Summary of Vital Statistics, 1980," *Pediatrics* 68 (1981): 755, 759.

World Health Organization. *World Health Report, 1995: Executive Summary.* Geneva, Switzerland: World Health Organization, 1995.

Zimmerman, Jack M. Quoted in the President's Commission for the Study of Ethical Problems in Medicine and Biomedical and Behavioral Research. *Deciding To Forego Life-Sustaining Treatment: A Report on the Ethical, Medical and Legal Issues in Treatment Decisions.* Washington, DC: U.S. Government Printing Office, 1983.

Directory of Organizations

S ignificant organizations involved in the end-of-life debate are listed in alphabetical order. Every effort has been made to include key organizations on both sides of the issue—the right to life as well as the right to die.

Many of those listed here are headquartered in the United States. Some foreign organizations have been included as well. Updated information about additional organizations can be accessed through the Euthanasia Resource Guidance Organization (ERGO) via its World Wide Web site (see ERGO listing below).

American Association of Suicidology (AAS)
4201 Connecticut Avenue, N.W., Suite 310
Washington, DC 20008
(202) 237-2280
Fax: (202) 237-2282
E-mail: BERM101W@wonder.em.cdu.gov
Director: Alan L. Berman

The American Association of Suicidology (AAS) is a nonprofit organization founded in 1986 by Edwin Shneidman to help people and organizations understand and prevent suicide. It provides public awareness programs as well as education and training for professionals and volunteers. It also serves as a national clearinghouse for information on suicide and sponsors an annual conference for professionals, survivors, academicians, and other interested parties.

Publications: Two newsletters, the quarterly *Surviving Suicide* and the membership update *Newslink*; several books, *The Suicidal Patient: Clinical and Legal Standards of Care, Preventing Elderly Suicide,* and *Suicide in Later Life*; and a pamphlet, *Suicide of Older Men and Women.*

American Chronic Pain Association (ACPA)
P.O. Box 850
Rocklin, CA 95677
(916) 632-0922
Fax: (916) 632-3208
Executive Director: Penny Cowan

The American Chronic Pain Association (ACAPA) is a nonprofit, self-help organization, which has operated internationally since 1980. It provides support for those who suffer from chronic pain and is a good resource for people who need support and education to deal with chronic pain associated with a terminal illness.

Publications: The quarterly newsletter *ACPA Chronicle, The ACPA Member Workbook Manual,* and a manual, *Staying Well, Advanced Pain Management for ACPA Members.*

American Life League (ALL)
P.O. Box 1350
Stafford, VA 22555
(703) 659-4171
Fax: (703) 659-2586
President: Judie Brown

Founded in 1982, this pro-life service organization currently has more than 250,000 members. American Life League (ALL) provides educational materials, books, flyers, and programs for local, state, and national pro-life, pro-family organizations. Its special fields of interest include euthanasia, abortion, organ transplantation, population, and world hunger. ALL produces *Celebrate Life!*, a weekly nationwide television program.

Publications: Various newsletters, the bimonthly journal *All about Issues,* the magazine *Choice in Matters of Life and Death,* and a book, *The Living Will.*

American Medical Association (AMA)
515 N. State Street
Chicago, IL 60010
(312) 464-5000
Executive Director: Dr. P. John Seward

The American Medical Association (AMA) was founded in 1847 to promote the science and art of medicine and the betterment of public health. It established a code of ethics and minimum requirements for medical education and training, and it provides information about physicians practicing medicine in the United States, including when they were licensed, area of specialization, and if they are board certified. The AMA has an active ethics committee, the Council on Ethical and Judicial Affairs. The AMA opposes physician-assisted death and has been a powerful influence against its legalization in the United States.

Publications: The weekly, professionally reviewed *Journal of the American Medical Association* and numerous other publications.

Americans for Death with Dignity
624 Ocotillo Avenue
Palm Springs, CA 92264
(619) 327-7967
Fax: (619) 322-3562
President: Anita Rufus

Founded in 1986 as Americans Against Human Suffering by attorney Robert W. Risely, this organization changed its name to Americans for Death with Dignity in 1993. The organization sponsored ballot initiatives on physician aid-in-dying in the state of California in 1986 and 1992. Both failed, but the organization continues to work for legal reform in California. It is funded by public subscription.

Publication: Occasional newsletter.

Americans United for Life
343 Dearborn, Suite 1804
Chicago, IL 60604
(312) 786-9494
President: Paige Cunningham

Founded in 1971, this pro-life legal and educational organization focuses on protecting human life at all stages of development. It conducts legal and legislative activities, including giving testi-mony and presenting legal briefs in cases involving euthanasia and abortion. It lobbies for the reversal of *Roe v. Wade.*

Publication: A monthly newsletter, *AUL Forum.*

Association pour le Droit de Mourir dans la Dignité
103 Rue de la Fayette
75010 Paris
France
33-1-4285-1222
Fax: 33-1-4596-0050
Executive Director: Henri Caillavet

Association pour le Droit de Mourir dans la Dignité, or the "Association for Death with Dignity," was founded in April 1980. Its objective is to promote the legal and social right to make deci-sions regarding one's own life and manner of death in a free and conscious manner in order to live the final stages of life under the best possible conditions. More than 25,000 active members belong to 83 regional chapters throughout Europe. The main office is located in Paris, where a board of six individuals coordinate the work of three main committees: Legal, Medical, and Commu-nications. The group holds meetings, organizes conferences, and participates in regional radio and television broadcasting.

Publications: A quarterly newsletter and an informational flyer. Also has published a book: *les Droits des vivants sur la fin de leur vie* and the proceedings of a 1994 colloquium that featured Dutch participation: *L'euthanasie volontaire: la situation aux Pays-Bas.*

Center for Bioethics at the Clinical Research Institute of Montreal
110 Pine Avenue, W.
Montreal, QC H2W 1R7
Canada
(514) 987-5617
Fax: (514) 987-5695
E-mail: royd@ircm.umontreal.ca
Director and Founder of Center for Bioethics: David J. Roy
Director of Cancer Ethics Program: Dr. Neil MacDonald

This institute performs in-depth studies of the long-term impact of biomedical developments on individuals and on society in general. It brings ethical issues to public attention and participates in professional forums to further educate citizens and professionals about medical conflicts in contemporary society. It is funded by donations, gifts, and grants. In addition to providing workshops and lectures, the institute maintains a documentation center that covers a wide range of bioethical issues and is open to the public.

Publications: A quarterly journal, *The Journal of Palliative Care*; up-to-date research papers in the field of hospice/palliative care; *Bioethics in Canada*, a comprehensive overview of bioethics and the controversies that have occurred in Canada; and *Medicine, Ethics and Law: Canadian and Polish Perspectives*, a book that contains several articles on euthanasia.

Center for Christian Bioethics
Loma Linda University
Griggs Hall, Room 221
Loma Linda, CA 92350
(909) 824-4956
Fax: (909) 824-4856
E-mail: gsample@ccmail.llu.edu
Theological Codirector: David R. Larson, D.Min., Ph.D.

The Center for Christian Bioethics was founded in 1983 to enhance education and research in the area of Christian biomedical ethics. It sponsors a monthly "Medical Ethics Grand Round," in which participants explore medical ethics from diverse points of view, as well as conferences and speakers.

Publications: A newsletter, *Updates*; the books *Bioethics Today: A New Ethical Vision* and *Remnant and Republic: Adventist Themes for Personal and Social Ethics*; and audio and videocassettes of "Medical Ethics Grand Round" sessions.

The Center for the Rights of the Terminally Ill, Inc.
P.O. Box 54246
Hurst, TX 76054-2064
(817) 656-5143
Executive Director: Julie A. Grimstad

Founded in 1986 by Anna Belle Lincoln and Julie Grimstad, the center campaigned for the repeal of the Montana Living Will Act. It opposes euthanasia and assisted suicide and works to promote compassion and respect toward patients who wish to "live with dignity." It provides information to patients, students, physicians, nurses, attorneys, pro-life organizations, and disability groups to help secure the right to competent, professional, compassionate, and ethical health care for the elderly, the handicapped, and the sick and dying. The center develops materials and conducts educational programs designed to highlight the humanity of all individuals. It lobbies for a federal conscience clause law that would allow health care personnel to decline to perform any act of omission or commission that would cause or hasten the death of a patient.

Publications: A quarterly newsletter, *CRTI Report*; a booklet, *Can Cancer Pain Be Relieved?*; and various pamphlets.

Children's Hospice International (CHI)
2202 Mount Vernon Avenue, Suite E3
Alexandria, VA 22301
(800) 24-CHILD
(703) 684-0330
Fax: (703) 684-0226
Founding Director: Ann Armstrong-Dailey

Children's Hospice International (CHI) provides support for terminally ill children and their families. It also connects families with research programs, support organizations, and educational programs involving the care of terminally ill children.

Publications: Numerous, including manuals on home care and pain management for children: *Home Care for Seriously Ill Children: A Manual for Parents; Palliative Pain*, and *Symptom Management for Children and Adolescents*; and a book, *Hospice Care for Children* by Ann Armstrong-Dailey and Sarah Zarbock.

Choice in Dying (CID)
200 Varick Street, 10th Floor
New York, NY 10014-4810
(800) 989-WILL
(212) 366-5540
Fax: (212) 366-5337
E-mail: CID@CHOICES.ORG
Executive Director: Karen O'Kaplan

Choice in Dying (CID) was founded in 1938 by Rev. Charles Potter as the Euthanasia Society of America to lobby for the right of "incurable sufferers" to choose to die. In 1967 the Euthanasia Society added an educational arm called the Euthanasia Educational Fund. The society focused on the legal and legislative aspects of the issues, while the Educational Fund concentrated on educating the public. The Euthanasia Society became the Society for the Right to Die in 1975, and the Educational Fund changed its name to Concern for Dying. In 1979 these two organizations severed their relationship. Both organizations continued to work throughout the 1980s to bring about advances in the law and to educate the public. In September 1991 the two organizations once again found they shared similar goals and merged as Choice in Dying. With more than 160,000 members and a staff of 28, CID is now the largest right-to-die group in America, funded primarily by public subscription. It educates the public about advance directives, living wills, and other issues involving end-of-life decisions.

Publications: The quarterly newsletter *Choices*; living-will documents for every state; books: *Advance Directive Protocols and the Patient Self-Determination Act, Advance Directives and Community Education, Advance Directives and End-of-Life Decisions,* and *Artificial Nutrition/Hydration*; plus videocassettes and pamphlets.

Citizens United in Resisting Euthanasia (CURE)
812 Stephen Street
Berkeley Springs, WV 25411
(304) 258-LIFE
Fax: (304) 258-5420
E-mail: CUREltd.@ix.netcom.com
Director: Earl Appelby Jr.

Citizens United in Resisting Euthanasia (CURE) was founded in 1981 by Madeleine Appelby, a firsthand witness to the Nazi Euthanasia Programme in Germany. This pro-life group works to educate people about the questionable side of the euthanasia movement. It assists and counsels families taking care of their loved ones, and it participated in the Third Annual International Pro-Life Conference sponsored by the Vatican in October 1995.

Publication: Life Matters, a quarterly journal.

Colorado Collective for Medical Decisions, Inc.
777 Grant Street, Suite 206
Denver, CO 80203
(303) 832-3003
Fax: (303) 832-2887
Director: Donald J. Murphy, M.D.
Project Coordinator: Beth Barbour

This is a collective of health care professionals and community members who work with other groups throughout the United States to develop community standards for intensive-care patients considered "futile." Although based in Denver, members work in association with groups in at least 25 other states.

Publication: GUIDE, a biannual publication.

Compassion in Dying
P.O. Box 75295
Seattle, WA 98125-0295
(206) 624-2775
Fax: (206) 624-2673
Executive Director: Ralph Mero, M.Div, D.D.

Compassion was founded in Seattle, Washington, in April 1993 as a nonprofit organization to assist terminally ill patients who are considering hastening death to end their suffering. It offers information, counseling, and emotional support for dying patients and their families. Members include physicians and other trained persons willing to be present at the time of death. To receive information on hastening death, patients must meet a set of criteria set forth in the organization's *Guidelines and Safeguards*. Compassion challenges the constitutionality of state laws that prohibit patients from receiving self-administered prescription medications to hasten death. It is governed by an elected board of directors with an advisory committee that includes professional nurses, doctors, ministers, and counselors.

Publication: The *Compassion in Dying* newsletter.

Death with Dignity Education Center
P.O. Box 1238
San Mateo, CA 94401-0816
(415) 344-6489
Fax: (415) 342-6615
E-mail: ddec@aol.com
Executive Director: Charlotte Ross

Founded in 1994 as the educational arm of Americans for Death with Dignity, the Death with Dignity Education Center is funded primarily by the Gerbode Foundation. The center fosters communication between right-to-die groups through summit meetings.

Deutsche Gesellschaft für Humanes Sterben (DGHS) e.V.
Lange Gasse 2-4
86152 Augsburg
Germany
49-821-50 23 50
Fax: 49-821-5 02 35 55
President: Prof. Dr. Med. Hermann Pohlmeier
Executive Director: Dr. Kurt F. Schobert

Deutsche Gesellschaft für Humanes Sterben (DGHS) was founded in November 1980 to promote the improvement of conditions of dying people in the public health care system. It leads what it considers a civil rights movement to guarantee the right to self-determination through the final moments of life. It represents citizens who wish to safeguard their right to shorten the process of dying for humanitarian reasons and has taken the lead in preparing consent forms that meet German Penal Code (§ 226a StGB) requirements and drafting legislation. The DGHS is independent of all political parties; cooperates on an international level with like organizations; organizes conferences, congresses, and seminars; promotes scientific research; and provides personal counseling.

Dying with Dignity
188 Eglinton Avenue East, #705
Toronto, Ontario M4P 2X7
Canada
(416) 486-3998
Fax: (416) 489-9010
Web: http://www.web.apc.org/dwd
Executive Director: Marilynn Seguin

Founded in 1980 this charitable society seeks to improve the quality of dying for Canadians in keeping with their individual wishes, values, and beliefs. It provides education, counseling, advocacy, living wills, and powers of attorney for health care, and it promotes public support for physician aid-in-dying. The organization also supports a research library and offers speakers.

Publications: A quarterly newsletter, *Dying with Dignity*; legal forms including "Enduring Power of Attorney for Personal Care" and "Voluntary Euthanasia Declaration"; and a book, *Gentle Death*, by Marilynn Seguin.

Euthanasia Research and Guidance Organization (ERGO)
24829 Norris Lane
Junction City, OR 97448-9559
(503) 998-3285
Fax: (503) 998-1873
E-mail: ergo@efn.org
Web: http://www.enf.org/ergo
President: Derek Humphrey

The Euthanasia Research and Guidance Organization (ERGO) was founded in 1992 by Derek Humphrey (author of *Final Exit*) to conduct research into aspects of voluntary euthanasia and develop euthanasia guidelines, to provide information for families or individuals experiencing an imminent end-of-life situation, and to provide resources for scholars and the media on the historical and ethical issues surrounding euthanasia.

Publications: Occasional newsletter; several books including *Deciding To Die: What You Should Consider, Assisting a Patient To Die: A Guide for Physicians*, and *Self-Deliverance from an End-Stage Terminal Illness by Use of a Plastic Bag*; and additional information available via the World Wide Web site.

EXIT A.D.M.D. Suisse Romande
Association pour le Droit de Mourir dans la Dignité
Case Postale 100
CH-1222 Vésenaz
Genève CCP: 12-8183-2
Switzerland
41-022-735-77-60
Fax: 41-022-735-77-65
Executive Director: Jeanne Marchig

Founded in 1983 to serve the French-speaking area of Switzerland, EXIT currently has more than 6,000 members.

Publication: A biannual journal in French.

Fondation Responsable Jusqu'a la Fin
10150, rue de Bretagne
Québec G2B 2R1
Canada
(418) 843-8807
Fax: (418) 845-2661
President: Yvon Bureau

This foundation does not promote euthanasia and assisted suicide per se, but instead it supports the use of living wills and

durable power of attorney documents in the province of Quebec
and French-speaking Canada. It undertakes activities that help
ensure a quality end of life and seeks to help individuals die
without suffering.

Fundación Pro Derecho a Morir Dignamente
Carrera 11, No. 73-44, Of. 508
A.A. 88900
Bogotá, Colombia
57-1-345-4065
Fax: 57-1-313-1607
Executive Director: Isabel Mejia de Camargo

This is a nonprofit organization founded in 1979 to help individuals exercise their right, already established in Colombia, to
decide whether to receive treatment in the case of terminal illness, with the goal of avoiding the useless prolongation of life
and unnecessary suffering. It helps individuals complete living
wills and is attempting to make this document legally binding.
The group works with health care professionals to encourage
changes in the treatment of the terminally ill. It also distributes
living wills and holds conferences and seminars.

Publications: Several monographs and the biannual *Reflexiones en
Torno del Derecho a Morir Dignamente.*

The Hastings Center
255 Elm Road
Briarcliff Manor, NY 10510
(914) 762-8500
Fax: (914) 762-2124
President: Daniel Callahan

The Hastings Center was founded in 1969 to help people understand and resolve the many ethical questions raised by advances
in the biomedical sciences. It currently has more than 11,500
members and a staff of 28. Comprising lawyers, physicians, scientists, professors, government officials, and business leaders, this
organization provides education to health care professionals, students, corporate officials, journalists, and international scholars. It
conducts research on issues relevant to ethics and offers consulting services. Members have been asked to testify before legislators on issues as diverse as AIDS, test-tube babies, organ
transplantation, and end-of-life decisions. Members also help
write legislation, offer speaking services, and sit on congressional
panels. The center houses a library used by government officials,

researchers, and visiting scholars. Conferences and workshops are frequently held at the facility. Current research projects include: *Good Medicine, Good Society; Decisions near the End of Life;* and *Ethical and Policy Issues in Hospice Care.*

Publications: Two bimonthly journals, *Hastings Center Report* and *IRB: A Review of Human Subjects Research,* plus a series of reports and educational supplements.

The Hemlock Society USA
P.O. Box 101810
Denver, CO 80250
(800) 247-7421
(303) 639-1224
E-mail: hemlock@privatei.com
Head of Information Services: Cindy Putnam

The Hemlock Society was founded in 1980 in Los Angeles by Derek Humphrey, Ann Wickett, Gerald Larue, and Richard S. Scott. It moved from Eugene, Oregon, to Denver in 1996. The society reports that it has more than 57,000 members and 80,000 supporters. It was founded on the belief that terminally ill people should have the right to self-determination in all end-of-life decisions and that a reverence for life demands that the dying be able to retain their dignity, integrity, and self-respect. Hemlock encourages public acceptance of active voluntary euthanasia for the terminally ill through a program of education and research and advocates changes in the law to allow voluntary physician aid-in-dying for the terminally ill. To this end, it provides speakers, maintains a collection of research materials, sends out information on aid-in-dying upon request, provides crisis intervention over the phone for callers who need help locating resources, acts as a clearinghouse for information involving legislation and court cases, and encourages members to become involved in local political processes involving dying with dignity. The Hemlock Society sponsors an annual national "Dying with Dignity" conference. It has nearly 50 state and local chapters throughout the United States and is supported by membership fees, donations, and the sale of educational materials.

Publications: Books by founder Derek Humphrey, including *Final Exit, Let Me Die before I Wake,* and *The Right To Die,* as well as books by other authors; a bimonthly newsletter, *Timelines,* plus reprints of the 1988 "Drug Dosage Table" and "A Letter to My Physician" (a document that can be used by individuals to help them communicate their end-of-life desires to their physician).

Hospice Association of America
228 Seventh Street, S.E.
Washington, DC 20003
(202) 546-4759
Fax: (202) 547-9559
Web: http://www.nahc.org
Executive Director: Janet E. Neigh

The Hospice Association of America is a membership organization founded in 1985 to promote quality care for hospice patients, preserve the rights of caregivers, represent hospice providers, and make hospice care a central part of health care delivery. It is now the largest lobbying group for hospice care in the United States, representing more than 2,000 hospices nationwide.

Publications: Hospice Forum, a biweekly newsletter focusing on legislative, regulatory, and legal updates; *Caring Magazine* and the *Homecare News* newspaper, both monthly; and books including *Hospice: A Consumer's Guide, The Tao of Dying: A Guide to Caring,* and *The National Homecare and Hospice Directory.*

HospiceLink
Hospice Education Institute
190 Westbrook Road, #2
Essex, CT 06426
(800) 331-1620
Fax: (860) 767-2746
Executive Director: Michael Galazka

HospiceLink provides information about hospice care, refers patients to hospice programs, and maintains an up-to-date computerized directory of hospices and related care services throughout the United States. It provides callers with an understanding of hospice care, offers free advice to persons who wish to develop a hospice in their community, and offers consultations, continuing education for health care professionals, and seminars around the world.

Publications: Booklets: *Notes on Symptom Control in Hospice and Palliative Care, Letting Go: Caring for the Dying and Bereaved, How Many Times Can You Say Good-Bye, The Hospice Movement,* and *Being There: Pastoral Care in Time of Illness.*

Human Life International
7845 Airpark Road, Suite E
Gaithersburg, MD 20879
(301) 670-7884

Fax: (301) 869-7363
President: Paul Marx

Founded in 1981, Human Life International serves as a research, educational, and service program offering positive alternatives to what the group calls the "anti-life/anti-family movement." It lists more than 500,000 members and has a staff of 85. It explores and comments on natural family planning, population issues, abortion, infanticide, and euthanasia, and it sponsors symposia and an annual conference.

Publications: The monthly newsletter, *HLI Reports*; the bimonthly newsletter *PRI Review*; the quarterly magazine *Escoge la Vida*; books such as *Death without Dignity* and *Confessions of a Prolife Missionary*; and special reports.

Institute for Jewish Medical Ethics
645 14th Avenue
San Francisco, CA 94118
(800) 258-4427

This is a membership organization that sponsors an annual international conference on the subject of medical ethics as it specifically relates to the Jewish religion. The group also provides information in book and tape form for those interested in learning more about conference topics.

Publications: Audiocassettes of conference proceedings on topics such as "Science, Technology and Jewish Ethos," "Advance Directives for Health Care: Prospects and Pitfalls," "Fateful Choices at Bedside: A Comparative Analysis of the Pressures To End Life in Pre-Holocaust Nazi Germany and in Present Day Medicine"; also numerous books and pamphlets, including *Medicine and Jewish Law, Modern Medicine and Jewish Ethics,* and *Time of Death.*

International Anti-Euthanasia Task Force (IAETF)
University of Steubenville
P.O. Box 760
Steubenville, OH 43952
(614) 282-3810 or (510) 689-0170
Fax: (614) 282-0769 or (510) 687-2943
Executive Director: Rita Marker
Public Information Director: Kathi Hamlon

Formed in 1987, this human rights group and educational network is a division of the Family Living Council and is supported by donations. IAETF brings together individuals and organizations that oppose euthanasia; provides information on euthanasia, suicide, assisted suicide, and related issues; draws attention to the pressure to "get out of the way" placed on individuals who are chronically ill, terminally ill, dependent, or disabled; and promotes and defends the right of all persons to be treated with respect, dignity, and compassion. The organization resists attitudes, programs, and policies that are thought to threaten the lives and rights of those who are medically vulnerable.

Publications: A bimonthly newsletter, *IAETF Update;* brochures on "Euthanasia Practice in Holland," "The Waiting Room A.D. 2020," and "The Facts about Jack Kevorkian"; and a protective identification card identifying the signer as someone who opposes euthanasia and assisted suicide. Videos available for purchase include *Euthanasia: False Light; California Debate "Aid in Dying"; A Matter of Death and Life—The Future?;* and *Coffee and Conversation.*

International Life Services, Inc.
2606 1/2 W. 8th Street
Los Angeles, CA 90057
(213) 382-2156
Fax: (213) 382-4203
Executive Director: Sr. Paula Vandegaer S.S.S.

Founded in 1985, this Judeo-Christian–oriented research and educational association works to promote the pro-life movement and to foster respect for human life from the moment of conception until natural death. It recognizes only God as having legitimate power over life and death and promotes alternatives to abortion and euthanasia. Each spring the organization sponsors an annual Learning Center conference.

Publications: Several periodicals including an occasional *ILSI Newsletter*, quarterly *Living World*, and biennial *Pro-Life Resource Manual*, as well as teaching materials and audiotapes.

Israeli Society for Dying with Dignity
P.O. Box 439
Herzliya B46103
Israel 6127
972-3-561-2892
Contact Person: Rivka Hochhoiser

This organization is a member of the World Federation of Right to Die Societies.

Japan Society for Dying with Dignity
Watanabe Building, 202, 229-1
Hongou, Bunkyo-Ku
Tokyo No. 118
Japan
03-3518-8503
Fax: 03-9818-8552
Executive Director: Ken Minami
CEO: Kaoru Narita

Founded in 1976, the Japan Society for Dying with Dignity works to help promote living wills, which are not currently accepted by the physician's association of this country. The organization has six chapters with 74,000 members and provides telephone consultation to members and nonmembers alike. Originals of living wills are kept on file by the organization to make it possible to negotiate with physicians who refuse to acknowledge the document.

Publication: A quarterly newsletter in Japanese, which is also excerpted in English.

Kennedy Institute of Ethics
Georgetown University
Box 571212
Washington, DC 20057-1212
(202) 687-2099
Fax: (202) 687-8089
Director: Dr. Robert M. Veatch
Director of Library Services: Doris Goldstein, M.L.S., M.A.

The Joseph and Rose Kennedy Institute of Ethics was established at Georgetown University in 1971. A teaching and research center, it offers moral and ethical perspectives on major policy issues. It is the largest university-based group of scholars in the world devoted to the research and teaching of biomedical ethics. The institute also houses the most extensive ethics library in the world, with more than 20,000 books and 100,000 articles. It offers seminars and courses on bioethics.

Publications: The quarterly *Kennedy Institute of Ethics Journal*; an online medical ethics database, "BIOETHICSLINE," and its annual print version, *Bibliography of Bioethics*; and two series: *New Titles in Bioethics* and *Scope Note Series*.

Landsforeningen Mitt Livestement
Lybekkv 9 b,
11182 Oslo, Norway
47-2-1456-30
Secretary: Unni Bohmer

Landsforeningen Mitt Livestement is a member of the World
Federation of Right to Die Societies.

MacLean Center for Clinical Medical Ethics
University of Chicago
MC 6098
5841 S. Maryland Avenue
Chicago, IL 60637-1470
(312) 702-1453
Fax: (312) 702-0090
E-mail: krainey@medicine.bsd.uchicago.edu
Web: http://ccme-mac4.bsd.uchicago.edu/CCME.html
Director: Mark Siegler, M.D.

Founded in 1984, the MacLean Center provides training and
education for physicians, as well as consultation services for
patients and their families. The faculty (physicians, nurses, legal
scholars, philosophers, and social scientists) explores medical-
ethical concerns and provides ethics programs—tailored for
individual institutions—that include education, assessment of
current mechanisms for addressing ethical concerns, suggestions for improvement, and consultation on individual cases.
Areas of expertise include limiting or withdrawing treatments,
DNR orders, artificial nutrition and hydration, brain death,
advance directives, nondiscrimination, and disclosure of errors.
The center houses an extensive medical ethics library.

Publication: The newsletter *Doctor-Patient Studies* on the World
Wide Web.

National Chronic Pain Outreach Association (NCPOA)
7979 Old Georgetown Road, Suite 100
Bethesda, MD 20814
(301) 652-4948
Fax: (301) 907-0745
President: William Hurwitz

A nonprofit, membership organization funded by dues, grants,
and gifts, National Chronic Pain Outreach Association (NCPOA)

was established in 1980. It maintains a computerized registry of chronic pain support groups in the United States and Canada, provides referrals to medical and psychological services, and supplies support group starter kits to those interested in developing a group in their community.

Publications: A quarterly newsletter, *Lifeline,* and several pamphlets: *Pain Research, Yesterday and Today; Prescribing Opiods: The Physician's Dilemma;* and *Myths and Misconceptions about Chronic Pain.*

National Citizen's Coalition for Nursing Home Reform (NCCNHR)
1424 16th Street, N.W., Suite 202
Washington, DC 20036
(202) 332-2275
Fax: (202) 332-2949

Founded in 1975, this nonprofit consumer advocacy organization works to ensure quality long-term care for residents of nursing homes. It reviews and distributes information on legal, legislative, and regulatory issues related to long-term care and tracks government enforcement activities. The coalition intervenes on behalf of consumers, helps ensure that decisions made by the courts are implemented in nursing home settings, and educates medical professionals and consumers about the status of current laws regarding long-term care issues.

Publications: A bimonthly newsletter, *Quality Care Advocate,* and several books: *Consumer Perspective on Quality Care: The Residents' Point of View; Restraints—Chemical or Physical; Avoiding Drugs Used as Chemical Restraints;* and *Avoiding Physical Restraint Use.*

National Conference of Catholic Bishops
Secretariat for Pro-Life Activities
3211 4th Street, N.E.
Washington, DC 20017-1194
(202) 541-3070
Fax: (202) 541-3054

This group joins in the Vatican's opposition to all forms of euthanasia and promotes awareness of that opposition throughout the Catholic community.

Publication: Life at Risk, a magazine published ten times a year.

National Electronic Archive of Advance Directives (NEAAD)
Department H
11000 Cedar Avenue
Cleveland, OH 44106-3052
(800) 379-6866
President: Ron Buford

Advance directives registered with the National Electronic Archive of Advance Directives (NEAAD) can be retrieved by family members or health care providers as needed via fax within 15 minutes of a request. Directives stored in the electronic registry are reviewed by Choice in Dying's legal staff to make sure they comply with relevant state laws. Registration cost: $24, plus a $12.50 annual renewal fee.

National Hospice Foundation (NHF)
1901 N. Moore Street, Suite 901
Arlington, VA 22209
(703) 516-4928
Fax: (703) 525-5762
Hospice Helpline: (800) 658-8898

Formed in 1978 to make hospice care an integral part of the health care system in the United States, the National Hospice Foundation (NHF) provides education, training, speakers, and technical expertise. The foundation works to influence health programs and public policy as these affect the terminally ill and those who care for them. It houses a comprehensive library of books, videotapes, audiotapes, and directories related to hospice care and sponsors several conferences each year on a wide range of subjects, including "Bereavement Care," "Volunteerism," "Spiritual Care," "Psychosocial Aspects," and "Physical Care Issues."

Publications: NHF Newsline, HOSPICE Magazine, Guide to the Nation's Hospices; technical manuals: *Hospice Operations Manual, Standards of a Hospice Program of Care*, and *Volunteer Training Curriculum*; plus numerous pamphlets, brochures, books, videos, and gift items.

National Right to Life Committee (NRLC)
419 7th Street, N.W., Suite 500
Washington, DC 20004-2293
(202) 626-8800

Web: http://www.nrlc.org/euthanasia/willtolive/index.html
Fax: (202) 737-9189 or (202) 347-5907
Executive Director: David N. O'Steen, Ph.D.

Founded in 1973, this is the largest pro-life group in the United States, with about 3,000 chapters. It works to protect lives threatened by abortion, infanticide, and euthanasia; provides a state-specific "Will To Live" to those who send a stamped, self-addressed envelope to the Will To Live Project (NRLC); opposes both passive and active euthanasia; and works to protect life through lobbying and legislative efforts on the federal and state levels.

Publications: The biweekly *NRL News* and "Will To Live."

Nederlands Vereniging voor Vrijwillige Euthanasie (NVVE)
Postbus 75331, Leidsegracht 103, 2d Floor
1070 AH Amsterdam
The Netherlands
31-20-420-5208
Fax: 31-20-420-7216
Contact Person: Jean Roell

Founded in 1973, Nederlands Vereniging voor Vrjwillige Euthanasie (NVVE), or the "Netherlands Society for Voluntary Euthanasia," currently has more than 85,000 members. It was an active participant in the debate process that led to the acceptance of physician-assisted death in the Netherlands. It promotes social acceptance and legalization of euthanasia in the Netherlands.

Publications: Numerous publications in Dutch.

Park Ridge Center
211 E. Ontario, Suite 800
Chicago, IL 60611-3215
(312) 266-2222
Fax: (312) 266-6086
President and CEO: Laurence O'Connell

Founded in 1985, Park Ridge is an interreligious, multidisciplinary institute for the study of health, faith, and ethics. The center fills what its members perceive to be a worldwide need for the study of religious aspects of human well-being, especially as related to prevention and treatment of disease, interpretation of illness and health, and similar concerns. It serves as an international forum for exchange and debate among experts in health care, religion, law, and ethics.

Publications: The quarterly magazine *Second Opinion* and several books, including *Caring and Curing, Healing and Restoring, Health and Medicine in the Faith Traditions,* and *Healthy People 2000—A Role for America's Religious Communities.*

Right to Die Society of Canada (RDSC)
P.O. Box 39018
Victoria, BC V8V 4X8
Canada
(604) 380-1112
Web: http://www.rights.org/~death
Fax: (604) 386-3800
E-mail: rights@islandnet.com
Executive Director: John Hofsess

The Right to Die Society of Canada was founded in 1991 to give Canadians a practical means of changing the law to permit choice-in-dying. It commissioned a national preelection poll in 1993 on voter attitudes toward right-to-die issues. This is the organization that initiated the Sue Rodriguez legal challenge in 1992, which has opened the doors of the physician-assisted death battle to provide an equal right to die for those who are physically incapable of committing suicide. RDSC has a Canadian focus but is international in the range of services it provides.

Publications: The journal *Last Rights*; two books: *Beyond Final Exit* and *Departing Drugs*; the website, DeathNET.

SAVES—The Living Will Society
P.O. Box 1460
Wandsbeck 3631
Republic of South Africa
27-031-266-8511
Fax: 27-031-867-0092
Director: Brigid Raw

Founded in 1974, SAVES—The Living Will Society currently has approximately 32,000 members. It supports passive euthanasia only. There are currently no laws governing end-of-life decision making in South Africa. SAVES promotes the use of living wills and supports the right to refuse heroic measures and other extraordinary treatment.

Publication: A landmark paper on all aspects of euthanasia was published in 1996.

The Voluntary Euthanasia Society
13 Prince of Wales Terrace
Kensington, London W8 5PG
England
44-171-937-7770
Fax: 44-171-376-2648
E-mail: ves.london@dial.pipex.com
Executive Director: John Oliver

Founded in 1935 by a group of doctors, the Voluntary Euthanasia Society lobbies to change the law so that incurably ill adults who are suffering unbearably can receive medical assistance in achieving a peaceful death at their own considered request. The society also distributes advance directives for the refusal of unwanted life-prolonging treatment. It is a member of the World Federation of Right to Die Societies.

Publications: A newsletter, information sheets on right-to-die issues, and an educational video.

World Federation of Right to Die Societies
61 Minterne Avenue
Norwood Green
Southall, Middlesex
England UB2 4HP
44-181-574-3775
Fax: 44-181-893-5986

and

P.O. Box 162
Francestown, NH 03043
Web: http://www.efn.org/~ergo/rights.news.html
Secretary: Malcolm Hurwitt

This federation represents most major right-to die groups and has member organizations in Australia, Belgium, Britain, Canada, Colombia, Finland, France, Germany, India, Israel, Japan, Luxembourg, the Netherlands, New Zealand, Norway, South Africa, Spain, Sweden, Switzerland, and the United States. It sponsors a biannual World Conference, which was held in Melbourne, Australia, in October 1996.

Publication: Quarterly *Newsletter.*

Selected Print Resources

6

A lthough death has always been a popular literary subject, within the past 30 years the virtual explosion of written material on end-of-life issues has mirrored the rapid escalation of interest and concern worldwide. Euthanasia, bioethics, philosophy of dying, living wills, and assisted suicide are some of the significant topics in this growing body of contemporary literature.

This chapter contains the most significant and unique of these materials available in print format. Accessibility was taken into account during the difficult selection process. General books and reference sources are included to provide background information. These are followed by specialized nonfiction sources, which are divided into the three categories used throughout the book: Medical-Bioethical, Spiritual-Social-Cultural, and Legal-Political. Listings are alphabetical within each of these sections, and all are annotated. Several recent works of fiction that have helped bring euthanasia into the cultural foreground are then listed, followed by selected periodicals. Only periodicals that deal primarily with the issues surrounding euthanasia and assisted suicide are listed.

Books: General and Reference

Atkinson, David, and David H. Field, eds. **The New Dictionary of Christian Ethics and Pastoral Theology.** Downers Grove, IL: Intervarsity Press, 1995. 918 pp. ISBN 0-85110-650-1.

This dictionary covers a broad range of Christian ethics, with entries on euthanasia, the ethics of medical care, coma, consent, the double effect, and quality of life. Information is presented from a Christian point of view. This reference book is a good point of departure for people who wish to gain an understanding of the issues raised by those opposed to euthanasia and assisted suicide.

Beresford, Larry. **The Hospice Handbook.** Boston, MA: Little, Brown, 1993. 165 pp. ISBN 0-316-09138-3.

The Hospice Handbook offers a wealth of end-of-life resources for patients who wish to know more about hospice care. It provides readers with a clear understanding of what hospices can and cannot offer to patients with chronic care needs. It provides a history of hospice care, requirements for enrollment, an explanation of services, a description of the team approach taken by caregivers, and several personal accounts. Commonly asked questions are also addressed in sections on insurance coverage and legal issues associated with hospice care, such as advance directives. Additional chapters cover what hospice care can offer AIDS patients and children. Elisabeth Kübler-Ross provides a foreword.

Cox, Donald W. **Hemlock's Cup.** Buffalo, NY: Prometheus Books, 1993. 311 pp. ISBN 0-087975-808-2.

Cox documents the history of the euthanasia movement in the United States. Legislation from a number of states is examined, as are patient case histories and descriptions of court cases against doctors accused of murdering their patients. Comprehensive through the early 1990s, this key source offers a clear understanding of the many factors that have affected the legal-political debate.

Duncan, A. S., et al., eds. **Dictionary of Medical Ethics.** New York: Crossroad, 1981. 496 pp. ISBN 0-8245-0338-5.

This well-referenced dictionary provides an excellent introduction to the new field of bioethics and is accessible to the lay reader.

Euthanasia: Opposing Viewpoints. San Diego: Greenhaven Press, 1989. 312 pp. ISBN 1-56-510-244-4 (hardcover), 1-56510-243-6 (paperback).

This book presents euthanasia as seen though the eyes of 25 leading authorities in the field. Contributors include Dr. Timothy Quill, Jack Kevorkian, Daniel Callahan, Derek Humphrey, and Edmund Pellegrino. A good source for those who seek a variety of perspectives on the debate.

Farberow, Norman L., ed. **Suicide in Different Cultures.** Baltimore, MD: University Park Press, 1975. 286 pp. ISBN 0-8391-0843-5.

This compilation of articles offers unique views on suicide from a number of world cultures. Chapters on the Netherlands, the United States, India, and Japan are particularly interesting and help illuminate cultural taboos regarding intentional dying around the world.

Fulton, Gere B., and Eileen K. Metress. **Perspectives on Death and Dying.** Boston: Jones and Bartlett, 1995. 505 pp. ISBN 0-86720-926-7.

This widely used college textbook covers all aspects of death and dying among the young and the old. It contains many useful illustrations, including maps and photographs.

Humphrey, Derek, and Ann Wickett. **The Right To Die: Understanding Euthanasia.** Eugene, OR: The Hemlock Society, 1990. 372 pp. ISBN 0-06-091411-4.

Originally published by Harper & Row in 1986, this landmark book provides an in-depth historical-cultural background of the euthanasia debate, as well as a discussion of its legal and religious development dating back to ancient Greece. *The Right To Die* offers clarification of the terminology used and an analysis of the various forms of euthanasia and suicide. The poignant and provocative stories behind several key legal cases are also presented. This volume is one of the most comprehensive sources available, both in scope and in terms of the number of resources cited. An excellent reference source through the 1980s.

Kohl, Marvin, ed. **Beneficent Euthanasia.** Buffalo, NY: Prometheus Books, 1975. 255 pp. ISBN 0-8797-7504-2.

This book contains 19 essays arguing in favor of both passive and active euthanasia, each addressing a different aspect of the issue. Although the book has a definite bias, potential problems and safeguards are suggested. An annotated bibliography is included.

————, ed. **Infanticide and the Value of Life.** Buffalo, NY: Prometheus Books, 1978. 353 pp. ISBN 0-87975-100-2.

Infanticide and the Value of Life examines the question of what the editor terms *benevolent infanticide,* in which steps are taken to help or minimize the suffering of severely deformed infants. The writers explore the limits of the value of human life and discuss the protective measures needed for society's most vulnerable members. The book is divided into the following subject areas: religious/ethical, medical/anthropological, and psychological, legal, and ideological/philosophical.

Landau, Elaine. **The Right To Die.** Danbury, CT: Watts, 1993. 96 pp. ISBN 0-531-13015-0.

This is a comprehensive survey of the right-to-die debate for younger readers, providing a balanced examination of issues such as denial of treatment for disabled infants, young adult rights, and various forms of suicide and euthanasia.

Mullens, Anne. **When Timely Death? A Consideration of Our Last Rights.** Toronto: Knopf Canada, 1996.

Mullens is an award-winning Canadian medical reporter. An Atkinson Foundation Award for Public Policy allowed her to spend a full year thoroughly researching right-to-die issues in Canada, the United States, and around the world, including the Netherlands. The results of her preliminary research were first published as a series of articles in *Last Rights* magazine (Winter 1995). This book is an integrated review of the numerous in-depth interviews she conducted with individuals who have never before told their stories. This is certain to become a very important book in the field.

Nolan, Anita L., and Mary Coutts, eds. **International Directory of Bioethics Organizations.** GA: National Reference Center for Bioethics Literature, 1994. 371 pp. ISBN 1-883912-11-X.

This annotated directory lists more than 300 organizations in 40 countries involved in the emerging field of bioethics. Listings are arranged by country in alphabetical order.

Reich, Warren T., ed. **Encyclopedia of Bioethics.** Rev. ed. New York: Macmillan, 1995. ISBN 0-02-897355-0.

A comprehensive source of information on a broad range of bioethical issues.

Steinbock, Bonnie, and Alastair Norcross. **Killing and Letting Die.** 2d ed. New York: Fordham University Press, 1994. 320 pp. ISBN 0-8232-1563-6.

This highly respected collection of essays contains virtually all of the major essays published prior to 1994 on the subtle distinction between killing someone and allowing that person to die. It also includes an excellent bibliography on the topic, which provides a crucial distinction to further illuminate concepts noted in many laws and ethical guidelines.

Veatch, Robert M. **Death, Dying and the Biological Revolution: Our Last Quest for Responsibility.** New Haven, CT: Yale University Press, 1976. 323 pp. ISBN 0-300-01949-1.

Veatch provides a comprehensive look at death, including medical, moral, and political aspects of how we die in contemporary times. The right to die is studied from numerous perspectives, offering readers a wealth of information on this complex topic.

Nonfiction Resources

Medical-Bioethical

Armstrong-Dailey, Ann, and Sarah Zarbock. **Hospice Care for Children.** New York: Oxford University Press, 1993. 289 pp. ISBN 0-19-507312-6.

Written by the founder of Children's Hospice International, this book provides enormous insight into the care of terminally ill children. The roles of family, health care providers, and volunteers are all explored.

Asch, D. A., et al. **"Decisions To Limit or Continue Life-Sustaining Treatment by Critical Care Physicians in the United States: Conflicts between Physician Practices and Patients' Wishes."** *American Journal of Respiratory and Critical Care Medicine* 151 (1995): 288–292.

This article summarizes a survey of 879 physicians in the United States aimed at revealing the practice of limiting life-sustaining treatment or making decisions to forego treatment. The researchers explore ways in which patients' wishes are respected or ignored in this process.

Barnard, Christiaan. **Good Life/Good Death.** Englewood Cliffs, NJ: Prentice Hall, 1980. 146 pp. ISBN 0-13-360370-9.

Written by the world-famous heart surgeon who performed the first human heart transplant, this book is as pertinent today as it was when it was published. Dr. Barnard uses examples from his practice to illuminate with warmth and wisdom the struggles that lead some patients to contemplate euthanasia or suicide. He provides a step-by-step look at the decision-making process from the physician's point of view and offers a closer look into the world of the modern physician, in which the death of a patient is considered a professional failure.

Battin, Margaret Pabst. **The Least Worst Death: Essays in Bio-ethics at the End of Life.** New York: Oxford University Press, 1994. 320 pp. ISBN 0-19-508265.

This book explores the end-of-life decision-making process from a bioethical point of view, rather than an emotional or personal perspective. The lack of painless alternatives in many instances becomes clear as essay follows upon essay.

————. **"Age Rationing and the Just Distribution of Health Care: Is There a Duty To Die?"** *Ethics* 97 (January 1987): 317–340.

Battin questions the wisdom of expending a large percentage of health care dollars on end-of-life treatment and explores several key ethical issues raised by this thorny topic.

Battin, Margaret, and Arthur J. Lipman, eds. **Drug Use in Assisted Suicide and Euthanasia.** Binghamton, NY: Pharma-ceutical Products Press, 1996. 376 pp. ISBN 1-56024-814-9 (hard-cover), 1-56024-843-2 (paperback).

The health profession's own version of *Final Exit*. Edited jointly by professors of philosophy and pharmacology, each chapter is written by a different expert. This book explores the potentially important role of the pharmacist in assisted suicide and eutha-nasia, and points out that fewer than 10 percent of all patients who contact Compassion in Dying (Seattle) to make serious inquiries about rational suicide actually meet that organization's criteria and are helped. Another chapter provides very valuable information about how doctors help patients die in the Nether-lands. An extremely comprehensive book aimed at health care professionals.

Beauchamp, Tom L., and James F. Childress. **Principles of Biomedical Ethics: A Clinical Textbook and Reference for the Health Care Profession.** Oxford, England: Oxford University Press, 1994. 560 pp. ISBN 0-1950-8537-X.

One of the first philosophical discussions of biomedical ethics, this textbook takes principles used in general ethics and applies them to the field of health care. It presents a provocative analysis of ethics in the health care arena.

Belkin, Lisa. **First, Do No Harm.** New York: Simon & Schuster, 1993. 270 pp. ISBN 0-671-68538-4.

Belkin, a *New York Times* reporter, spent three years (1988–1991) sitting in on meetings of the Ethics Committee of Hermann Hospital in Houston, Texas. Her book is based on interviews, meetings, and regular attendance at actual decision-making sessions involving physicians and their patients. The true stories recorded here put human faces on the end-of-life decision-making process, providing readers with a visceral sense of how these difficult decisions are made. Belkin reports on the actions of individuals and institutions but allows the reader to decide where to draw the line in the shifting sands of these emotional questions.

Callahan, Daniel. **Setting Limits: Medical Goals in an Aging Society.** New York: Simon & Schuster, 1987. 256 pp. ISBN 0-671-22477-8.

Callahan, cofounder and director of the Hastings Center, questions medicine's goals for a rapidly aging population in a time of limited resources. He argues that we are not serving the needs of the elderly by prolonging their lives without giving them better quality of life, and he asserts that medical practice should be oriented toward offering preventive care and better quality of life for the elderly while they are living and relief of suffering as they are dying. *Setting Limits* is one of three nonfiction books nominated in 1987 for a Pulitzer Prize.

Cohen, Cynthia B., ed. **Casebook on the Termination of Life-Sustaining Treatment and the Care of the Dying.** Bloomington: Indiana University Press, 1988. 176 pp. ISBN 0-253-212-07-03.

Twenty-six actual cases in which life-sustaining treatment was terminated illuminate the many questions raised by our ability to use medical technology to prevent death. Each case study explores these questions from the perspectives of patients, family members, physicians, nurses, lawyers, and health care administrators.

Cundiff, David. **Euthanasia Is Not the Answer: A Hospice Physician's View.** Totowa, NJ: Humana Press, 1992. 190 pp. ISBN 0-89603-237-X.

This book presents an interesting counterpoint to Dr. Timothy Quill's groundbreaking book *Death and Dignity: Making Choices and Taking Charge*. Although these two physicians share a similar professional experience with terminally ill patients, they arrive at strikingly different conclusions regarding the role physician-assisted death should play in end-of-life decision making.

Duff, Raymond S., and A. G. M. Campbell. **"Moral and Ethical Dilemmas in the Special Care Nursery."** *New England Journal of Medicine* 289 (1973): 890–894.

This was one of the first articles to explore the ethical issues raised by the increasing ability of high-tech interventions to saves the lives of severely deformed infants.

Emanuel, E., and L. Emanuel. **"The Economics of Dying: The Illusion of Cost Savings at the End of Life."** *New England Journal of Medicine* 330 (1994): 540–544.

The authors examine various ways to calculate the cost of end-of-life care, shedding light on the impact of managed care on the delivery of health care.

Fletcher, Joseph. **Humanhood: Essays in Biomedical Ethics**. Buffalo, NY: Prometheus Books, 1979. 204 pp. ISBN 0-8797-5123-1.

Humanhood is a classic work of general medical ethics by the father of the bioethics movement.

Gaylin, Willard, and Ruth Macklin. **Who Speaks for the Child? The Problem of Proxy Consent.** New York: Plenum Press, 1982. 301 pp. ISBN 0-306-40860-0.

Cowritten by a past president of the Hastings Center, this work represents one of the first attempts to determine guidelines for when a child is ready to take part in medical decision making.

Hanson, Mark J. **Voices in the Wilderness: Theological Voices in Medical Ethics.** Grand Rapids, MI: William B. Erdmans, 1993. 256 pp.

Voices in the Wilderness brings together the theological voices that have contributed to the bioethics movement, including: Paul Ramsey (a Roman Catholic theologian), James Childress (a Quaker religious educator), Immanual Jakobovits (a Jewish rabbi), and Richard McCormick (a Roman Catholic priest). Together these essays, all originally published elsewhere, provide a comprehensive picture of the development of bioethics since the 1960s, clarifying important shifts in thinking. The writers examine several assumptions basic to the discussion, including the idea that no decision is absolutely and permanently right. They also provide an important theological exploration of bioethics.

Harvard Medical School, Ad Hoc Committee of the Harvard Medical School to Examine the Definition of Brain Death. **"A Definition of Irreversible Coma."** *Journal of the American Medical Association* 205 (1968): 337–340.

This report lays the biomedical foundation for much of the current policy and law regarding withdrawal of life support and passive euthanasia in the United States.

Humber, James M., R. F. Almeder, and Gregg A. Kasting, eds. **Physician-Assisted Death.** Totowa, NJ: Humana Press, 1993. 155 pp. ISBN 0-8960-3265-5.

Physician-Assisted Death presents the topic of physician-assisted death from several points of view. Each chapter is written by an authority in the field of ethics, philosophy, biomedical ethics, or medicine. The book includes discussions of doctors' attitudes toward the practice and the constitutionality of physician-assisted death, as well as ethical questions, and covers terminology, arguments, polls, and whether euthanasia is necessary today given recent advances in pain control. The final chapter tells the story of Thomas Donaldson, a patient with an inoperable brain tumor. His unusual legal request to be killed and cryogenically frozen presents a unique problem that indicates the directions in which this debate is likely to develop.

Humphrey, Derek. **Final Exit: The Practicalities of Self-Deliverance and Assisted Suicide.** Eugene, OR: The Hemlock Society, 1991. 192 pp. ISBN 0-9696030-3-4.

This controversial book has been called everything from the terminal patient's Bible to a suicide manual. It is the first book about suicide and euthanasia to make the best-seller list, but it also has been widely condemned as irresponsible and a hazard to emotionally vulnerable individuals. Groups in Australia, New Zealand, and the United States tried unsuccessfully to ban this book, while France has done so.

Institute of Society, Ethics and the Life Sciences, Task Force on Death and Dying. **"Refinements in Criteria for the Determination of Death."** *Journal of the American Medical Association* 221 (1972): 48–53.

This article documents some of the earliest attempts at redefining death as required by increased knowledge of how the human body functions and the then-new technological advances that made it possible to sustain the lives of those who would otherwise have died.

Kevorkian, Jack. **Prescription Medicine: The Goodness of Planned Death.** Buffalo, NY: Prometheus Books, 1991. 268 pp. ISBN 0-8797-5872-4.

This autobiographical book provides an interesting look at Dr. Kevorkian from his own point of view. Kevorkian explains his motives in helping individuals die and documents his struggles with the medical and legal systems, beginning with his attempts to provide death row inmates with peaceful deaths so they could donate their organs. Kevorkian also chronicles the development of his suicide machines.

Koop, C. Everett. **The Right To Live, The Right To Die.** Wheaton, IL: Tyndale House Publishers, 1981. 160 pp. ISBN 0-919225-02-0.

This book has become a classic since its publication in the 1970s. Koop was and is a voice of moderation in this emotional debate. He explores the major issues in accessible language and presents arguments that remain valid today in a well-organized manner.

National Conference Steering Committee. **"Standards for Cardiopulmonary Resuscitation (CPR) and Emergency Cardiac Care (ECC)."** *Journal of the American Medical Association* 227 (1974): 837–864.

This landmark paper declared that CPR should be initiated in any situation where medically indicated, excepting only those patients who were already dying and whose condition was considered irreversible.

President's Commission for the Study of Ethical Problems in Medicine and Biomedical and Behavioral Research. **Deciding To Forego Life-Sustaining Treatment: A Report on the Ethical, Medical and Legal Issues in Treatment Decisions.** Washington, DC: U.S. Government Printing Office, 1983. 554 pp. ISBN 0-3181-1774-6.

This landmark report contains numerous surveys, voluminous data, and expert testimony and analysis on questions regarding end-of-life care. It is an essential document in the end-of-life debate.

Quill, Timothy E. **"Death and Dignity: A Case of Individualized Decision Making."** *New England Journal of Medicine* 324 (1991): 691–694.

With this famous article Quill became one of the first physicians to publicly admit to assisting a patient to die. The former hospice physician's account of his experience with "Diane" caused a storm of protest as well as some very healthy debate within the health care profession about this widely practiced but rarely discussed medical course of action.

―――. **Death and Dignity: Making Choices and Taking Charge.** New York: W. W. Norton, 1993. 255 pp. ISBN 0-393-03448-8.

This book further documents Dr. Quill's professional journey with the patient "Diane," whom he helped to die. Quill provides an intimate look at the end-of-life decision-making process, as well as a clear and rational look at the careful choices that need to be made to maintain a trusting doctor-patient relationship in the face of unrelenting, terminal suffering. Dr. Quill writes with great skill and compassion about his patients and the choices he has made with them to end their suffering. He also provides readers with a clear understanding of the choices and pitfalls physicians face as they struggle to come to terms with the ambiguity of a legal system that offers little in the way of clear, professional direction. The book includes the texts of his often cited articles in the *New England Journal of Medicine* and a sample living will and health care proxy. Sherwin Nuland, author of *How We Die*, predicts this work will "prove to be a reference point on the compass of medical ethics."

Reiser, Stanley J., ed. **Ethics in Medicine: Historical Perspectives and Contemporary Concerns.** Boston: MIT Press, 1977. ISBN 0-2626-8029-7.

This comprehensive history of medical ethics includes numerous documents, 103 articles, and a number of sample cases addressing many concerns, including the doctor-patient relationship, human experimentation, public health, suffering, and death.

Rothman, David J. **Strangers at the Bedside: A History of How Law and Bioethics Transformed Medical Decision Making.** New York: Basic Books, 1991. 303 pp. ISBN 0-465-08209-2.

Rothman presents a unique and important perspective on the current debate by examining developments from 1966 to 1976, a critical decade in which medical decision making in the United States was radically altered. He offers substantial historical background on the doctor-patient relationship and the relationship between medicine and culture.

Roy, David J., John R. Williams, and Bernard M. Dickens. **Bioethics in Canada.** Ontario: Prentice Hall Canada, 1994. 499 pp. ISBN 013-328097-7.

This book distinguishes the field of bioethics from philosophical, theological, and applied ethics perspectives and takes readers on an intimate, real-life exploration of science and medicine. It covers the history of bioethics, the Canadian health care system, and the doctor-patient relationship. It also presents discussions of the contemporary issues that have dominated the field for the past 15 years, including euthanasia, transplantation ethics, and withholding or withdrawing treatment.

Seltzer, Richard. **Raising the Dead: A Doctor's Encounter with His Own Mortality.** New York: Penguin Books, 1993. 128 pp. ISBN 0-1402-3489-6.

In this first-person account of his own experience in the hospital after he nearly died of pneumonia, Dr. Seltzer gives readers a guided tour of serious illness from an insider's point of view. He richly describes the indignities he suffered in the ICU, hooked up to a ventilator and comatose, at the hands of "a flock of white birds stooping to peck at my arms, groin, beaking my mouth, rectum, everywhere," and then the daily routine of his recovery.

By stripping away the gloss and bringing readers into the recovery room with him, Seltzer gives a human face to the issue of medical suffering in contemporary times.

Spiritual-Social-Cultural

Alecson, Deborah Golden. **Lost Lullaby.** Berkeley: University of California Press, 1995. 207 pp. ISBN 0-520-08870-0.

This moving account describes the struggle a mother and father undergo when their daughter suffers severe brain damage during birth. The quality of life their daughter would enjoy is taken into consideration; the hospital and medical ethics committee stance on the plight of the infant; and the love, grief, and anger of the parents are all explored in an unsensational manner.

Aly, Gotz, Peter Chroust, and Christian Pross. **Cleansing the Fatherland: Nazi Medicine and Racial Hygiene.** Baltimore, MD: Johns Hopkins University Press, 1995. 295 pp. ISBN 0-8018-4824-5.

This extensively researched book presents a wealth of information on the Nazi euthanasia program from a German perspective. Exploring the attitudes of the Nazis and their slide down the "slippery slope," the authors take a hard look at the role played by the complacency of the German people.

Aronheim, Judith, and Doron Weber. **Final Passages: Positive Choices for the Dying and Their Loved Ones.** New York: Simon & Schuster, 1992. 285 pp. ISBN 0-671-78025-5.

Aronheim and Weber explore the hard questions that must be asked about assisted suicide. They question whether medical options that could help patients go on living more comfortably have been fully explored and whether anyone is trying hard enough to have true empathy for the suffering of the terminally ill. They assert that the desire to legalize the right to die poses a "serious health threat."

Baird, Robert, and Stuart E. Rosenblum, eds. **Euthanasia: The Moral Issues.** Buffalo, NY: Prometheus Books, 1989. 182 pp. ISBN 0-87975-555-5.

This book is part of a series on *Contemporary Issues in Philosophy*. Each chapter is written by a well-known authority on a different aspect of euthanasia. C. Everett Koop writes about Karen Ann

Quinlan, James Rachels addresses active and passive euthanasia, and Pieter Admiraal writes about what he calls justifiable active euthanasia in the Netherlands. The writers offer many unique philosophical perspectives on euthanasia.

Barry, Robert Laurence. **Breaking the Thread of Life: On Rational Suicide.** Rutgers, NJ: Transaction Publications, 1994. 353 pp. ISBN 1-56000-142-9.

Robert Barry, a Dominican priest and professor of religious studies, looks at suicide from a historical and religious perspective. He questions whether suicide can ever really be a rational, voluntary act and claims that the right-to-die movement is biased against women.

Battin, Margaret P. **Ethical Issues in Suicide.** 2d ed. NJ: Prentice Hall, 1994. 256 pp. ISBN 0-13-304668-0.

A provocative series of essays by a well-known philosopher. The chapter on physician-assisted suicide is particularly informative. This book is essential reading for every student exploring this field.

Berger, Arthur S., and Joyce Berger, eds. **To Die or Not To Die? Cross-Disciplinary, Cultural, and Legal Perspectives on the Right To Choose Death.** New York: Praeger, 1990. 194 pp. ISBN 0-275-39585-X.

The Bergers asked experts from a number of countries, religions, and professions to address the right to die. Islamic, African, Japanese, Indian, British, and Dutch perspectives are examined. Appendices offer a digest of United States case law decisions, sample forms, and a select bibliography.

Betzhold, Michael. **Appointment with Dr. Death.** Troy, MI: Momentum Books, 1993. 341 pp. ISBN 1-879094-37-1 (harcover), 1-879094-42-8 (paperback).

Written by a reporter who has covered Dr. Kevorkian for the press, this book provides an in-depth look at a very complex and pivotal figure in the euthanasia debate, including the views of detractors and supporters. Betzhold chronicles Kevorkian's medical career and the paths that have led to his current line of work. This information is interspersed with vignettes about the people he assisted and his courtroom experiences. Betzhold also profiles Kevorkian's outspoken lawyer, Geoffrey Fieger, and documents the methods of the right-to-life groups that oppose

Kevorkian's actions. In a unique twist of fate, the author discovers that his own cousin was one of the women assisted by Kevorkian.

Burleigh, Michael. **Death and Deliverance—"Euthanasia" in Germany c. 1900–1945.** Cambridge, England: Cambridge University Press, 1994. 382 pp. ISBN 0-521-41613-2.

Burleigh focuses on the Weimar Republic's eugenics program and the cultural-historical context that allowed this horrifying public policy to be established. It describes the planning and execution of the euthanasia program, pointing out that the vast majority of victims were placed in institutions by their families and were not removed even after the nature of the program became apparent. The role of the medical profession is also explored. Many of the same questions and concerns being raised today were confronted during this period of Germany's history.

Carrick, Paul. **Medical Ethics in Antiquity.** Philosophy and Medicine, vol. 18. Dordrecht, Holland: D. Reidel Publishing, 1985. 242 pp. ISBN 90-277-1825-3 (hardcover), 90-277-1915-2 (paperback).

In this authoritative and intimate look at the philosophies, treatment, day-to-day lives, and ways of thinking about illness and health prevalent in ancient Greece and Rome, the author provides an in-depth examination of the Hippocratic Oath (the authorship of which scholars continue to debate) and the many views held by physicians and philosophers during this period. Doctors were considered craftsmen, not professionals, Carrick points out. This work clearly demonstrates that euthanasia has been debated since antiquity.

Chirban, John T., ed. **Ethical Dilemmas: Crises in Faith and Modern Medicine.** Lanham, MD: University Press of America, 1994. 172 pp. ISBN 0-8191-9338-0.

Various authors examine five key realms in which religion and medicine intersect. Sections on euthanasia, bioethics, and end-of-life decisions explore the more spiritual aspects of the euthanasia debate from a Christian perspective.

Colt, George Howe. **The Enigma of Suicide.** New York: Summit Books, 1991. 575 pp. ISBN 0-671-50996-9.

This comprehensive examination of suicide in its many forms covers its history, from ancient Greece through modern times, fleshing out the historical and cultural attitudes that underlie the issue today. An entire chapter is devoted to the right-to-die movement, with particular emphasis on the Hemlock Society.

Eareckson, Joni. **Joni.** Grand Rapids, MI: Zondervan Press, 1976. 208 pp. ISBN 0-3102-1149-2.

Joni is the first-person account of a young Christian woman's fight to survive after an accident that left her paralyzed.

Fairbairn, Gavin J. **Contemplating Suicide.** London: Routledge, 1995. 209 pp. ISBN 0-415-10605-2.

Fairbairn explores suicide from a broad perspective, providing a rich view of the history and current models of self-harm. He also examines euthanasia and assisted suicide in relationship to other forms of self-harm.

Fletcher, Joseph. **Morals and Medicine.** Ann Arbor, MI: Books on Demand, 1954. 267 pp. ISBN 0-8357-4198-2.

Dr. Fletcher presents five moral problems, including a patient's right to know the truth and the right to die. This book is considered an important first step into the arena of medical ethics.

Hamel, Ron P., ed. **Choosing Death: Active Euthanasia, Religion and the Public Debate.** Philadelphia: Trinity Press International, 1991. 192 pp. ISBN 1-5633-8031-5.

Providing numerous case studies and historical landmarks, as well as a question-and-answer section, *Choosing Death* is a good overview of the contemporary debate.

Humphrey, Derek. **Let Me Die before I Wake.** Eugene, OR: The Hemlock Society, 1986. 132 pp. ISBN 0-4405-0477-5.

Originally published in 1984, this groundbreaking book includes several case histories that illuminate the tragic circumstances some people face in their attempts to self-deliver, which is the general term for euthanasia preferred by many proponents. The narratives illustrate several effective suicide methods.

————. **Final Exit: The Practicalities of Self-Deliverance and Assisted Suicide for the Dying.** New York: Carol Publishing, 1991. 192 pp. ISBN 0-9606030-3-4.

Perhaps the most controversial book written about the right to die, *Final Exit* has been translated into nearly a dozen languages and is banned in France. At the end of 1991 it was among the five best-selling nonfiction books in the United States. In it, Derek Humphrey offers frank information about self-deliverance and ways to handle discussions with health professionals in order to obtain lethal doses of drugs. A 1992 edition contains additional information, as well as warnings against abuse.

————. **Lawful Exit: The Limits of Freedom for Help in Dying.** Junction City, OR: Norris Lane Press, 1993. 165 pp. ISBN 0-9637280-0-8.

In *Lawful Exit*, Humphrey discusses how the legal system in the United States has thus far failed to adequately address the right to die. He explores the semantics of the debate, as well as the role of the medical profession in defining the issues. The Model Death with Dignity Act is reproduced in full, as are the unique legal guidelines set up in 1993 by the Dutch Parliament. Humphrey calls physician aid-in-dying "the ultimate civil liberty, the freedom to select one's own manner of dying without interference from others, but with help if we choose. If we cannot die by our choice, then we are not free people."

Irish, Donald P., Kathleen F. Lundquist, and Vivian Jenkins Nelson, eds. **Ethnic Variations in Death and Dying.** Washington, DC: Taylor and Francis, 1993. 250 pp. ISBN 1-5603-2277-2.

One of the first books to thoroughly explore cultural differences in attitudes toward death and dying, *Ethnic Variations* offers readers clear and sometimes heart-wrenching insights into the ways in which these differences affect patients and their families in the hospital, and into the ways they perceive and mourn death. It is an important book for those who recognize the need to address multicultural issues in end-of-life legislation, as well as for medical professionals and funeral directors.

Jamison, Stephen. **The Final Acts of Love: Families and Assisted Dying.** New York: Putnam, 1996. 288 pp. ISBN 0-87477-816-6.

A social psychologist in San Francisco who has closely experienced assisted suicides, primarily in the context of AIDS patients. He lists what to do and what not to do when helping another person to die so that the person assisting is left emotionally strong after the experience.

Kliever, Lonnie D., ed. **Dax's Case.** Dallas, TX: Southern Methodist Press, 1989. 221 pp. ISBN 0-87074-277-9.

This collection of essays about Dax Cowart's desire to die after being seriously burned in an accident includes fascinating commentary from physicians, lawyers, and ethicists addressing the complexities of the case.

Kübler-Ross, Elisabeth. **On Death and Dying.** New York: Simon & Schuster, 1993. 260 pp. ISBN 0-0208-9141-5.

This groundbreaking book was the first to identify a number of universal stages of grieving suffered by humans faced with loss. It is an excellent treatise on Western attitudes toward death.

Larue, Gerald A. **Euthanasia and Religion: A Survey of the Attitudes of World Religions to the Right-To-Die.** Los Angeles: The Hemlock Society, 1985. 154 pp. ISBN 0-9606030-3-4.

Based on a survey conducted by Larue—cofounder and past president of the Hemlock Society—to generate more information on the role of religion in end-of-life issues, this book examines passive euthanasia, assisted suicide, pastoral counseling about euthanasia, and burial issues as they pertain to terminally ill patients, as well as other pertinent topics. It is organized by denomination.

Logue, Barbara J. **Last Rights: Death Control and the Elderly in America.** New York: Lexington Books, 1993. 372 pp. ISBN 0-669-27370-8.

In her in-depth look at aging trends, Logue discusses the ways in which the process of aging has changed and how these changes have led many people to make desperate choices. She explores the sociopolitical, economic, and technological reasons why certain people want to die or help others die; suggests ways to communicate end-of-life wishes to family members, friends, and physicians; and examines the pros and cons of various types of directives. Looking to the future, Logue sheds light on the risks and burdens of solutions that are currently being proposed. A chapter on the elderly and ethnic groups provides a much needed look at the special concerns of these vulnerable populations. *Last Rights* contains a wealth of statistical, historical, and legal information.

McKenzie, Nancy F., Ph.D. **Beyond Crisis: Confronting Health Care in the United States.** New York: Penguin Books, 1994. 550 pp. ISBN 0-4520-1028-4.

Beyond Crisis is an easy-to-read look at the changing face of health care today and future needs that threaten to evolve into abuses, should physician-assisted suicide become legal.

Marker, Rita. **Deadly Compassion.** New York: Avon, 1995. 310 pp. ISBN 0-3807-2332-8.

Marker illustrates the complexity of end-of-life issues from an antieuthanasia perspective. Based on interviews with Derek Humphrey's dying ex-wife, Ann Wickett, *Deadly Compassion* is Marker's account of Wickett's life with the then-president of the Hemlock Society and the bitter end of that marriage. Unfortunately, in her attempts to expose the dark side of Humphrey and the right-to-die movement through an examination of his personal life, Marker seems to have become a pawn in a marital dispute. However, the book does provide another view of the man behind the Hemlock Society, as well as an understanding of the need for supportive counseling for the terminally ill.

Morris, Jennifer. **Pride against Prejudice: Transforming Attitudes toward Disability.** Philadelphia: New Society, 1991. 208 pp. ISBN 0-8657-1279-4.

Written by a disability rights activist, *Pride against Prejudice* provides an analysis of the experiences of people with disabilities, including the prejudices they encounter in various aspects of their lives. Morris explores with conviction and compassion such topics as mercy killing, abortion, and institutionalization as they relate to the disabled community.

Munley, Anne. **The Hospice Alternative.** New York: Basic Books, 1983. 349 pp. ISBN 0-465-03060-2.

In this overview of the hospice movement, its origins, and current practices, case histories lend a sense of intimacy and illuminate the bigger picture of terminal care today. The book addresses the physical and psychological aspects of pain, fear, financial worries, and family dynamics. A look at the future of the hospice movement offers much food for thought, as well as a sense of how far the movement has come in this country.

Nuland, Sherwin B. **How We Die: Reflections on Life's Final Chapter.** New York: Random House, 1993. 278 pp. ISBN 0-6797-7424-1.

Nuland provides lay readers with a bedside view of the emotional, physical, and social issues that emerge during the final stage of life. Passages on the physiology of death offer background information that is usually available only to those who have studied medicine and witnessed death firsthand. This lays the groundwork for later chapters on dying from Alzheimer's, heart disease, cancer, and AIDS. *How We Die* presents death as a biological process as well as an emotional transition and provides a unique understanding of the futility of treating terminally ill patients. Death by suicide is explored from a number of perspectives, including the plastic bag method recommended in *Final Exit.* By describing in graphic detail what these deaths "look like," Nuland emphasizes the value of physician-assisted death. This book fills in the blanks for a generation separated from death by high-tech interventions that limit access to and understanding of the dying process. It won the 1994 National Book Award for a nonfiction best-seller.

Osgood, Nancy J. **Suicide in Later Life: Recognizing the Warning Signs.** New York: Lexington Books, 1992. 167 pp. ISBN 0-669-21214-8.

This book illustrates the tragedy of growing old in the United States today by examining ageism and the loneliness that is all too often the fate of elders in contemporary society. Osgood includes an important chapter on depression among the elderly, describing societal factors that contribute to suicide and exploring the concept of eldercide. She questions whether societal hostility to elder populations causes individuals to end their lives prematurely.

Rachels, James. **The End of Life: Euthanasia and Morality.** Oxford, England: Oxford University Press, 1986. 204 pp. ISBN 0-19-217746-X.

Rachels argues in favor of the moral and philosophical value of euthanasia. Making no effort to disguise his point of view, he does an admirable job of pulling apart the questions and looking at their components in light of historical fact, logic, psychological reasoning, and spiritual practice. Distinguishing between the biological and biographical aspects of a life, Rachels shows why judging the worth of a life is difficult, discusses the moral rules against killing, and explores the difference between ordinary and extraordinary treatment, the duty of the physician to the patient, religious arguments against the practice of euthanasia, and how the law treats those accused of mercy killing. These are rich, thought-provoking perspectives on the many questions raised by death and dying.

Rinpoche, Sogyal. **The Tibetan Book of Living and Dying.** San Francisco: Harper, 1992. 428 pp. ISBN 0-06-250793-1.

By combining a Buddhist perspective with current research on death and dying, Rinpoche, a Buddhist meditation master, has created a guide to understanding and dealing with death that is meaningful to people of any faith. His description of the ideal, peaceful death contrasts sharply with the death process common in most hospitals today and suggests that medical technology stands between the patient and a spiritual passage from this life.

Rollin, Betty. **Last Wish.** New York: Random House, 1977. 240 pp. ISBN 0-5171-4935-4.

Poignantly telling the story of her mother's battle with ovarian cancer, the author illustrates how the suffering and pain associated with this form of cancer can so seriously diminish the quality of life that life is no longer worth living. After attempts at therapy failed, Rollin's mother died at the age of 76 from an overdose of pills provided by her daughter.

Shavelson, Lonny, M.D: **A Chosen Death: The Dying Confront Assisted Suicide.** New York: Simon & Schuster, 1995. 240 pp. ISBN 0-6848-0100-0.

This is a good introduction to the personal end-of-life issues faced by the handicapped and the terminally ill. *A Chosen Death* documents the lives of five patients over a period of several years, illustrating with each story a different set of concerns surrounding choice in dying.

Shneidman, Edwin. **Voices of Death.** New York: Harper & Row, 1980. 209 pp. ISBN 0-06-014023-2.

A pioneer in the field of thanatology, Shneidman uses interviews, suicide notes, and other personal documents to provide readers with a unique and visceral understanding of the thought processes of a person facing death. He explores the lack of perspective, or "tunnel vision," that sets in once a person makes the decision to commit suicide and questions whether anguish rules out the mental competency needed for one to make a rational choice to die. This is a thought-provoking book.

Singer, Peter. **Rethinking Life and Death: The Collapse of Our Traditional Ethics.** New York: St. Martin's Press, 1996. ISBN 0-312-11880-5 (hardcover), 0-312-14401-6 (paperback).

Singer is one of the founders of the animal rights movement and a professor of philosophy at Monash University in Melbourne, Australia. He points out that Christian ethics have for centuries failed to prevent murder, genocide, and other atrocities, and that Christians who use the "sanctity of life" argument to oppose euthanasia are thus being hypocritical. Derek Humphrey's review of this controversial book claims that Singer "brilliantly debunks old concepts and introduces honesty to modern medical ethics." *Rethinking Life and Death* is likely to spark great debate, even among those who thought they agreed on fundamental life-and-death issues.

Sosby, Dick. **Violence and Abuse in the Lives of People with Disabilities: The End of Silent Acceptance?** Baltimore, MD: Paul H. Brooks, 1994. 480 pp. ISBN 1-5576-6148-0.

Sosby sheds light on the often hidden issue of abuse of the disabled, questions why abuse of this population is so prevalent, and explores what can be done to help stop it. This book is an important resource for people concerned about the abuse and coercion of vulnerable citizens in regard to euthanasia.

Tada, Joni Eareckson. **When Is It Right To Die? Suicide, Euthanasia, Suffering, Mercy.** Grand Rapids, MI: Zondervan, 1992. 189 pp. ISBN 0-310-58570-8.

The author is a deeply religious woman who suffered an accident that left her a quadriplegic. She asserts that many people skip over the most meaningful aspects of dying when they choose to end their lives prematurely, and she examines the more spiritual aspects of the right-to-die and assisted-suicide debates.

Tivnan, Edward. **The Moral Imagination: Confronting the Ethical Issues of Our Day.** New York: Simon & Schuster, 1995. 334 pp. ISBN 0-671-74708-8.

A good, easily understood introduction to modern ethical dilemmas. Written by a philosopher, this book explores the issues of abortion, suicide, euthanasia, and capital punishment, as well as racial injustice and affirmative action. Tivnan provides some history on these issues, summarizes the pros and cons of each, and then makes a case for tolerance and understanding of opposing viewpoints.

Westly, Dick. **When It's Right To Die: Conflicting Voices, Difficult Choices.** Mystic, CT: Twenty-Third Publications, 1995. 224 pp. ISBN 0-8962-2609-3.

A professor of philosophy at Loyola University, Westly makes a case for active, voluntary euthanasia. He asks readers to consider whether religious beliefs and a desire to have the right to die must remain mutually exclusive.

Legal-Political

Annas, George J. **"Nancy Cruzan and the Right To Die."** *New England Journal of Medicine* 323 (1990): 670–673.

This analysis of the landmark Cruzan case by one of the most respected health-law experts in the United States provides unique legal insights into this historic battle to allow a beloved daughter to die.

———. **Standard of Care: The Law of American Bioethics.** New York: Oxford University Press, 1993. 291 pp. ISBN 0-19-507247-2.

In this medico-legal exploration of the euthanasia debate, George Annas examines the conflicts between a doctor's respect for patient autonomy and the fear of malpractice litigation. Using specific legal cases to explore the issues of euthanasia, organ transplantation, rationing, and genetic research, Annas offers a unique jury-box perspective on the choices that are made, sometimes unintentionally, as solutions to difficult ethical questions are hammered out. He provides legal analysis of the cases involving Karen Ann Quinlan, Baby Doe, and Nancy Cruzan, exposing intricacies of the law and the complexity of the issues.

Cantor, Norman L. **Advance Directives and the Pursuit of Death with Dignity.** Bloomington: Indiana University Press, 1993. 228 pp. ISBN 0-2533-1304-X.

Written by a Rutgers University law professor, this book traces the legislation and case law behind advance directives. It also provides state-by-state information about existing laws.

Dworkin, Ronald. **Life's Dominion: An Argument about Abortion, Euthanasia, and Individual Freedom.** New York: Alfred A. Knopf, 1993. 273 pp. ISBN 0-394-58941-6.

This book by a New York University law professor provides fresh insight into the intention of the U.S. Constitution regarding euthanasia and abortion. It addresses the questions faced by state legislators as they struggle to come to terms with writing laws about such deeply personal matters and provides insight into why people feel so strongly about these issues and how these feelings impact law.

Final Report of the Netherlands State Commission on Euthanasia: An English Summary. *Bioethics* 1 (1987): 163–174.

This report is an abridged version of the legal policy on euthanasia in the Netherlands. It is one of the few sources of this information in English.

Goldfluss, Howard E. **Living Wills and Wills.** New York: Wings Books, 1994. 247 pp. ISBN 0-5171-0145-9.

Although he is a former New York State Supreme Court judge, Goldfluss uses easy-to-understand language to clarify for the layperson how wills work. He lists the legal paperwork required for end-of-life issues and describes landmark legal cases that have helped forge the laws in place today.

Gomez, Carlos F., M.D. **Regulating Death: Euthanasia and the Case of the Netherlands.** New York: The Free Press, 1991. 172 pp. ISBN 0-02-912440-9.

Proponents of euthanasia frequently point to the Netherlands as an example of a civilized society that allows euthanasia, but these people seldom examine or discuss the laws and practices that exist behind the scenes there. Gomez interviewed Dutch physicians and translated into English the laws and restrictions as they are currently written. What his effort reveals is a disturbing lack of safeguards in the law and an even more frightening tendency among doctors to ignore the rules that do exist. Gomez provides the most comprehensive body of information available in English about euthanasia as it is practiced in the Netherlands.

Hoefler, James M., with Brian E. Kamoie. **Deathright: Culture, Medicine, Politics and the Right To Die.** Boulder, CO: Westview Press, 1994. 291 pp. ISBN 0-8133-1701-0.

Presenting the right to die as a public policy issue, *Deathright* examines the history of the right-to-die movement and how public interest has been a factor in developing public policy. The authors state that policy making involves restraint (denial of mortality prevents public discussion), activism (technological developments, media attention, and fear spurs discussion), and mediation (activism overcomes restraint, allowing policy to be shaped). They get beyond polarized opinions to a rational exploration of the debate. This is a fascinating overview of the history of the doctor-patient relationship that explores how shifts in methods of delivering and accessing medical care have affected the right to die. It is an important book for those who feel social policy should have nothing to do with the individual's right to make a decision.

Humphrey, Derek. **Dying with Dignity.** New York: Random House, 1995. 215 pp. ISBN 0-5171-4342-9.

In this book Humphrey uses a simple question-answer format to provide short case histories and summaries of landmark legal cases, as well as a chronology of legislative activity.

In the Matter of Karen Ann Quinlan: The Complete Legal Briefs, Court Proceedings, and Decision in the Superior Court of New Jersey. Arlington, VA: University Publications of America, 1975.

This is a comprehensive source of information on and documentation of the Quinlan case.

Lewin, Tamar. **"Ruling Sharpens Debate on 'Right To Die.'"** *New York Times*, 8 March 1996, A8.

This is an excellent analysis of the many implications of the Ninth Circuit Court of Appeals decision affirming the right to die and permitting physician-assisted suicide.

Rodwin, Marc A. **Medicine, Money and Morals.** New York: Oxford University Press, 1993. 395 pp. ISBN 0-1950-9647-9.

Rodwin examines conflicts of interest within the medical profession and the faith that is placed in a profession that is allowed to function under less clearly defined boundaries than would be considered acceptable in business or government. A must-read for those who don't understand the fear with which some people regard the prospect of legalized euthanasia, or who don't see the inherent dangers involved in leaving life-and-death issues in the hands of doctors.

Rosenblatt, Stanley M. **Murder or Mercy.** Buffalo, NY: Prometheus Books, 1992. 352 pp. ISBN 0-8797-5772-8.

Documenting the case of his client, Dr. Peter Rosier, who was accused of murdering his wife, Patricia, Stanley Rosenblatt provides an inside view of a legal defense and raises unsettling questions about the U.S. legal system. Rosenblatt unabashedly revels in his ability to manipulate a jury, reveals the seamier side of the right-to-die issue—underlining family tensions, legal wrangling, and manipulation—and provides ample incentive to establish clear public policy on the issue of euthanasia.

Urofsky, Melvin L. **Letting Go: Death, Dying and the Law.** New York: Charles Scribner's Sons, 1993. 204 pp. ISBN 0-684-19344-2.

Urofsky examines the concepts of personal autonomy and public control in the arena of death and dying, using key legal cases and documents as illustration.

Fiction

Cook, Robin. **Fatal Cure.** New York: Berkeley Books, 1995. 449 pp. ISBN 0-425-14563-8.

Cook uses an all-too-possible scenario to address the role managed care could play in leading an unsuspecting population down the slippery slope to involuntary euthanasia. This chilling tale is set in a state-of-the-art community hospital in Vermont. A husband and wife medical team uncover a stealthy euthanasia program engineered to cut health care costs.

Delbanco, Nicholas. **In the Name of Mercy.** New York: Warner Books, 1995. 310 pp. ISBN 0-446-51711-9.

The plot of this well-written and thoughtful novel addresses many perspectives on euthanasia. A physician helps his cancer-wracked wife to die, and then similarly aids several patients. But then the deaths multiply and extend well beyond those who wish to end their lives. Mercy quickly turns sinister.

Michener, James A. **Recessional.** New York: Ballantine Books, 1994. 532 pp. ISBN 0-449-22345-0.

In this thoughtful and sweeping saga, Michener illuminates the challenges of aging. In the process, end-of-life issues are unavoidably addressed in the context of a modern assisted-living center. Pro-life forces are portrayed as radical activists, but their infiltration of the center serves as a catalyst for realistic discussions about choice-in-dying and suffering.

Quindlen, Anna. **One True Thing.** New York: Dell, 1995. 400 pp. ISBN 0-4402-2103-X.

This moving novel by a Pulitzer Prize–winning journalist involves many of the issues raised by assisted dying. *One True Thing* is a good read, emotionally touching, but also quite realistic. It deserves its best-seller status.

Snodgrass, Steven. **Lethal Dose.** Orlando, FL: Icam, 1996. 350 pp. ISBN 0-964263-1-7.

A chilling tale of what could happen should voluntary euthanasia be legalized. Religious zealots attack the medical staff of a hospital authorized to help suffering patients die following careful consultation and evaluation. They murder several doctors, blow up a car, and finally bomb the hospital. The plot is intentionally reminiscent of the recent abortion clinic bombings. This is a medical thriller with a strong plot and a disturbingly gutsy realism.

Solomon, Andrew. **A Stone Boat.** New York: Faber & Faber, 1994. 241 pp. ISBN 0-4522-7498-2.

Set in America and England, this is the story of a young man who assists his mother to die to bring to an end her battle with cancer. The main character in this obviously semiautobiographical first novel has doubts about his sexual orientation at the same time as he—with family—helps his cancer-stricken mother to die.

Tolstoy, Leo. **The Death of Ivan Illyich.** New York: Bantam Books, 1981. ISBN 0-4515-2508-6.

This is a collection of the short stories and essays by Tolstoy that address the issues surrounding death and dying. These provide a valuable look at the classic, universal issues surrounding death, without the overlay of modern issues, such as managed care.

Periodicals

ACPA Chronicle
American Chronic Pain Association (ACPA)
P.O. Box 850
Rocklin, CA 95677

This quarterly newsletter is a good source of information about the types of support and educational programs available to deal effectively with the chronic pain that is often associated with terminal illness and that can play a decisive role in end-of-life decision making.

Caring Magazine
Hospice Association of America
228 Seventh Street, S.E.
Washington, DC 20003

Feature articles in this monthly magazine focus on quality of care for hospice patients, the role of hospice in caring for the terminally ill, and palliative care and pain control.

Choices
Choice in Dying (CID)
200 Varick Street
New York, NY 10014

Choice in Dying's quarterly newsletter provides up-to-date, accurate information about advance directives, living wills, and other issues affecting end-of-life decisions.

Compassion in Dying
Compassion in Dying
P.O. Box 75295
Seattle, WA 98125-0295

Compassion in Dying's newsletter focuses on the legal aspects of assisted suicide and also provides sources and information for support, emotional and otherwise, sought by the terminally ill.

CRTI Report
The Center for the Rights of the Terminally Ill, Inc.
P.O. Box 54246
Hurst, TX 76054

This quarterly newsletter features articles that argue against euthanasia and assisted suicide, instead promoting compassion and respect toward patients who wish to "live with dignity."

Dying with Dignity
Dying with Dignity
188 Eglinton Avenue East, #705
Toronto, Ontario M4P 2X7
Canada

Articles in this quarterly newsletter are aimed at improving the quality of dying and generating support for physician aid-in-dying in Canada.

The Hastings Center Report
The Hastings Center
255 Elm Road
Briarcliff Manor, NY 10510

The Hastings Center's bimonthly journal documents research conducted at the center and provides professional discourse for many bioethics scholars worldwide. It is an excellent source of information on issues at the forefront of the debate.

Home Care News
Hospice Association of America
228 Seventh Street, S.E.
Washington, DC 20003

This monthly newspaper offers a wealth of valuable information on comfort care for home care providers and those who care for ill family members.

Hospice Forum
Hospice Association of America
228 Seventh Street, S.E.
Washington, DC 20003

This biweekly newsletter contains information on ways to improve the quality of care for hospice patients and champions the cause of hospice caregivers. It is a good source of information about hospice alternatives for the terminally ill.

HOSPICE Magazine, Guide to the Nation's Hospices
National Hospice Foundation (NHF)
1901 North Moore Street, Suite 901
Arlington, VA 22209

This comprehensive quarterly is published by the largest hospice organization in the nation. Its articles on hospice care inform, educate, inspire, and encourage.

IAETF Update
International Anti-Euthanasia Task Force (IATEF)
University of Steubenville
P.O. Box 760
Steubenville, OH 43952

Articles in this bimonthly newsletter are designed to draw attention to the pressures placed on individuals to end their lives too soon because they are chronically ill, terminally ill, dependent, or disabled. It presents viewpoints opposing euthanasia, suicide, and assisted suicide and includes analysis of legal-political developments, taking a special interest in medically vulnerable populations.

The Journal of Palliative Care
Center for Bioethics Clinical Research Institute of Montreal
110 Pine Avenue, W.
Montreal, Quebec H2W 1R7
Canada

This quarterly journal contains reports on current research in the field of hospice/palliative care. It raises ethical issues in an effort to further educate individuals and professionals about medical conflicts in contemporary society.

Kennedy Institute of Ethics Journal
Kennedy Institute of Ethics
Georgetown University
Box 571212
Washington, DC 20057-1212

The Kennedy Institute's quarterly journal reports on research that informs moral and ethical perspectives on major policy issues, often involving biomedical ethics.

Last Rights
Right to Die Society of Canada
P.O. Box 39018
Victoria, British Columbia V8V 4X8
Canada

This quarterly journal is one of the premier publications of the right-to-die movement. It serves as a forum for the many activities of the Right to Die Society of Canada, including the results of original research and the legal and political efforts undertaken by this organization. The initial results of Anne Muller's groundbreaking research on right-to-die issues in Canada was first published here.

Life at Risk
National Conference of Catholic Bishops
Secretariat for Pro-Life Activities
3211 Fourth Street, N.E.
Washington, DC 20017-1194

This newsletter, published ten times a year, offers articles promoting alternatives to euthanasia and espousing the Catholic opposition to the right to die.

Lifeline
National Chronic Pain Outreach Association (NCPOA)
7979 Old Georgetown Road, Suite 100
Bethesda, MD 20814

Lifeline is a quarterly newsletter containing current information on the latest pain control methodologies. It also reports on and promotes community support groups.

NRL News
National Right to Life Committee, Inc.
Suite 500
419 Seventh Street, N.W.
Washington, DC 20004-2293

This biweekly newspaper goes out to members of the largest pro-life group in the United States. Articles present opposition to abortion, infanticide, and euthanasia, both passive and active. *NRL News* is a good source of information on right-to-life issues and how they affect the assisted-suicide debate.

Omega: Journal of Death and Dying
Baywood Publishing Co., Inc.
26 Austin Avenue, Box 337
Amityville, NY 11701

Omega is a two-volume annual guide for clinicians, social workers, and health care professionals dealing with problems in crisis management such as terminal illness, fatal accidents, catastrophes, suicide, and bereavement.

Quality Care Advocate
National Citizen's Coalition for Nursing Home Reform
(NCCNHR)
1424 Sixteenth Street, N.W., Suite 202
Washington, DC 20036

National Citizen's Coalition for Nursing Home Reform puts out this bimonthly newsletter focusing on legal, legislative, and regulatory issues related to long-term care, especially those affecting nursing home residents. The publication closely follows government enforcement activities and is an excellent source of information about the current status of laws governing long-term care issues.

Surviving Suicide
American Association of Suicidology (AAS)
4201 Connecticut Avenue, N.W., Suite 310
Washington, DC 20008

This quarterly newsletter contains articles intended to help readers understand and prevent suicide.

Timelines
The Hemlock Society USA
P.O. Box 101810
Denver, CO 80250

In its bimonthly newsletter, the Hemlock Society advocates self-determination for the terminally ill and runs articles promoting dignity, integrity, and self-respect during the end-of-life process. It is an excellent source of information for those who want support in making a decision to die.

Selected Nonprint Resources

7

S everal nonprint formats are covered in this chapter, including fiction and nonfiction videos, movies made for television, CD-ROMs, and various Internet resources. The nonfiction videos are divided into the three familiar topic groups used throughout the book (Medical-Bioethical, Spiritual-Social-Cultural, and Legal-Political) to provide readers with a sense of the focus of the materials.

Nonfiction Videotapes

Medical-Bioethical

An Act of Self-Determination

Type: VHS
Length: 21 min.
Date: 1992
Cost: $89.95
Source: Choice in Dying
200 Varick Street
New York, NY 10014
(212) 366-5540

Studies have shown that many patients want their doctors to raise the subject of advance planning and that many physicians would like to offer this assistance but are uncertain about how to do so. This video was produced to close the communication gap by offering caregivers a clearer understanding of the needs of their patients. The video uses actual discussions between health care providers and their patients and also includes advice about how to raise issues in a sensitive way. Footage of a dramatic bedside encounter in an ICU illustrates the need for family involvement in end-of-life decision making.

An Appointment with Death
A Health Quarterly/Frontline Special
Type: VHS
Length: 60 min.
Date: 1994
Cost: $69.95
Source: PBS Video
1320 Braddock Place
Alexandria, VA 22314-1698
(800) 344-3337

Frontline and the *Health Quarterly* travel to Holland to examine what the Dutch have learned during the 20 years in which euthanasia has been allowed. Interviews with Dutch doctors reveal the difficult questions they face.

Born Dying
Type: VHS
Length: 20 min.
Date: 1983
Cost: $250
Source: Baxley Media Group
110 W. Main
Urbana, IL 61801
(800) 421-6999 or (217) 384-4838

This is the story of a couple whose baby is dying in the neonatal ICU. Nurses, parents, doctors, grandparents, a right-to-life representative, an advocate for the handicapped, and a hospital administrator all voice their various concerns about whether or not the baby should be treated. This is an effective springboard for discussion, particularly for college ethics classes and in medical settings.

Bringing Hospice Home
Type: VHS
Length: 14 min.
Date: 1992
Cost: $195 purchase; $65/3 days or $100/5 days rental

Source: Baxley Media Group
            110 W. Main
            Urbana, IL 61801
            (800) 421-6999 or (217) 384-4838

Produced by the SIU School of Medicine, *Bringing Hospice Home* is a valuable introduction to hospice. Interviews with members of the home hospice team and scenes from the homes of their clients illustrate this innovative program's focus on total care. The needs of both the patient and the family are considered, and quality of life is the central issue for the team. Although this video is intended for health care providers, social workers, and volunteers, it provides an objective, no-nonsense look at what it takes to provide the best possible environment at home for a loved one who is dying.

Death and Dying
Type: VHS
Length: 59 min.
Date: 1980
Cost: N/A
Source: Available only through library collections

Hosted by a past president of the Hastings Center, Dr. Willard Gaylin, this video provides a historical overview of the ways in which death has been viewed by different cultures and cultural resistance to facing death and dying. It explores the changes caused by the recent life-extending advances in medical technology. Philosopher Joseph Fletcher, Dr. George Annas, and Eric Cassell express opinions on the terminology of death, choices, patient autonomy, transplantation, and quality of life. A particularly powerful scene takes place in Dr. Cassell's office as he informs a patient of a possibly cancerous tumor that requires immediate surgery. Viewers take part in a very intimate and frightening moment, and it is suddenly not hard to understand why conversations between doctors and patients can be so difficult. Because this particular video was made prior to the Cruzan case and the Patient Self-Determination Act, the legal information provided is no longer up-to-date. This video is part of the *Hard Choices* series created by KTCS-TV in Seattle.

Death and Dying: The Physician's Perspective
Type: VHS
Length: 29 min.
Date: 1981
Cost: $69

Source: Fanlight Productions
47 Halifax Street
Boston, MA 02130
(800) 937-4113 or (617) 524-0980

This video does not deal specifically with euthanasia but consists of interviews with physicians regarding their attitudes about death and dying. A range of responses to death is exhibited by these doctors, who say their medical training does little to prepare them for the realities of their job. This is a provocative springboard for those who argue against physicians assisting with death.

The DNR Dilemma
Type: VHS
Length: 43 min. (2 parts)
Date: 1988
Cost: Part 1 or 2—$295 purchase; $65/
3 days or $100/5 days rental
Set—$495 purchase; $125/
3 days or $150/5 days rental
Includes 17-page Leader's Guide
Source: Baxley Media Group
110 W. Main
Urbana, IL 61801
(800) 421-6999 or (217) 384-4838

The DNR Dilemma examines some of the difficulties faced by physicians when communicating with patients and families about do-not-resuscitate orders. It explores the conflicts that all too often arise among health care providers faced with this issue. Part I, *When the Time Comes* (18 min.), dramatizes the anxieties and concerns of an oncologist who is reluctant to discuss resuscitation options with his terminally ill patients. Part II, *Professional Perspectives* (25 min.), annotates portions of part I with commentary by health care professionals who are directly affected by DNR orders. This is an excellent film which, although primarily directed toward health care professionals and administrators, works well for students.

A Fate Worse than Death
Type: VHS
Length: 50 min.
Date: 1990
Cost: $245

Source: Fanlight Productions
47 Halifax Street
Boston, MA 02130
(800) 937-4113 or (617) 524-0980

This video presents many perspectives on withholding or withdrawing artificial life supports. From doctors to patients, from senators to ethicists, a multitude of opinions are expressed and considered. PVS, or persistent vegetative state, is clearly explained, and there is a touching interview with a nurse who left the profession after being asked to remove feeding tubes.

The Heart of the New Age Hospice
Type: VHS
Length: 28 min.
Date: 1988
Cost: $195 purchase; $65/3 days or $100/5 days rental
Source: Baxley Media Group
110 W. Main
Urbana, IL 61801
(800) 421-6999 or (217) 384-4838

This moving video examines the full spectrum of hospice services and offers a valuable model for other organizations to follow when caring for the terminally ill. The heart of any hospice is the team of professionals that carries out treatment plans. Through candid interviews with these doctors, nurses, chaplains, social workers, home health aides, and volunteers, the program provides an inside look at the cooperation needed to provide a dying patient with the best possible care. Intended for hospice workers; suitable for nonprofessionals.

The Kevorkian File
A Frontline Special
Type: VHS
Length: 60 min.
Date: 1994
Cost: $69.95
Source: PBS Video
1320 Braddock Place
Alexandria, VA 22314-1698
(800) 344-3337

Frontline was granted special access to Dr. Jack Kevorkian, his family, friends, and survivors of the people he has assisted. This program provides fascinating insights into the man who has kept physician-assisted suicide in the news.

The Right To Die

Type: VHS, Beta, 3/4 in.
Length: 19 min.
Date: 1986
Cost: $385
Source: Baxley Media Group
110 W. Main
Urbana, IL 61801
(800) 421-6999 or (217) 384-4838

Intended for health care professionals, this program takes a thorough look at the questions surrounding a patient's right to be removed from artificial life supports. It is good background information for those interested in knowing some of the criteria used by health care professionals when advising families about the withdrawal of artificial supports.

To Choose No Harm

Type: VHS (open-captioned available)
Length: 45 min.
Date: 1996
Cost: $195 purchase; $50 rental
Source: Fanlight Productions
47 Halifax Street
Boston, MA 02130
(800) 937-4113 or (617) 524-0980

This powerful documentary explores a range of end-of-life issues by examining two cases in which health care teams must resolve conflicts between the wishes of their patients and the patients' families, and their own beliefs and clinical judgments. The first case involves a terminally ill AIDS patient who demands the continuation of treatments that the team has concluded will be both futile and expensive. The second case highlights the dilemmas posed when the end-of-life wishes of an elderly cancer patient and those of her husband differ, and how the health care team deals with the ethical problems this poses. Each case is followed by a panel discussion that includes a hospital ethicist, a nurse manager, a physician, a medical resident, and a hospital administrator. Suitable as an educational tool for students and those discussing end-of-life issues.

Spiritual-Social-Cultural

Born Dying

Type: VHS
Length: 20 min.
Date: 1983
Cost: $250 purchase; $65/3 days or $100/5 days rental
Includes 17-page Leader's Guide
Source: Baxley Media Group
110 W. Main
Urbana, IL 61801
(800) 421-6999 or (217) 384-4838

Born Dying poignantly portrays the agony of a couple who suddenly find themselves the parents of a dying baby, as well as that of the intensive care nurse who must provide care for the infant until a treatment decision is made. A hospital room confrontation provides a broad spectrum of viewpoints and is interwoven with neonatal ICU scenes that document the baby's decline. The film does not attempt to resolve the treatment/no treatment dilemma, but is meant to be used as a springboard for discussion of this sensitive area of health care.

Care beyond Cure: Hospice Helping Physicians Treat the Terminally Ill

Type: VHS
Length: 30 min.
Date: 1994
Cost: $14.95 plus postage
Source: National Hospice Foundation
1901 North Moore Street, Suite 901
Arlington, VA 22209
(800) 646-6460 or (703) 516-4928

Created as a tool to help physicians learn about end-of-life challenges and hospice care, this video is also appropriate for the lay viewer. The program begins with a doctor interviewing a terminally ill woman. He asks, "What do you want doctors to know?" She demands honesty of physicians. The rest of the program, hosted by Brad Stuart, M.D., medical director of the Home Hospice of Sonoma County, consists of doctors and patients discussing end-of-life issues and exploring why dealing with terminally ill patients is often very difficult for doctors and what can be done to make the process easier. The program exposes the emotional ups and downs of a terminal diagnosis, with one patient discussing her "utterly suicidal" feelings after her diagnosis. This is a good reminder that dying is not a medical condition but a personal experience that should be treated as such, even by medical personnel.

Dax's Case: Who Should Decide?

Type:	VHS
Length:	58 min.
Date:	1985
Cost:	$89.95
Source:	Choice in Dying
	200 Varick Street
	New York, NY 10014
	(212) 366-5540

This documentary covers ten years in the life of Dax Cowart, a man who was severely burned in an explosion that killed his father. Then in his twenties, he was blinded, disfigured, helpless, and in constant pain. He asked to die, but his wishes were not respected by his mother, who signed the consent papers for him to be treated, or by his physicians, who treated him against his will. The circumstances under which severely injured patients have the right to refuse treatment are explored. Family, friends, doctors, and nurses offer their perspectives on this issue. Cowart made progress in his recovery, married, and started his own business, but all along he has maintained that he should have been allowed to choose to die. The video provides an excellent springboard for discussion of right-to-die issues. It won an award at the American Film Festival in 1985.

Euthanasia in the 90s

Type:	VHS
Length:	40 min.
Date:	1995
Cost:	$19.95
Source:	Ignatius Press
	15 Oakland Avenue
	Harrison, NY 10528-9944
	(914) 835-4216

A sermon by Monsignor William Smith presents the Catholic viewpoint. He discusses the questions brought up by various key cases and also discusses the changes in terminology that occur when social change begins to alter the way we look at a concept. He points out that, prior to 1980, the definition of the word euthanasia was "mercy killing." After 1980 the definition became "an easy, painless death."

False Light
Type: VHS
Length: 14 min.
Date: 1995
Cost: $24.95
Source: International Anti-Euthanasia Task Force
           University of Steubenville
           P.O. Box 760
           Steubenville, OH 43952
           (614) 282-3810

False Light begins with a woman sitting alone and frightened in a dark room. A man walks down a hallway to her room, where he prepares a syringe with poison to inject into her. This ominous dramatic sequence implies that legalizing physician-assisted suicide will lead to this scene. The rest of the video utilizes a short-clip interview style to present the most common arguments made by those who believe that physician-assisted death is really killing. The impossibility of making a firm diagnosis is illustrated by the story of Denny Brace, who was told by his physician that he would be dead within a year. Three years later, he appears in this video. Inadequate pain relief, lack of physician training in dealing with end-of-life concerns, and depression are all discussed by other patients, a doctor, and a hospice nurse. Sound bites such as "doctors make mistakes" probably do more to frighten than to educate, but some meaningful issues are raised.

From Patient to Person
Type: VHS
Length: 22 min.
Date: 1987
Cost: $25 for members
Source: American Chronic Pain Association
           P.O. Box 850
           Rocklin, CA 95677
           (916) 632-0922

This intimate interview with Penny Cowan, founder and president of the American Chronic Pain Association, does not deal directly with end-of-life issues, but instead addresses the devastating effects of chronic pain on the individual, family members, and physicians. Cowan talks about physicians who give up on patients they cannot cure and gives advice on learning to deal with chronic pain, figuring out what causes pain, knowing what to expect, and taking personal responsibility—subjects that can be very difficult for patients whose doctors don't believe in their pain, don't deal honestly with them, or refuse to validate their experience. Cowan shows that many people with chronic pain are "people pleasers" who don't understand they can say no and therefore decide to do what would be best for others and not for themselves.

Help Me Die
Type: VHS
Length: 48 min.
Date: 1990
Cost: $195
Source: Fanlight Productions
            47 Halifax Street
            Boston, MA 02130
            (800) 937-4113 or (617) 524-0980

This is a compilation of programs focusing on Oregon and the right to die. It covers hospice care, advances in the treatment of pain, and the hard questions that many people must address in making end-of-life decisions. The video features the stories of several terminally ill patients, their families, and others who care for them, including Derek Humphrey (founder of the Hemlock Society) and the husband of Janet Adkins (the first person Dr. Jack Kevorkian assisted, using his suicide machine). One of the most powerful aspects of this video is that it shows how people's thinking can shift. Some who wanted to die no longer want to by the end of the program; others have moved toward a greater acceptance of some forms of euthanasia after heartrending experiences with family members.

Living Choices
Type: VHS (open-captioned available)
Length: 16 min.
Date: 1991
Cost: $250 purchase; $65/3 days or $100/5 days rental
Source: Baxley Media Group
            110 W. Main
            Urbana, IL 61801
            (800) 421-6999 or (217) 384-4838

This brief video uses believable characters in everyday situations to answer common questions about advance directives:

Who needs an advance directive? What is a durable power of attorney? How difficult is the paperwork? Does it require an attorney? What is meant by quality of life? *Living Choices* clears up common misconceptions and reinforces the importance of advance directives. Satisfies both the spirit and letter of the Patient Self-Determination Act.

Living with Dying
Type: VHS, Beta, 3/4 in.
Length: 19 min.
Date: 1974
Cost: $295
Source: Professional Research, Inc.
1560 Sherman, #100
Evanston, IL 60201
(800) 421-2363 or (708) 328-6700

Revealing medical, social, and emotional dilemmas experienced by the terminally ill, several patients explain how they cope with dying.

Living with Dying
Type: VHS
Length: 28 min.
Date: 1992
Cost: Not available for purchase; Available through libraries and interlibrary loan
Source: Indiana University Media and Teaching Resources
Franklin Hall, Room 004
Bloomington, IN 47405
(812) 855-2853

This story of how Albert and Margaret Kerestes deal with the impending death of their son, Albert, covers many aspects of terminal care and the emotional stresses that accompany the loss of a loved one.

Time To Die—Who Decides?
Type: VHS, Beta
Length: 28 min.
Date: 1988
Cost: $285
Source: Churchill Media
6901 Woodley Avenue
Van Nuys, CA 91406
(800) 334-7830 or (818) 778-1978

In this poignant documentary, three individuals face death from terminal illnesses with dignity and courage.

To Touch a Grieving Heart
Type: VHS
Length: 40 min.
Date: 1992
Cost: $29.95
Source: Baxley Media Group
110 W. Main
Urbana, IL 61801
(800) 421-6999 or (217) 384-4838

Sensitive, practical insights are captured in this enlightening and highly acclaimed program. Explains how to touch grieving hearts in healthy ways. This program is useful for classrooms, support groups, families, and individuals. One of the best video-tapes available on grief.

Legal-Political

Choices 1995
Type: VHS
Length: 13 min.
Date: 1995
Cost: $89.98
Source: Choice in Dying
200 Varick Street
New York, NY 10014
(212) 366-5540

Narrated by Art Ulene, this poignant video explores the issues related to end-of-life decisions and focuses on advance direc-tives. By allowing viewers to sit in on conversations with indi-viduals facing these decisions, the program helps viewers explore their own values. The video was produced by Southwest Productions in collaboration with the Institute of Public Law at the Center for Health Law and Ethics at the University of New Mexico. It won the silver award at the 1995 National Mature Media Awards Program.

Choosing Death
A Health Quarterly/Frontline Special
Type: VHS
Length: 120 min.

Date: 1993
Cost: $125
Source: PBS Video
           1320 Braddock Place
           Alexandria, VA 22314-1698
           (800) 344-3337

Examining physician-assisted suicide in Holland and the impact the Dutch experience is having on legislative efforts in the United States, journalist Roger Mudd moderates a discussion among physicians, medical experts, and religious experts before a live audience.

The Death of Nancy Cruzan
A Frontline Special
Type: VHS
Length: 90 min.
Date: 1992
Cost: $69.95
Source: PBS Video
           1320 Braddock Place
           Alexandria, VA 22314-1698
           (800) 344-3337

This program chronicles the eight-year legal saga of the Cruzan family following the automobile crash that left Nancy Cruzan in a persistent vegetative state. It also documents developments during the final days before Nancy died.

Eskimo Ice Cream Shoes
Type: VHS
Length: 15 min.
Date: 1990
Cost: $99 (includes 9-page Leader's Guide)
Source: Baxley Media Group
           110 W. Main
           Urbana, IL 61801
           (800) 421-6999 or (217) 384-4838

The cycle of healing that the bereaved need to experience is outlined in drama form. A young woman is grieving the loss of her husband when a mysterious ice cream vendor helps her find ways to channel her grief. This short video addresses the problem of prolonged grieving in a unique, caring and nonthreatening way, and is suitable for all ages.

Final Choices

Type:	VHS
Length:	30 min.
Date:	1988
Cost:	$39.95 home use, $89.95 institutional use
Source:	KCET Public Television
	4401 Sunset Boulevard
	Los Angeles, CA 90027
	(213) 666-9541

This National Media Owl Award–winning video explores the effects of medical technology on end-of-life decision making for medical professionals, patients, and families. It includes several excellent interviews.

In Sickness or in Health

Type:	VHS
Length:	33 min.
Date:	1990
Cost:	$89.95
Source:	Choice in Dying
	200 Varick Street
	New York, NY 10014
	(212) 366-5540

In this overview of decision making for long-term care, commentary and legal analysis is provided by ethicist and attorney Nancy Dubler. Two nursing home residents are featured. One is capable of making her own health care decisions, while the other is not. Three versions of the video are available: for residents, for family members of residents, and for long-term care staff.

Life Support Decisions

Type:	VHS
Length:	59 min.
Date:	1994
Cost:	$110
Source:	Choice in Dying
	200 Varick Street
	New York, NY 10014
	(212) 366-5540

An informative discussion about end-of-life decisions from the lay and professional points of view includes family members, lawyers, ethicists, and health care workers. Personal stories illuminate the difficulty and pain involved in making end-of-life decisions.

No Heroic Measures

Type: VHS
Length: 23 min.
Date: 1986
Cost: $250 purchase or rental
Source: Baxley Media Group
110 W. Main
Urbana, IL 61801
(800) 421-6999 or (217) 384-4838

This video follows the story of Claire Conroy and her niece's struggle to have Conroy's feeding tube removed. Hearings in the nursing home and in the courtroom are shown, and the more emotional aspects of the decision are revealed through the people who care for Conroy. The story is a good introduction to the concept of substituted judgment.

The Right To Die

Type: VHS
Length: 19 min.
Date: 1985
Cost: $250 purchase or rental
Source: Baxley Media Group
110 W. Main
Urbana, IL 61801
(800) 421-6999 or (217) 384-4838

Legal, ethical, and emotional issues arise when a patient asks to have a ventilator removed. The story is told to a hospital ethics committee from three different points of view: that of the patient's physician, a spouse, and a nurse. The film was created to bring the issues into focus and to initiate discussion; it does not take a particular stance.

The Right To Die

Type: VHS, Beta
Length: 23 min.
Date: 1993
Cost: $295
Source: Lucerne Media
37 Ground Pine Road
Morris Plains, NJ 07950
(800) 341-2293 or (201) 538-1401

A panel of professionals discusses several facets of the right-to-die controversy, including the legal implications of the battle fought by the family of Nancy Cruzan.

The Right To Die: Considering the Ethical and Legal Issues
Type: VHS
Length: 28 min.
Date: N/A
Cost: $285
Source: American Journal of Nursing Company
             Educational Services Division
             555 W. 57th Street
             New York, NY 10019-2961
             (800) 225-5256 or (212) 582-8820

Made for nurses and nursing students, this video provides a valuable explanation of the 1991 Patient Self-Determination Act and its implications in health care settings. Medical and nonmedical professionals discuss the impact of this act on the patient's right to use advance directives. Another topic is the ethics committee's role as consultant in issues such as self-determination, professional mandates, benefit vs. burden of treatment, and the evaluation of a patient's condition. A study guide is included.

The Sovereign Self: Right To Live, Right To Die
Type: VHS
Length: 60 min.
Date: 1984
Cost: No longer available for purchase;
             Available through libraries and interlibrary loan
Source: Films Inc.
             5547 N. Ravenswood Avenue
             Chicago, IL 60640-1199
             (800) 323-4222 or (312) 878-2600

This tenth episode of the series *The Constitution: That Delicate Balance* brings together a panel of 20 people including members of Congress, medical ethicists, religious leaders, lawyers and judges, physicians, and popular media personalities to discuss the right to sovereignty as it relates to the Constitution. In Philadelphia's Congress Hall, the panelists answer questions about a hypothetical patient who has refused medical interventions that would save his life. The patient's age, medical condition, family relationships, and circumstances change as the discussion continues. Physician-assisted death, voluntary suicide, and euthanasia are discussed, providing valuable insights into the difficulties faced when attempts are made to balance personal choice and privacy with the best interests of society. The second half of the program focuses on the question of abortion and the "tragic newborn," providing a broader base of discussion for those asking end-of-life questions.

A Time To Choose
Type: VHS
Length: 20 min.
Date: 1990
Cost: $89.95
Source: Choice in Dying
            200 Varick Street
            New York, NY 10014
            (212) 366-5540

This introduction to living wills and health care proxies was taped at the primary care clinic of a major urban hospital and is intended to educate the ill, but not acutely ill, patient. A discussion between an elderly couple about their wishes should either of them become incapacitated nicely illustrates end-of-life questions. The two are guided in their discussion by a lawyer ethicist, and two physicians join the discussion later in the program.

Your Money and Your Life: America's Managed Care Revolution
Type: VHS
Length: 60 min.
Date: 1995
Cost: $69.95
Source: WNET/Thirteen Non-Broadcast
            356 W. 58th Street
            New York, NY 10019
            (212) 560-3045

Harvard University law professor Arthur Miller moderates a roundtable discussion on the impact of health care cost cutting and managed care on a variety of ethical questions. Participants examine the potential effect of health care policy reform on a wide range of issues.

Fiction Videotapes

Many of these videos are available through video rental stores and libraries or can be requested through them.

Dark Victory
Type: VHS, Beta, LV (close-captioned)
Length: 106 min.
Date: 1939
Cost: $19.95
Source: MGM/UA
           2500 Broadway
           Santa Monica, CA 90404-6061
           (310) 449-3000

This story of a woman who is dying of a brain tumor and the assistance she receives from her doctor is directed by Edmund Goulding and stars Bette Davis, Humphrey Bogart, and Ronald Reagan.

A Matter of Life and Death
Type: VHS
Length: 98 min.
Date: 1981
Cost: No longer available for purchase; Available through libraries and interlibrary loan
Source: Lorimar Home Video
           15838 N. 62nd Street, #100
           Scottsdale, AZ 85254
           (602) 596-9970

This movie is based on the story of Joy Ufema, a nurse who dedicated her life to improving the treatment of the terminally ill. Directed by Russ Mayberry, it stars Linda Lavin and Tyne Daly.

Murder or Mercy?
Type: VHS
Length: 78 min.
Date: 1974
Cost: $49.95
Source: Worldvision Home Video, Inc.
           1700 Broadway
           New York, NY 10019-5905
           (212) 261-2700

The still timely story of a famous doctor accused of killing his terminally ill wife features courtroom drama and focuses on the morality of mercy killing. It was directed by Harrey Hart and stars Melvin Douglas and Bradford Dillman.

On Goldon Pond

Type:	VHS, Beta, LV
Length:	109 min.
Date:	1981
Cost:	$14.95
Source:	Karol Video
	P.O. Box 7600
	Wilkes Barre, PA 18773
	(717) 822-8899

This award-winning motion picture starring Henry and Jane Fonda does an excellent job of exploring and portraying the emotional challenges of old age and terminal illness. Directed by Mark Rydell.

Pride of the Yankees

Type:	VHS, Beta, LV
Length:	128 min.
Date:	1942
Cost:	$19.98
Source:	CBS/Fox Video
	1330 Avenue of the Americas
	New York, NY 10019
	(800) 800-2369 or (212) 373-4800

Gary Cooper and Babe Ruth star in this drama based on the true story of Lou Gehrig and his death from amyotrophic lateral sclerosis (ALS), which later came to be known as Lou Gehrig's disease. Directed by Sam Wood.

Soylent Green

Type:	VHS, Beta, LV
Length:	95 min.
Date:	1973
Cost:	$19.98
Source:	MGM/UA
	2500 Broadway
	Santa Monica, CA 90404-6061
	(310) 449-3000

In this sci-fi thriller starring Charlton Heston, the greenhouse effect and a resulting shortage of resources in the twenty-first century make euthanasia and cannibalism attractive options. Directed by Richard Fleischer.

When the Time Comes
Type: VHS (closed-captioned)
Length: 94 min.
Date: 1991
Cost: $79.98
Source: Republic Pictures Home Video
          5700 Wilshire Boulevard, #525
          Los Angeles, CA 90036
          (213) 965-6900

A woman who is suffering from cancer wants to take her own life, but when her husband refuses to assist her, she seeks the help of a male friend.

Whose Life Is It, Anyway?
Type: VHS, Beta
Length: 118 min.
Date: 1981
Cost: $79.95
Source: MGM/UA
          2500 Broadway
          Santa Monica, CA 90404-6061
          (310) 449-3000

Richard Dreyfuss portrays a man who is paralyzed from the neck down and struggles to have his life support disconnected. Rife with black humor, this movie was directed by John Badham and also stars John Cassavetes.

A Woman's Tale
Type: VHS (closed-captioned)
Length: 94 min.
Date: 1992
Cost: $79.98
Source: Orion Home Video
          1888 Century Park E.
          Los Angeles, CA 90067
          (312) 282-0550

Paul Cox directed this story of a woman with cancer (Sheila Florence) and her determination to have a good death.

CD-ROMs

CD-ROM databases are often available for use in libraries and schools. These sources are useful for research purposes. Keywords for searches on these CDs might include *euthanasia, right-to-die, bioethics, suicide,* and *physician-assisted death.*

BIOETHICSLINE
Source: Silverplatter Publishing
100 River Ridge Drive
Norwood, MA 02062
(800) 343-0064

Maintained by the U.S. National Library of Medicine and the Kennedy Institute of Ethics at Georgetown University, this database includes citations from 1973 to the present. It focuses on ethical and public policy questions in the fields of health care and biomedical research. The 35,000 available records cover topics such as euthanasia, organ transplantation, allocation of health care resources, patient rights, and codes of professional ethics.

MEDLINE
Source: Silverplatter Publishing
100 River Ridge Drive
Norwood, MA 02062
(800) 343-0064

These CD-ROM disks contain comprehensive bibliographic medical references with abstracts. The standard database includes information from 1966 to the present and currently consists of 18 disks containing 8.4 million records. More than 380,000 additional records are added annually. The database covers topics such as health care, nursing, and psychiatry, and it is updated monthly. All information comes from the U.S. National Library of Medicine, 8600 Rockville Pike, Bethesda, MD, 20894, 800-272-4787.

PsycLIT
Source: Silverplatter Publishing
100 River Ridge Drive
Norwood, MA 02062
(800) 343-0064

The information in this database is provided by the American Psychological Association, 750 First Street, N.E., Washington, DC 20002-4242, (202) 336-6062. It covers 1974 to the present and is updated quarterly. The database's two disks contain 760,000 bibliographic records and abstracts covering topics related to education, medicine, psychiatry, psychology, and sociology. More than 52,000 new records are added annually.

WESTLAW

Source: West Publishing
620 Opperman Drive
P.O. Box 64770
St. Paul, MN 55164-0779
(800) 328-9352
E-mail: webmaster@westpub.com

WESTLAW's three CD-ROM libraries—Federal, State, and Topical—contain extensive information about legal cases. These are updated at least quarterly, with more information from advance sheets input for state case law. For the most current information, the WESTLAW online legal research service contains more than 8,000 databases. This is available through many law libraries.

Internet

The Internet has, in many ways, revolutionized the way information is accessed. Many public and university libraries now provide patrons with access to the Internet. These libraries may themselves be accessed through accounts at schools, homes, or offices.

Because the Internet provides users with a vast array of resources and convenient access, it is quickly becoming a very popular research tool. Nearly anyone with Internet access can search by topic or keyword to find information on a multitude of subjects. Be warned: Searching the Internet changes constantly as software is refined and systems are updated.

Some caveats are in order for those who are interested in using the Internet for serious research purposes. Keep in mind the following source criteria.

Authority

When you are directed to a site on the Internet, it is important to check the authority of the information provided by looking at the address (the universal resource listing, or URL). This lets you know where the information is coming from—a university or research institute, for instance. Look also at the authorship of the page to ascertain if the person writing the information is a recognizable authority in the field of study you are pursuing. If they are not, they should indicate their authority on the page. If you find a site and you cannot determine authority or the address, you would be wise to question any information found there. You may want to back up your research using more traditional sources. Internet users must be careful to remember that anyone can put information on the Internet. Our tendency as readers is to regard information we find as factual.

Janet Carabell, Internet librarian at the Boulder (Colorado) Public Library explains: "People see something in print and they believe it is fact. When they see online information—print *and* pictures—they *really* believe it." Much of the information on the Internet looks very authoritative, but looks can be deceiving, and serious researchers must be careful to look past the packaging to the content.

Currency

Determine how current the information provided by each site is by looking for dates on the documents you review and on the site itself. The currency of the site can be determined by the date listed as the last time the site was updated. If the site has not been updated recently, pursue other sites. Internet sites often "move," so addresses may not always be a reliable way of returning to your source. Always print information so that you have a hard copy to work from and refer to later.

Viewpoint

Who is the intended audience for this information? Information intended for entertainment or personal communication is not the same as that disseminated for research and academic study. Also look for any bias. Who is writing and why? Take note of the other sites linked to the site as well.

Scope

How thorough is the information and how well is it referenced? Are authoritative sources cited? Is the information primary data (generated by the site itself) or secondary information (links to information at other sites)?

Use these criteria to help determine the validity of the information and send e-mail or write the site if you have additional questions. Reliable sites usually provide an address so that users may contact them with questions or comments.

Information is not provided on the following types of online/Internet resources because they are not reliable sources of factual information.

Listserves

Listserves are e-mail–based discussion groups. Many are moderated, which means that someone is paying attention to make sure that the content of the discussion is relevant to the topic being addressed. Information that is not relevant is discarded. Moderation in no way implies that the content is factual.

Newsgroups

Newsgroups are provided by Internet services and therefore require an Internet account. These, too, are arranged by topic but they are not moderated—they are just people talking to people. All of the information gleaned from newsgroups must be considered testimonial, not factual.

Chat Groups

Commercial online services allow users to enter into chat groups wherein they may participate in real-time online discussions on particular topics. Like newsgroups, these have no authority whatsoever.

Sites of Interest on the Internet

A few key sites that were available as this book was being compiled are listed below. These sites merely provide a point of departure for further research on right-to-die topics. Perform your own Internet search as well by using keywords such as:

- *Right to die*
- *Euthanasia*
- *Physician-assisted suicide*
- *Bioethics*

Note that the Internet is case-sensitive. When typing in addresses, be sure to type them exactly as they appear below.

CNN Interactive
http://www.cgi.cnn.com/US/

Maintained by CNN, this site provides daily news updates on a multitude of topics and also contains a searchable index that allows users access to information reported by the press. Keywords: *physician-assisted death, Kevorkian, euthanasia,* etc.

ERGO
http://www.enf.org/ergo
Maintained by Derek Humphrey's organization, the Euthanasia Research and Guidance Organization (ERGO), this site provides numerous news updates, a glossary of common terms, extensive bibliographic information, and addresses of organizations around the world involved in right-to-die issues.

LifeNET
http://www.awinc.com/partners/bc/commpass/lifenet/lifenet.html
At this pro-life–oriented site, the Euthanasia Roundtable Web site offers links to a variety of organizations, position papers, legislation, and international news involving euthanasia.

MedWeb: Bioethics
http://www.cc.emory.edu/WHSCL/medweb.bioethics.html
Maintained by Emory University, this site provides links to numerous sites involving the study of bioethics. Users have access to conferences, bibliographies, documents, and electronic journals.

National Right to Life
http://www.clark.net/nrlc
Maintained by the pro-life National Right to Life Committee, this site offers position papers on right-to-die issues, fact sheets on assisted suicide, and links to other organizations with similar views, including the disability rights community.

VESS, the Voluntary Euthanasia Society of Scotland
http://www.netlink.co.uk/users/vess/index.html
Maintained by the society of the same name, this site is notable because it provides users with numerous links to other euthanasia-related sites. It also provides information about the history of the debate in the British Isles and a "Students' Page" to help students who are researching the issue.

Internet-Related Reference Books

Learn more about using the Internet by reading one of many text-based resources such as:

Krol, Ed. **The Whole Internet Users Guide & Catalog,** 2nd ed. Sebastopol, CA: O'Reilly & Associates, April 1994. 574 pp. ISBN 1-56592-063-5.

If you do use electronic information for research, the following reference provides information about citing electronic sources:

Li, Xia, and Nancy B. Crane. **Electronic Style: A Guide To Citing Electronic Information**. Westport, CT: Meckler, 1993. 65 pp. ISBN 0-88736-909-X.

Glossary

acquit To relieve of legal responsibility for an alleged crime.

active euthanasia Taking intentional action to speed the time of death via use of drugs or other means, including a lethal injection, by an individual or a physician.

acute illness A rapid change in health status that can cause high stress because of its sudden onset (i.e., automobile accident, heart attack, etc.).

advance directive A document that allows individuals to make known their desires in the event of grave illness or a serious accident. Indicates whether they wish physicians to forego treatment.

advance declaration *See* **advance directive.**

advance heath care directive *See* **advance directive.**

ageism A word that was coined by Dr. Robert Butler in 1967 to describe discrimination against the elderly.

agent A person who makes decisions for the patient through the power of a health care proxy document. Also known as a surrogate or a health care proxy. *See also* **health care proxy.**

aporregnymi bion Phrase coined by Euripedes, meaning "to break off life."

appeal To ask for a review of a case by a higher (appellate) court.

appellate court A court that has jurisdiction to review cases from other lower courts. The Supreme Court is at the top of the hierarchy of appellate courts in the United States.

artificial nutrition and hydration Food and water provided via feeding tube.

artificial respiration *See* **ventilator.**

assault A threat made by one person to another's body without actual contact.

assisted suicide The act in which one person helps hasten the death of another by making the means available with full knowledge that the person plans to commit suicide. *See also* **physician-assisted death.**

attending physician The doctor charged with the primary responsibility for a patient. A patient can have more than one attending physician.

attention sticker An adhesive label used on medical records to indicate that the patient has an advance directive or a living will.

authority The right to act on behalf of another. Authority is expressly given in a power of attorney.

autocheiria A first-century B.C. Greek term for suicide; translated into English as "an act with one's own hand."

autoktonia Common Greek word for suicide coined in the second century A.D., meaning "self-killing."

auto-euthanasia The act of ending one's own life without any outside assistance. *See also* **rational suicide.**

autopsy Examination of a deceased person to determine the cause of death. Performed by a pathologist.

battery Use of unwanted or unprovoked physical force on another person.

bereavement Process of dealing with feelings generated by the death of a loved one.

best-interests standard The standard used to determine care for a legally incompetent patient who, prior to becoming incompetent, gave no indications as to their beliefs and desires concerning medical treatment or nontreatment.

biazesthai heauton Aristotle's word for suicide, translated as "to flee living."

bioethics An area of study formally recognized in 1971. In medical contexts, includes the study of sociology, psychology, philosophy, law, and medicine.

brain death Loss of cerebral function while the heart continues to function. A patient must be monitored for brain waves for a full 30 minutes before he or she may be legally declared brain dead.

capacity The ability to understand one's own actions and their repercussions, particularly in the legal sense.

capitation A managed care term indicating that a health care provider is paid a set fee per patient enrolled in a health plan. This fee is paid whether or not the patient receives treatment and is not dependent on the amount of care received. Usually applies to a "gatekeeper," or primary care physician. The cost of care provided by specialists to whom the primary care physician refers the patient may or may not be deducted from the capitation fee.

cardiopulmonary resuscitation (CPR) A medical procedure intended to restart the heart after it has stopped beating. May only be applied to a patient who is not breathing. CPR usually involves short puffs of breath and manual pressure, but can also include electric shock applied to the chest or intravenous drugs to restart the heart.

case law A law that is based on another court ruling, rather than on legislation.

chief justice The primary judge in a court where there are three or more judges ruling on a case. The Supreme Court and appeals courts have chief justices.

chronic illness A long-term illness or disease for which there is no known cure.

circuit court A court that hears cases from several jurisdictions or counties.

civil action A legal term describing a case brought to court to remedy an invasion of a private right or a wrong that is not a criminal act.

clinical death A period of time during which the biological functions that sustain the body have ceased but rescue is still possible.

clinical physician A doctor whose work is performed at the bedside of the patient, as opposed to in the laboratory or in an academic setting.

clinician *See* **clinical physician.**

coercion The use of threats, intimidation, or force to persuade another person to act.

coma A state of unconsciousness from which the patient cannot be awakened. Not the same as **persistent vegetative state.**

comfort care *See* **palliative care.**

competence The ability to function competently; to be able to make sound decisions regarding health care issues.

compos mentis Latin term for "of sound mind."

concurring physician   A physician other than the attending physician who is brought in to agree with the attending physician.

conflict of interest   When a person's private interests conflict with a public duty to act in a particular manner.

consent   The voluntary permission given by a person able to make a competent decision.

consent to CPR   Every person admitted to or receiving treatment in a hospital is legally assumed to desire CPR unless a DNR order directs otherwise. *See also* **do not resuscitate.**

conservator   A person appointed by the court to take responsibility for another who is not competent.

constitutional right   A right guaranteed a person by the U.S. Constitution. May not be violated by any act of legislation.

coroner   A person who investigates the cause of death in cases in which suspicious circumstances warrant investigation.

criminal negligence   A crime resulting from a lack of reasonable care or action.

curare   A drug used during surgical procedures for the purpose of paralyzing the muscles.

custody   Having guardianship, but not ownership, of another person.

death   The cessation of life.

death certificate   The legal document that must be filled out by the attending physician of a patient who dies. The death certificate minimally states the time and cause of death.

depression   Persistent feelings of sadness or hopelessness. Often seen as an inability to enjoy life, and is frequently accompanied by changes in sleeping and eating patterns. There are various levels and types of depression, ranging from mild to chronic.

depressive suicide   Suicide that is the result of a patient's depressed state, rather than a well-considered decision. *See also* **rational suicide.**

determination   A final decision in a case handed down by a court of law.

dispute mediation system   A hospital committee charged with mediating any disputes that involve patients having an advance directive.

dissenting opinion   A judge's documented arguments against the ruling opinion in a court case.

district court   A federal trial court covering a specific geographic area.

DNR   *See* **do not resuscitate.**

do not resuscitate (DNR)   Medical orders initiated by a patient that indicate to the medical team that the patient does not desire CPR or other extreme life-saving measures.

double effect   The impact on a patient when a medical treatment has a dual effect. Often describes situations in which the amount of medication a patient must use to alleviate pain has the simultaneous effect of ending or endangering that patient's life.

durable power of attorney   The legal document that allows one person to designate another person to represent him or her and make legally binding decisions in the event the appointing person becomes incompetent.

dying   The process by which life ends.

emergency card   A card that can be carried in a wallet that summarizes the information in a person's living will.

endotracheal tube   A tube placed in a patient's trachea through an opening cut in the throat to establish an airway for artificial respiration.

ethics   A common body of principles that directs the actions of a person or a group.

ethics committee   *See* **terminal care team.**

eugenics   A process of selection that alters human evolution by eliminating persons with unwanted characteristics (negative) or promoting the gene contributions of those members with wanted characteristics (positive).

eulogos exagoge   A suicide term used by the Stoics in ancient Greece; translates into English as "sensible removal."

euthanasia   From the Greek, *eu+thanatos,* meaning "good death." Historically, a wide range of interpretations have been attributed to this term.

euthanasiac   When used as an adjective, this term describes substances and devices that can facilitate euthanasia. When used as a noun, usually refers to a drug suitable for the purpose of euthanasia.

felo de se   A Spanish term meaning "self-murder," used during the second and third centuries to describe suicides. Used in legal documents in jurisdictions in which suicide is a felony.

force feeding   Forcing a patient to ingest food against his or her wishes, for the purpose of keeping the patient alive.

force majeure   French term meaning a higher force or a natural, unavoidable force. Used in the euthanasia debate in the Netherlands to describe choices made in situations where there is no clearly defined correct choice.

forum shopping   A term coined in the United States to describe a person's search for a state or county in which to perform an act because it is legal in that "forum," but is not necessarily legal in the place where the person resides.

gastronomy tube   A tube placed directly in the stomach to provide artificial nutrition and hydration.

haireo thanaton   Greek, meaning "to seize death."

health care power of attorney   *See* **health care proxy.**

health care proxy   A legal document that allows a person to be appointed by the patient to make health care decisions should the patient become unable to do so.

hekonein haidou   A term coined by Plato, meaning "to voluntarily go to Hades."

home care   Medical or support care following hospitalization that takes place in the patient's home.

homicide   The purposeful and intentional taking of another person's life.

hospice   A facility or service that provides palliative care to terminally ill patients and their families. The modern hospice movement began in England to provide consistent pain control and emotional support for the terminally ill. In the United States, a patient must be diagnosed as likely to live six months or less to qualify for many types of hospice care. *See also* **palliative care.**

iatrogenic illness   Illness resulting from a physician's treatment of a patient or from hospital conditions or procedures. Implies the illness could have been avoided had the physician been more judicious, the hospital properly maintained and equipped, or had appropriate procedures been followed.

informed consent   A legal concept meaning that each patient has the right to any known information about the nature and risks associated with procedures or medications, as well as the right to refuse any type of unwanted care.

injunction   A court order for a person or group to discontinue a particular act.

inpatient care   Medical care that requires a patient to remain overnight in a medical facility.

inquest   A legal procedure to determine the cause of a suspicious death.

intensive care unit (ICU)   A section of the hospital designed to provide constant monitoring and support for patients with life-threatening conditions.

intravenous (IV)   Administered via the body's circulatory system. Refers to a method of administering medications, glucose, nutrition, anesthesia, etc.

intubation To insert a tube into a body canal, usually the airway, to provide respiratory support.

joint suicide When two people commit suicide together.

life support Medical interventions to maintain life when the body is incapable of supporting basic life functions.

life-sustaining *See* **life support.**

living will *See* **advance directive.**

malpractice Misconduct of a physician through negligence and/or lack of skill or careful consideration.

mechanical support Describes the use of a respirator to force air in and out of the lungs of a patient who is unable to breathe independently. Air reaches the lungs through a tube inserted into the windpipe.

medically futile Describes attempts to resuscitate a patient that will fail to sustain life for any length of time. Death is considered inevitable.

medico-legal Relating to both medicine and the law.

mental capacity *See* **competence.**

mercy killing Ending a person's suffering by ending his or her life. This differs from voluntary euthanasia, in which a person has clearly stated the wish to die.

microencephaly A condition characterized by an abnormally small brain.

natural death Death that proceeds without heroic measures or attempts to sustain life.

negotiated death A death resulting when family members instruct medical staff to disconnect life-support systems.

next of kin The nearest blood relative of a patient.

outpatient care Medical care that does not require the patient to stay in a medical facility overnight.

palliative care Medical care that provides pain relief and attempts to make the patient as comfortable as possible, regardless of possible long-term detrimental side effects. Hospice programs champion this type of care for the terminally ill.

parasuicide A failed suicide attempt that constitutes a cry for help from a person who is suicidal. This is common among young people who are distressed. *See also* **suicide gestures.**

parenticide The act of murdering one's parent or parents.

passive euthanasia Euthanasia that relies on lack of treatment, rather than on active measures that would cause death. This includes withholding or withdrawing treatment, including CPR and mechanical respiration.

pathologist A doctor who practices in a laboratory, primarily researching causes of illness and disease. Usually consults with clinical physicians.

patholysis A word coined by Dr. Jack Kevorkian meaning assisted suicide to relieve suffering.

patient-controlled anesthesia (PCA) An intravenous drug delivery system designed to allow the patient to exercise some control over pain medication. The patient presses a button to deliver a preset dose when needed. A physician or nurse determines the number of doses that can be dispensed during a given time period to prevent overdosing.

persistent vegetative state (PVS) A state in which a person is at no risk of dying but has suffered irreversible brain damage. People can stay in a PVS for as long as several decades with medical intervention. This state differs from a coma in that the brain damage is considered so pervasive that there is virtually no possibility that the patient will ever spontaneously emerge, as sometimes happens when patients are comatose for long periods of time. A person in a PVS with a functional brain stem can have reflex responses, causing such muscular activity as the eyes opening and closing or convulsions.

physician aid-in-dying Physician participation in a patient's death by providing lethal drugs for patient administration or by actively ending a patient's life.

physician-assisted death The act in which a physician helps a patient hasten his or her death at the patient's request—not initiated by the physician—by making the means available or by administering them.

policy diffusion A policy-making term describing the process in which judicial opinions from one court are used to create decisions in another state. The opinions are usually introduced to the court through a lawyer's legal brief.

privacy The right to make personal decisions regarding health care, protected by law.

prognosis The expected outcome of an illness or disease.

prophylactic treatment Treatment that tries to prevent disease rather than cure it.

prosecution The process of bringing formal charges against someone suspected of an illegal act.

proxy Person authorized to act in another's stead.

pseudodementia When depression causes symptoms that mimic dementia, including apathy, confusion, memory problems, and an inability to care for oneself.

public policy That which is deemed good for the general public. Intended to prevent persons from committing acts that would result in harm to society.

rational suicide   The act of ending one's own life in a deliberate manner and without assistance while in a rational state of mind. *See also* **auto-euthanasia.**

religious freedom   A right guaranteed by the First Amendment of the U.S. Constitution. Allows each individual to worship according to his or her own religion and includes the right to not act in a way that goes against personal religious beliefs, with the proviso that all such actions fall within what is consistent with the social order.

restraining order   A court order that follows an application for an injunction and that forbids a person from performing a particular act until the court is able to review the injunction. *See also* **injunction.**

revoke   To cancel authority, power, or privileges, including power of attorney and physician licenses.

self-deliver   A euphemism for suicide or euthanasia. Emphasizes the decision by the individual to act or to have someone act on his or her behalf.

slippery slope   A hypothesis that states that once something becomes acceptable to society, it then will be encouraged as well. Often used to describe the German experience with the concept of so-called mercy killing during World War II.

substituted judgment   An ethics term meaning to use information gleaned from a patient to make a medical decision on his or her behalf.

suicide   The act of intentionally taking one's own life. Suicide can be depressive, irrational, or rational in nature.

suicide clause   A clause found in some life insurance policies that disqualifies beneficiaries if there is evidence that the death was the result of suicide.

suicide gestures   Attempted suicides using methods likely to be unsuccessful. Intended to draw attention rather than cause death.

suicide pact   A promise among two or more people to help one another commit suicide if one or the other becomes incapable of auto-euthanasia.

suicide sticker   A way to update a living will that indicates a patient has not changed his or her mind since the time the document was signed.

surrogate   *See* **agent** and **health care proxy.**

suspended sentence   Term of imprisonment for a convicted person that is recorded but not served.

terminal care team   A team made up of physicians, social workers, and administrators that reviews requests for euthanasia placed by patients in hospitals.

terminal illness An illness that will result in death; most often a chronic illness for which there is no cure.

thanatology The study of death.

thanatos Greek word for death. Also a proper name for the personification of death, who is the twin brother of Hypnos (sleep) in the Homeric Pantheon.

tube feeding The process in which a tube is inserted into the digestive system of a patient in order to provide nutrients when the patient is unable to eat or swallow independently. The tube is usually inserted through the nose (nasogastric tube), but can also be inserted directly into the stomach.

uniform In the legal sense, statutes or laws that are drafted and approved by the Commission on Uniform State Laws.

uniform determination of death State statutes that establish uniform criteria for physicians to follow when determining cessation of life.

uxoricide The killing of a wife by her husband.

ventilator A machine designed to provide oxygen to the lungs of a patient who is unable to breathe independently.

voluntary Acting of one's own free will without undue influence from others.

voluntary euthanasia When a competent patient requests help in hastening his or her own death.

ward of the court A person whose welfare is guarded by the court.

withdrawal of life supports The removal of devices and treatment initiated to sustain life. A form of passive euthanasia.

withholding of life supports The act of holding back any treatment that may prolong life in a case where death is anticipated. A form of passive euthanasia.

witness A person who is present for the purpose of observing the signing of a legal document.

wrongful death statute Allows survivors of a deceased family member to sue if negligence is believed to be involved in the death.

Index

337

C arolyn Roberts has written extensively on health-related issues and also in the fields of education and technology. Her work has appeared in local and national newspapers and journals. She is currently at work on a book on parenting and educating gifted children.

M artha Gorman is the author of *Environmental Hazards: Marine Pollution* (ABC-CLIO, Contemporary World Issues series, 1993) and is a nationally known health writer. She has authored a weekly health column since 1990 and is a contributing writer for *Podiatry Today* magazine. She has also worked extensively with the chiropractic profession. Other writing credits include *Ill, Not Insane—The Physiological Bases of Chronic Mental Illnesses* (New Idea Press, 1985), *Everybody for President—The 1984 Do-It-Yourself Presidental Compaign Kit* (Workman Publishing, 1984), and *Baby's Home Journal* (New Idea Press, 1989). She owns Health Horizons, Inc., a supplier of health copy for hospitals and health care providers. Her deep, personal interest in death by choice, or euthanasia, began in the 1970s, when her brother Tim was dying of muscular dystrophy.